Y SWIM LESSONS®

# the parent/child and preschool

## AQUATIC PROGRAM MANUAL

Produced Under A Grant From The Aquatic
Resources (Wallop-Breaux) Trust Fund
Administered By The U.S. Coast Guard

YMCA
We build strong kids,
strong families, strong communities.

YMCA of the USA.
The parent/child and preschool aquatic program manual/YMCA of the USA.
p. cm. — (YMCA swim lessons)
Includes index.
ISBN: 0-7360-0053-4
1. Swimming for children—Study and teaching. 2. Swimming for infants—Study and teaching. 3. Parent and child. I. Title. II. Series.
GV837.2.Y52 1999
797.2'1'083—dc21 98-37501
CIP

ISBN-10: 0-7360-0053-4
ISBN-13: 978-0-7360-0053-6
Published by the YMCA of the USA
Item no.: YPSAQ0404
Copyright © 1999 National Council of Young Men's Christian Associations of the United States of America

All rights reserved. Except for use in a review, the reproduction or utilization of this work in any form or by any electronic, mechanical, or other means, now known or hereafter invented, including xerography, photocopying, and recording, and in any information storage and retrieval system, is forbidden without the written permission of the publisher.

Parts of Chapter 9 reprinted with permission of Simon & Schuster from *Teaching Your Children Values* by Richard and Linda Eyre. Copyright © 1993 by Richard and Linda Eyre.

Other permission notices for material reprinted or adapted in this book from other sources can be found on page viii.

*Project Coordinator:* Laura J. Slane
*Writers:* Pat Sammann and Laura J. Slane
*Acquisitions Editor:* Pat Sammann
*Managing Editor:* Melinda Graham
*Copyeditor:* Amie Bell
*Proofreader:* Debra Aglaia
*Indexer:* Sharon Duffy
*Book Design and Composition:* Studio Montage
*Photographer (cover and interior):* Tracy Frankel
*Photo Editor:* Laura J. Slane
*Illustrator:* Cindy Wrobel
*Printer:* Premier Print Group

Printed in the United States of America 10 9 8 7 6 5

Copies of this book may be purchased from the YMCA Program Store.
www.ymcaprogramstore.com or 800-747-0089

The YMCA of the USA is a not-for-profit corporation that provides advice and guidance, but not rules of compliance, for member associations of the National Council of YMCAs.

# Contents

# Acknowledgments

**The YMCA of the USA would like to acknowledge the contributions of the following people to *The Parent/Child and Preschool Aquatic Program Manual.* Staff leadership for this project was coordinated by Laura J. Slane. We'd like to thank the USCG for their help and support for the development of the YMCA Swim Lessons program.**

**Pam Barrett**
Leesburg, VA

**Mary Carter**
Bethesda-Chevy Chase YMCA,
Bethesda, MD

**Kathi Cook**
West Park, NY

**Dr. Jerry DeMers**
California Polytechnic
State University,
San Luis Obispo, CA

**Diane Erb**
South Side/Carondelet YMCA,
St. Louis, MO

**Linda Garcia**
Wheeler Regional Branch YMCA,
Plainville, CT

**Theresa Hill**
Northbrook YMCA,
Northbrook, IL

**Marcia Humphrey**
Gwinnett Family YMCA,
Lawrenceville, GA

**Dr. Ralph Johnson**
North Greenville College,
Tigerville, SC

**Dr. Stephen Langendorfer**
Bowling Green State University,
Bowling Green, OH

**Marianne Mackey-Smith**
Bob Sierra Family YMCA,
Tampa, FL

**Karen Martrano**
YMCA of Metropolitan Detroit,
Detroit, MI

**Cami Ramo**
YMCA of Greater New Bedford,
New Bedford, MA

**Pat Sammann**
YMCA Program Store,
Champaign, IL

**Kay Smiley**
Town North YMCA, Dallas, TX

**Stephen Smith**
Schroeder YMCA,
Brown Deer, WI

**Debby Speck**
Lake County Central YMCA,
Painesville, OH

**Barb Straube**
Rich Port YMCA,
La Grange, IL

**John Wingfield**
United States Diving,
Indianapolis, IN

**Pat Wolfe**
Southwest Branch YMCA,
Saratoga, CA

**Linda Pourchot**
West County YMCA,
Chesterfield, MO

**Laura Slane**
**Barb Taylor**
**Lynne Vaughan**
**Mary Zoller**
YMCA of the USA

---

We would like to thank the staff and members of
**Chino Valley YMCA,**
Chino, CA

**Crescenta Canada YMCA,**
La Canada Flintridge, CA

**Deb Anderson,**
Chino Valley YMCA,
Chino, CA

**Georgia Harrison,**
Crescenta Canada YMCA,
Flintridge, CA
for their help and assistance with our photo shoot for this book.

We also would like to thank the following companies who donated the equipment and supplies listed for the book's photo shoot:

Adolph Kiefer and Associates (Phone: (847) 872-8866):
Polywog Tube (#600510), Mesh Water Polo Cap (#600028), Kiefer Synchro Nose Clip (#690200), Kiefer Kona Silicone Snorkel (#810485), Kiefer Lahaina Silicone Mask (#810815), CPR Basic Learning System (#HLS100), Visor with Lifeguard (#909500), Kiefer Fin (#810002, #810003, #810004), Workout Dumbell Waveeater (#650610), Kiefer Barbell (#650603), Vest Type II Toddler (#621307), Underwater Slalom Game Set (#643027), 3/pk Connector Water Log 9" (#650590), YMCA Rescue Tube (#620042Y), Diving Brick (#600044), Type II Child (#621107), Vest Type II Child (#621207), Vest Type II Univ Adult (#621007), #3 Water Polo Wetball Jr. Ball (#606603), Dive Toys Pool Pals Set of 5 (#651002)

Printworks, Inc. (Phone: (414) 421-5400):
YMCA Staff Tee (#43071), YMCA Staff Polo (#43082), J-Collar Theme Polo (#43112), Character Development Hot Top (#43505), Character Development Tee (#43123), Y Times 4 Tee (#43125)

Recreonics, Inc. (Phone: (502) 456-5706 or (800) 428-3254):
Water Woogles (#94071), Catalina Boat Kit (#94059), "Freddy Fish" Funny Float 29" (94124), Yellow Rubber Duckie (#94150), Dive F/The Tropical Fish Game (#94150), Dive Brick (#92260), Recreonics "Superboard" (Yellow #92212.Y, Red #92212.R, Blue #92212.B), Deluxe Junior Floating Fins (#92442, #92440), Advanced Tempered Glass Dive Mask and Snorkel Set (#92450), Infant's Head Ups Vest, Orange (#12284.O), Foam Type II Life Vest (#12279, #12280, #12281)

# Preface

**As the YMCA's current logo says, the Y builds strong kids, strong families, and strong communities. No Y program better illustrates this than The Parent/Child and Preschool Aquatic Program.**

**This program develops kids' skills and confidence; it strengthens the bonds between parents and children; and it not only provides valuable aquatic survival skills to community members, but it also helps promote positive values.**

*The Parent/Child and Preschool Aquatic Program Manual* is the course text for those who wish to be trained as aquatic instructors for children ages five and under and their parents. This program, formerly known as Y SKIPPERS, has two components:

- The Parent/Child Aquatic Program, in which the instructor works with parent/child teams and the children are between six-months and three-years-old.
- The Preschool Aquatic Program, in which the instructor usually works directly with children between three- and five-years-old who are unaccompanied by their parents.

The book reflects this feature of the program, as it is divided into three parts: an overview of the entire program, then a section on each of the two components.

Part I, which contains chapters 1 and 2, introduces you to the program. The first chapter explains the history of the program and why the YMCA is involved in teaching swimming as well as the purpose of the program. Chapter 2 gives you, as a new instructor, some valuable ideas on how to work with parents and children and make them comfortable in the aquatic environment.

The Parent/Child Aquatic Program is the focus of part II. Chapter 3 describes program goals and skills for parents and the relationship that you as the instructor should form with parents.

Chapter 4 provides information on the developmental characteristics of children between six-months and three-years-old. It also discusses teaching techniques and skill progression and covers the topics of IFDs, toys, and safety in the pool and around water. The program skills are listed and described in chapter 5 for each of the five program components: stroke development, personal growth, personal safety, water sports and games, and rescue. The last chapter in part II, chapter 6, explains how to take the skills from chapter 5 and incorporate them into session and lesson plans and offers tips on helping participants make the transition from the Parent/Child Aquatic Program to the Preschool Aquatic Program.

The last part, part III, is devoted to the Preschool Aquatic Program. Chapter 7 introduces you to the program, explaining the class components and skill objectives, providing developmental information on three- to five-year-olds, and outlining the role of the parent in this program. This is followed by information on session and lesson planning in chapter 8, which also includes ideas for class start-up and special events. The theme of chapter 9 is teaching character development; children in this program are now able to understand, at a basic level, what caring, honesty, respect, and responsibility mean. The last two chapters, chapters 10 and 11, include all skill objectives for the Preschool Aquatic Program, sample discussion guidelines for activities that meet those objectives, and performance criteria for each objective.

You can find helpful supplementary materials in the book's appendixes. Appendix A is the YMCA's Aquatic Program Guidelines for Children Under the Age of Three, which covers many important issues that concern working with this age group. A large number of activities, games, and songs for class use are found in appendix B.

The Parent/Child and Preschool Aquatic Program is special in that it reaches children and parents early in their relationship. Parents are given guidance on how to develop their children's abilities and how to protect their children from harm; children are given the chance to explore a new environment and to build skills that add to their self-confidence. Both benefit from taking part in an experience that lets them learn and have fun together. We hope that this manual will help you develop the skills and insight to work with parents and children effectively, so you can offer them this opportunity to learn aquatic skills and build their relationships at the same time.

# Credits

The aquatic readiness section in chapter 1 and the game, push against the wall, adapted, by permission, from Langendorfer, S., 1995, *Aquatic Readiness*, (Champaign, IL: Human Kinetics) 3, 73, 74, 166.

The section "Discipline and Young Children" in chapter 7 adapted, by permission, from *Time out for "time out,"* 1997, (Washington, D.C.: National Association for the Education of Young Children).

Information on jumping into a pool wearing a PFD adapted from the National Safe Boating Council and U.S. Coast Guard. 1997. *Wear Your Life Jacket! Boat Smart From the Start*. Washington, D.C.: Authors.
Passing the ball skill description in chapter 11 adapted from *United States Water Polo Wetball Coaching Manual: Junior Water Polo for Beginning Swimmers*. Bill Barnett and Bruce Wigo. 1996. Colorado Springs, CO: U.S. Water Polo.

Dribbling a ball and Push pass skill descriptions in chapter 10 adapted from *United States Water Polo Level One Coaching Manual*, Daniel Sharadin. 1993. Carmel, IN: Cooper Publishing Group.

Canoe scull skill description in chapter 11 adapted from *Coaching Synchronized Swimming Effectively*, Margaret Forbes. 1984. Champaign, IL: Human Kinetics.

# the parent/child and preschool

## AQUATIC PROGRAM MANUAL

# Overview of the Parent/Child and Preschool Aquatic Program

**The Parent/Child and Preschool Aquatic Program is the Y's aquatic program for children from six months up to five years of age. It has two separate parts:**

- The Parent/Child Aquatic Program, which promotes water enrichment and aquatic readiness activities for children from six months up to three years of age and their parents or other trusted adults.
- The Preschool Aquatic Program, which teaches water adjustment and basic swimming skills for children from three to five years of age. In most Ys these classes are held without parents, but some Ys do offer classes in which the parents participate with the children.

Although participants are divided into the two programs by age, they are assigned to specific levels within each program according to their developmental abilities or aquatic skills, which may or may not correspond to their chronological age. The parent/child portion of the program uses the following developmental ability guidelines for the following levels:

| | | |
|---|---|---|
| ***Shrimps*** | 6 to 8 months | Child can control the head and sit with support from the hands. |
| ***Kippers*** | 9 to 12 months | Child can sit without hand support and stand with support from the hands. |
| ***Inias*** | 3 to 18 months | Child can stand without support and walk with or without support or aid. |
| ***Perch*** | 19 to 36 months | Child can run and jump. |

The preschool portion of the program divides participants into the following levels according to their aquatic skills:

| | |
|---|---|
| ***Pike*** | Beginner I |
| ***Eel*** | Beginner II |
| ***Ray*** | Advanced Beginner I |
| ***Starfish*** | Advanced Beginner II |

In all levels the objectives of the Parent/Child and Preschool Aquatic Program are for participants to

- have fun,
- get exercise,
- receive parent education,
- learn safe water adjustment,
- learn boating safety, and
- learn the appropriate use of personal flotation devices (PFDs).

The skills taught in the Parent/Child and Preschool Aquatic Program center around five main components:

- Personal safety: Activities that help increase awareness of personal safety issues for both the child and the family, including boating safety
- Personal growth: Activities that help the child and the family grow in spirit, mind, and body, including character development
- Stroke development: Activities that help develop swimming abilities so participants can move in the water safely
- Water sports and games: Activities that help develop an appreciation of aquatic activities that may last a lifetime, including age-appropriate games and songs.
- Rescue: Activities that build awareness of how to help others in aquatic emergencies

The skills to be taught within each component are described in parts II and III of this manual. Part I, which includes chapters 1 and 2, provides you with an introduction to the program and its purpose and explains the role of the instructor in the Parent/Child and Preschool Aquatic Program classes.

CHAPTER *one*

# Introduction to The Parent/Child and Preschool Aquatic Program

**Many parents select the Y as the place for their young child's first introduction to water because the YMCA has a reputation for offering programs that are safe, that are educational for both child and parent, and that teach sound Christian values.**

**The Parent/Child and Preschool Aquatic Program was created with these three features in mind.**

In the Parent/Child and Preschool Aquatic Program, the developmental experiences of each child are used to build the child's self-confidence. Parents learn from the instructor's example how to guide their children through positive reinforcement and appropriate praise.

Another benefit of the Parent/Child and Preschool Aquatic Program is the social experiences it provides for both children and parents. Infant aquatic classes are a special, fun time for parents to interact with their children and with each other. Children three and over have the chance to socialize and play together.

This chapter acquaints you with the history of the Parent/Child and Preschool Aquatic Program and why the YMCA is involved with aquatic programs for young children. It also explains how the program introduces infants and young children to the water with aquatic readiness activities. Instead of offering false guarantees that teaching young children to swim will protect them from drowning, this program educates parents and children about aquatic hazards and ways to reduce drowning risks through proper supervision and other safeguards.

## History of The Parent/Child and Preschool Aquatic Program

Before 1972 the National YMCA Aquatic Program provided instruction and recreation for people eight years of age and over. As the constituency of the YMCA changed to include all members of the family, YMCAs created a variety of programs to serve the very young.

The original idea to provide aquatics for children five and under emerged as a result of a national survey. This survey prompted the 1970 National Aquatics Conference in Fort Lauderdale, Florida, to design a program for teaching swimming to children between the ages of three and five. This new program was called the "Tadpole Program," and a suitable testing level, emblem, and award card were developed. Like the National Aquatic Program, the Tadpole Program used flotation devices to teach preschool children how to swim. The original manual for the program, *Teaching the Very Young to Swim,* was co-authored by John deBarbadillo and Marjorie M. Murphy, chairpersons of the Preschool Committee of the YMCA. National and international YMCAs implemented the Tadpole Program with much success.

As interest in involving even younger children in aquatic programs increased, many YMCAs introduced their own local water programs for children under the age of three. In 1982 a survey of 200 YMCAs revealed that over 60,000 infants were participating in aquatic programs. The programs involved a wide variety of experiences, including actual swimming instruction for these very young participants. The YMCA recognized that a national program ensuring uniform guidelines for the safety of these children was needed.

In 1982, in conjunction with the Council for National Cooperation in Aquatics, the YMCA published aquatic program guidelines for young children under the age of three. These guidelines established the YMCA's Water Enrichment Program, a child/parent program providing a rewarding experience for both child and adult. Currently, the American Academy of Pediatrics recognizes the revised (1996) YMCA of the USA aquatic guidelines for parents who choose to have their children participate in swim programs for children under the age of three, and it continues to support the work of the YMCA in this area. (See "Aquatic Program Guidelines for Children Under the Age of Three" in appendix A.)

In 1984 the Y began development of its first program for both children under three and their parents and for preschoolers between three- and five-years-old. It was named Y SKIPPERS, and its development was supported by a grant from the United States Coast Guard. The program was released in 1987 and was used until the introduction of the present YMCA Swim Lessons program in 1999.The present Parent/Child and Preschool Aquatic Program Manual was supported by a Wallop-Breaux Trust Fund grant from the United States Coast Guard.

## The Y's Involvement in Swimming Instruction

The YMCA teaches swimming and water safety for several reasons. First, swim lessons serve as an avenue for building character. The Parent/Child and Preschool Aquatic Program incorporates discussion about and draws attention to four core values—caring, honesty, respect, and responsibility. Program activities are designed to help children accept and demonstrate these positive values.

Second, learning to swim and being safe around water are proven long term drowning prevention strategies. With less national and local emphasis today on water safety, many people are needlessly drowning or becoming involved in water-related accidents. YMCA swimming and water safety programs, such as The Parent/Child and Preschool Aquatic Program, can help solve this problem.

Third, learning to swim can help children build self-confidence and self-esteem and contributes to overall child development. Learning swimming skills develops children's abilities and their pride

in what they can do. The Parent/Child and Preschool Aquatic Program is especially appropriate for this development, as children who learn swimming readiness skills early have been found to be better swimmers later on.

Last, swimming programs provide people with avenues for social contacts and opportunities to strengthen family bonds. Classes bring people together in a casual, comfortable atmosphere, and Y instructors try to promote interaction among class members. The Parent/Child Aquatic Program within the Parent/Child and Preschool Aquatic Program emphasizes bonding between parents and their babies. In classes for the Preschool Aquatic Program, parent involvement is encouraged by frequent contacts with parents regarding their children's progress, parenting education through handouts and meetings, and handouts with activities for the whole family.

These reasons for offering swimming instruction are derived from the Y's larger purpose in presenting programs for adults and children. The Y always has seen its programs not as an end in themselves but rather as a means to help people develop and grow. The Y's mission is "to put Christian principles into practice through programs that build a healthy spirit, mind, and body for all." To do this, the Y has created the following seven program objectives. Every YMCA program should help people to

*Grow personally: Build self-esteem and self-reliance.*

- Develop self-esteem. People who are involved in YMCA programs gain a greater sense of their own worth. They learn to treat themselves and others with respect. High self-esteem helps people of all ages to build strong, healthy relationships and to overcome obstacles in life so that they can reach their full potential.

*Teach values: Develop moral and ethical behavior based on Christian principles.*

- Develop character. The YMCA has been helping people develop values for over 150 years. Founded originally to bring men to God through Christ, the YMCA has evolved into an inclusive organization that helps people of all faiths develop values and behavior that are consistent with Judeo-Christian principles. The YMCA believes the four values of caring, honesty, respect, and responsibility are essential for character development. Emphasis is on building a core set of values shared by the world's major religions and by people from all walks of life.

*Improve personal and family relationships: Learn to care, communicate, and cooperate with family and friends.*

- Support families. Today YMCAs are embracing families of all kinds and are more flexible in responding to their needs. Not only do Ys strengthen families through their own programs, but YMCA staff are also increasingly being trained to help families in need or in crisis find other community supports that can help. YMCAs now plan programs and events with today's busy, sometimes frantic, families in mind. Families also get involved in helping plan and run Y family programs. The idea is to program *with* families, not just *for* them.

*Appreciate diversity: Respect people of different ages, abilities, incomes, races, religions, cultures, and beliefs.*

- Reflect the diversity of the community. The country's diversity can be seen in terms of religion, race, ethnicity, age, income, abilities, and lifestyle. Today YMCAs must assess their membership to see if it reflects the diversity of their communities. Diversity is a source of strength. The YMCA will foster an environment where everyone is treated with respect and is able to contribute to the larger community. Diversity should be celebrated, not merely tolerated.

*Become better leaders and supporters: Learn the give and take necessary to work toward the common good.*

- Promote leadership development through volunteerism. The YMCA is driven by volunteer leadership, and today it has a renewed emphasis on providing meaningful volunteer opportunities for all kinds of people, especially youth and families. People are encouraged to move from program participation to deeper levels of involvement, including volunteer leadership. This enriches their lives, their YMCAs, and their communities.

*Develop specific skills: Acquire new knowledge and ways to grow in spirit, mind, and body.*

- Build life skills. YMCA programs, such as employment programs for teens and programs that support activities of daily living for seniors, help people succeed in their daily lives through programs that build self-reliance, practical skills, and good values.
- Have fun—enjoy life!

Fun, enjoyment, and laughter are essential qualities of all programs and contribute to people feeling good about themselves and the YMCA!

For more on the Y's mission and its program philosophy, see the Introduction in *Teaching Swimming Fundamentals.*

## Common Elements With the Youth and Adult Aquatic Program

Swimming instruction for school-age children up to and including adults is offered through the Youth and Adult Aquatic Program. That program has a number of elements in common with the Parent/Child and Preschool Aquatic Program:

- Both are based on the mission of the Y.
- Both have similar program objectives.
- Both work from a student-centered teaching philosophy.
- Both employ developmental approaches to swimming instruction.
- Both have similar program components.

## Aquatic Readiness

Before young children can learn to swim, they need to develop a foundation of interacting skills, attitudes, and understandings that is called aquatic readiness (Langendorfer & Bruya, 1995). These include but are not limited to the following:

- Psychomotor aquatic skills such as water entry, water balance, breath control, buoyancy, arm and leg movements, and coordination
- Attitudes such as showing respect for the water, following water safety principles, observing pool rules for safe participation, and obeying swimming instructors and lifeguards
- Cognitive understandings such as class procedures, pool rules, the language of instruction, games and activity rules, and basic mechanics (buoyancy, submersion)

The level to which each child can achieve readiness is based on his or her cognitive, psychomotor, attitudinal (affective), and social development. Achieving readiness early in the child's life helps him or her develop swimming skills more completely because early learning establishes a strong base.

When instructors understand the order in which swimming skills naturally develop, they can help guide children's experiences in the water. Teaching for aquatic readiness should be purposeful and goal directed, and these goals should be communicated to students and their parents so

they can better understand instruction. Good communication allows students and parents to vary their responses to do what works best for them individually and for the long term.

For example, if an instructor wanted an infant or young child to hold the breath before putting the face in the water, the instructor would first have to help the child to understand what holding the breath means and how to do it. One way to do this might be to blow in the child's face, triggering a breath holding or gasping response. Such an action merely sets off a reflex, however, and likely doesn't teach the child anything. A better approach would be for the instructor to use "1, 2, 3" or another verbal cue before asking the child to put the face into the water. If the cue is used consistently over time, the child learns to use the signal to anticipate being asked to hold his or her breath, thus developing a simple but voluntary movement routine.

## Drowning Prevention

Often parents register their young children in aquatic classes as insurance against drowning. Although the Parent/Child and Preschool Aquatic Program does offer instruction in skills that reduce the possibility of drowning over the long run, no program can guarantee that a child will never drown. We need to educate those parents who enroll their children about the risks and hazards of water as well as the benefits.

Most children are not afraid of water, especially after they have had a good time playing in it! They are too young, however, to fully comprehend the dangers of water. They cannot tell the difference between the shallow water in a tub and the water in a pool, even if they are able to swim a little. And even a small amount of water can drown a child—infants and toddlers have been known to drown in less than a foot of water.

Close supervision of young children is the best way to protect them from drowning. Through the Parent/Child and Preschool Aquatic Program, parents learn how to supervise children in the water, how to prevent accidents, and how to plan for emergencies. It has happened that both a parent and child have drowned when the parent jumped into deep water to rescue the drowning child. Both might have been saved if the parent had known basic rescue techniques.

**Reference**

Langendorfer, Stephen J., and Lawrence D. Bruya. 1995. *Aquatic readiness: Developing Water Competence in Young Children*. Champaign, IL: Human Kinetics.

CHAPTER two

# Role of the Parent/Child and Preschool Aquatic Program Instructor

**The Parent/Child and Preschool Aquatic Program is a unique expression of the YMCA program objectives in an aquatic program for children under the age of five.**

**As an instructor you will be the one to make those objectives come alive through your efforts. You will need to teach, coach, share, model, and always support every participant with a smile.**

With the information you gain from this course and your *Teaching Swimming Fundamentals* course, you can develop your own special way of presenting this program.

Your challenge as a Parent/Child and Preschool Aquatic Program instructor is to accomplish the following:

- Help parents and their young children relate to each other in healthy, enjoyable ways.
- Prepare children for swimming through aquatic readiness experiences.
- Educate parents and children in safe practices in or near water.
- Encourage participants to be positive and enthusiastic.
- Make sure every participant is safe and having fun.

To do this you will need to maintain a positive attitude toward parents and their children. You will be asked to provide quality instruction and to create a supportive, caring environment for class participants. Characteristics that will help you do this include being

- fond of all children,
- knowledgeable about swimming and children's development,
- safety conscious,
- gentle,
- perceptive,
- encouraging,

→ patient,

→ able to communicate with parents,

→ enthusiastic, and

→ creative.

Whether you are teaching a parent/child or a preschool class, the following tips will make your classes more fun for you and your students. Here are some practical suggestions on working with children and parents, a few pointers on how to make young children feel more comfortable in class, and some ideas on solving common class problems.

## Working With Parents and Children

Try the following ideas to develop an upbeat, positive atmosphere in your classes:

→ Talk and work with each child or child/parent team several times during each class. Make eye contact with each child/parent team when you talk. Know everyone's first names and use them frequently.

→ Accept and respect each child and parent as a unique, worthy person.

→ Express warmth and affection toward participants.

→ Listen with care and concern to what participants say, and accept their right—whether adults or children—to have their own feelings.

→ Remember that sustaining each person's sense of self-worth is much more important than teaching a skill or sticking to the day's lesson plan.

→ Help parents in your class to develop open, sharing relationships with each other. Assign them to perform some activities in pairs, and repeat their names often, to give them a chance to get to know each other. Encourage them to become friends.

→ Encourage parents to talk with you or other Y staff members after class or during the week if they have questions or issues to discuss.

→ Use volunteers to help you with the class. Volunteers might be a parent and child who previously attended your class, a grandparent, another adult, a member of your aquatic leaders' club, or a mature student. Extra eyes and hands are useful in the program.

→ Motivate your students and parents with praise and positive, constructive reinforcement. We learn by knowing that what we are doing is right, or nearly right. Some people are uncomfortable with being recognized in front of others; congratulate and praise each person individually, when possible, rather than in front of the group.

- Minimize children's fear and resistance by helping parents establish unique cues and signals for each activity. Through the use of familiar preparation cues, no activity comes as a surprise, and each develops special connections.
- Build the confidence of both children and their parents. Give them warm smiles and genuine praise. Explain goals and objectives simply. Provide a variety of ways to participate in activities successfully so that everyone can achieve some task in whole or in part. Tasks should be structured so that everyone can succeed at some level.
- Establish trust. Only promise those things that you can do, and always do what you promise. For example, don't tell a child that you won't let go of his or her hand and then let go. Encourage parents to establish trust with their children in the same way.
- Ask children to perform only those skills that they are physically and psychologically ready to perform. Reading the "Developmental Characteristics" section of chapter 4 for each level and doing supplemental reading may help you pinpoint the most appropriate activities for the children in your class. Be creative and experiment with different approaches to see what works best with each child.
- When you give feedback, use a "sandwich" approach: Make a positive statement, explain how the task can be performed better, then follow up with another positive statement.

- For children under three, instruct through the parents. For children at this age, the parent should be the child's teacher.
- When you demonstrate an activity or exercise to the whole group, "borrow" a willing child. A child from a more experienced group or a veteran parent/child team who are in the pool at the same time as your class may work well.
- Wear practical swimwear that will stay put despite a baby's clinging to the straps or untying a string, and wear brightly colored swimwear to help make the class more lively.

- Never wear a necklace or dangling earrings, as small children tend to grab them and can injure you or themselves.
- Be playful in the pool. Besides teaching safety and showing that you care, make your class fun.
- Always end the class on an upbeat note, with a fun song, game, or activity performed together. Such a consistent and standard conclusion helps children make the transition from class activities to the end of class. You may also want to have a standard class opening activity.

## Comfort Hints

Although children generally enjoy being in the water, the water environment may cause some of them physical discomfort for a number of reasons. Water is a dense, viscous medium that is very different from the normal land-air environment to which children are accustomed. Water affects a child in these ways:

- Changes the child's center of balance
- Reduces the child's heart rate
- Cools the child's skin/body temperature, both directly through conduction and indirectly through evaporation

- Provides increased resistance to movement
- Necessitates a change in breathing patterns
- May irritate or seem to irritate the skin, eyes, ears, nose, mouth, and lungs

These effects, along with other characteristics of the water, may make children feel not only physical but also psychological discomfort about being in the water. However, we need to tell parents, and to keep in mind ourselves, that a child's discomfort is real to the child, not imaginary. Neither you nor a parent should dismiss a child's fears, discomfort, or reluctance to be in the water, even when it is inconvenient, time consuming, or embarrassing. This section lists some of the more common reactions children may have to water, possible causes of those reactions, and suggestions for helping the children cope.

**Reaction:** Child is fearful or reluctant to enter the water and clings tightly to the parent or to the side of the pool. She may cry, scream, or show reluctance to come to class.

**Possible cause:** Child may not feel in control of her balance due to buoyancy and a raised center of balance.

**Possible solutions:**

- Let the child try shallower water, such as on the pool steps or a ramp, or in an auxiliary pool (could be a small plastic pool on deck).
- Allow a reluctant, fearful child more time to get used to the water.
- Have an adult hold the child, talking soothingly and quietly. Gradually give the child experiences in the water in which she can control her body position and balance.

**Possible cause:** Child doesn't like the coolness of water on his or her skin (or the lowered heart rate that accompanies submersion), or the increased pressure.

**Possible solutions:**

- Keep the pool water temperature as warm as possible (83°–86°F). Increase the air temperature an hour before class starts (2°–4°F above the water temperature).
- Keep the child in the water to reduce evaporation, which cools the skin.

- Place infrared heaters above the shallow end of the pool.
- Have the child wear a light t-shirt while in the water.
- Give the child a chance to get wet slowly, perhaps by starting in a warm shower.

**Possible cause:** Child has had a previous negative experience in or around water (near drowning, aspiration of water and choking, water or air that was too cold, being pushed too much).

**Possible solutions:**

- Eliminate negative associations with the pool (try a different pool, warm the water, keep the child's head above water).
- Give the child time to acclimate to the water slowly and at her own pace.
- Provide colorful, musical, or otherwise interesting toys as distractions.

**Reaction:** Child is shivering, his lips are blue, and/or the skin under his fingernails is blue.

**Possible causes:**

- Child has been chilled by water exposure (usually occurs with a thin or young child).
- Child's normal temperature regulation is not working well due to illness, hunger, fatigue, or individual differences.

**Possible solutions:**

- Remove the child from the water immediately. Dry the child off (especially his head and hair) and/or put the child in a warm shower. Dress the child warmly afterward, with a hat on his head.
- Warm the air or water further, or have the child wear a thin t-shirt in the water.

**Reaction:** Child is coughing, choking, or feels pain in her nose.

**Possible causes:**

- Child has aspirated water due to submersion or a breath control problem.

**Possible solutions:**

- Provide better cues and signals before the child submerges.
- Provide more practice and experience with breath control.
- Practice shipping (holding water in the mouth without swallowing or spitting it out) and spitting water to help the child understand the concept of expelling water rather than breathing it in or swallowing it.

- Encourage the child to breathe in and out mainly through her mouth rather than her nose. (Encourage blowing bubbles through the nose but not breathing in.)
- Have a parent gently press the child's nose with the thumb and index finger to relieve any pain. (Don't put anything in the child's nose, as it could be inhaled into the lungs.)

**Reaction:** Child rubs his eyes, and his eyes are red or swollen after submersion.

**Possible causes:**

- Eye allergy or eye infection
- Normal irritation from pool chemicals

**Possible solutions:**

- Suggest to the parent that the child with an eye allergy or infection see a health care provider.
- For the child with normal irritation, try the following:
  - Ask the child to blink his eyes rapidly instead of rubbing them.
  - Provide the child with a mask or goggles (do not use goggles for underwater swimming or diving).

  - Have the child place a small transparent container filled with cool water over his eyes; instruct the child to practice opening his eyes in the water.
  - Change the pH, alkalinity, or chloramine levels of the pool water.
  - Tell the parent or child not to submerge his eyes for a while.
  - Try very gently wiping the child's eyebrows from the bridge of the nose out, which should keep water from running into the eyes.

**Reaction:** Child with water in his ears complains about the discomfort and about the rumbling sound the water makes or experiences pain in his ears.

**Possible causes:**

- The child is not used to having water in his external ear canal.
- The child has "swimmer's ear" (otitis externa); a middle or inner ear infection (otitis media); or, rarely, a ruptured eardrum (tympanic membrane).

**Possible solutions:**

- If you suspect the child has an ear infection or a ruptured eardrum, or the child is experiencing pain, suggest to the parent that the child see a health care provider.
- If the child has normal discomfort, show him how to lean his head sideways to let the water drain out. (If water retention in the ears is increased by ear wax buildup, suggest to the parent that the child see a health care provider.)
- Have the child submerge with his head vertical, not tipped sideways.

*Note:* Very little evidence exists that infant and preschool swimming either causes, aggravates, or worsens middle ear infections. For many young children, such infections are chronic conditions during early childhood. In fact, much of the research indicates that swimming either doesn't affect these infections or actually helps to eliminate them. Always recommend to parents whose children have middle ear infections that a physician or pediatrician be consulted and that his or her recommendations be followed.

**Reaction:** Child has a distended stomach or produces large amounts of urine within an hour after swim lessons.

**Possible causes:**

- The child is swallowing large amounts of water when partially or fully submerged.

**Possible solutions:**

- Limit the child's number of submersions (see the Aquatic Program Guidelines for Children Under the Age of Three in appendix A).
- Limit the child's number of partial submersions (when the mouth is in or near the water).
- Take the child out of the pool and burp him or her to release air.
- Work with the child on breath control, especially exhaling and expelling water instead of swallowing it.

*Note:* A rare condition called *hyponatremia* (incorrectly called "water intoxication") can result from one of the following:

- Loss of body electrolytes and minerals (through vomiting or diarrhea)
- Ingestion of large amounts of fluid (more than 100 cc/kg or 1/4 cup /1 lb of body weight)
- A combination of both loss of electrolytes and increase in water drunk

Several case studies of hyponatremia related to infant swimming were reported in the medical literature in the early 1980s. Strictly following the Aquatic Program Guidelines will significantly reduce the already very low risk of hyponatremia in young children in YMCA aquatic programs.

**Reaction:** Child frequently requests permission to use the bathroom.

**Possible causes:**

- The child is ingesting or drinking water while submerging.
- The child has a bladder or urinary tract infection.
- The child is upset about some aspect of the swim lesson and is going to the bathroom to avoid it.

**Possible solutions:**

- If the child is ingesting or drinking water while submerging, try the same solutions as for the child who has a distended stomach or produces large amounts of urine.
- If the child seems to have a bladder or urinary tract infection, suggest to the parent that the child see a health care provider.
- If the child seems upset about some aspect of the swim lesson, talk to the child to try to determine the source of his or her distress.
- Regardless of the reason the child goes to the bathroom, he or she needs to shower again before reentering the pool.

## Common Class Problems

Many potential class problems can be anticipated and prevented before they become problems. Orienting participants thoroughly at the beginning of the program, so that everyone understands the goals and the methods to be used, is a good approach for avoiding problems. Another suggestion is to allow time during class for discussion of how the class is going. Airing concerns openly allows for necessary adjustments and encourages ongoing cooperation.

Remember that children and adults often behave the way we expect them to behave. If you expect children to cry, they probably will. Most of the parents and children who participate in the program come to class wanting to learn and expecting to do well and enjoy the experience. Sometimes, however, problems are unavoidable. Fortunately, most of the time these problems are manageable. Here are some problems that commonly occur and some suggestions for dealing with them.

**Problem:** A crying or upset child.

**Solutions:**

- → Help the parent to find out why the child is crying, if possible, and to remedy the cause. Crying can be either a protest or a simple expression of displeasure.
- → Accept the child's behavior; everyone has the right to protest a new or difficult situation.

- → Reassure the parent that everyone understands and still accepts the child.
- → Find an experienced parent/child pair to work with the upset child and his or her parent.

**Problem:** A parent or accompanying adult permits a child to demonstrate uncontrolled or inappropriate behavior.

**Solution:** Take the adult aside privately either during or after class. Explain your concern for the child's and the other children's safety. Encourage all adults to maintain contact with their children at all times when they are in the pool area or are entering or leaving the area.

**Problem:** An adult who deals with a child inappropriately, especially when it is in opposition to the YMCA philosophy and principles.

**Solutions:**

- → Accept the adult's right to his or her own convictions or methods.
- → Approach the adult privately after class to gain a fuller understanding of what he or she is doing. Both of you might learn something.
- → Provide a copy of the YMCA philosophy and principles and explain that these principles are being violated by the adult's actions.
- → If the adult's actions intrude on the class, ask the adult for cooperation and suggest discussing the situation after class.
- → Show the adult a way to work with the child that is more consistent with the program's philosophy and more caring.
- → Openly praise and reinforce acceptable or exemplary parental behavior.

**Problem:** A child who is being aggressive about getting some toy or equipment that is being used by another child.

**Solutions:**

- → Encourage the children's parents to handle the problem.
- → If a child is likely to be harmed, intervene to prevent harm, but talk to the aggressive child's parent immediately to explain the urgency in controlling the child's behavior.
- → Offer the child a special toy of his or her own, preferably one similar to the toy the child wants.
- → Teach all the children to share by taking turns.

**Problem:** A child has a bowel movement or vomits in the pool.

**Solutions:**

- → Make sure all children in the pool are wearing tight-fitting pants (preferably with a plastic cover). Swim diapers or training pants with rubber pants over them are possible options.
- → Encourage children to go to the bathroom just before class starts.
- → If an accident happens, know your state health department and YMCA regulations and enforce them.
- → Use a towel or a leaf strainer to remove the material, or brush it toward the pool gutter.

- If the material is on the deck, cover it with a towel, then make sure it is cleaned up immediately.
- Encourage the child to take a soap shower before reentering the pool.

**Problem:** A child appears to be extremely shy.

**Solutions:**

- Use the child's first name often.
- Smile at him or her with your eyes.
- Assign the child simple duties in the class.
- Ask the child conversational questions.
- Praise the child often.
- Draw the child into conversations with other children.
- Talk about the child's strengths and special skills.
- Make a request of the child to demonstrate a simple skill.
- Invite the child to participate (don't force him or her), even if he or she continues to refuse.
- Don't make a point of the child's shyness. If it comes up, say, "I think [name] will play too in a little while." Encourage the child's parents to treat the shyness in the same way.
- Exercise patience with the child.

**Problem:** A child demonstrates antisocial behavior.

**Solutions:**

- Reassure the child with affection.
- Praise the child when he or she does things right, and correct the child when he or she does something wrong. Always explain to the child what behavior you expect from him or her, and let the child know that it is the negative behavior you don't like, not the child.
- Show the child how to do something, then allow him or her to make comments or ask questions.
- Give the child small responsibilities.
- Keep the child busy.
- Make only a few rules, but enforce them.
- Be patient but firm, and be willing to listen.
- Find out what the child's interests are and try to appeal to them.
- Above all, encourage the other children to talk to and to show interest in this child.
- Let the child learn that positive attention comes from acceptable behavior.

**Problem:** A child who often shows off, especially to get attention from you or his or her peers.

**Solutions:**

- Ask the child to demonstrate something to the group. (Before the demonstration, make sure the child understands how to demonstrate properly whatever skill you have asked to be demonstrated.)
- Encourage the child to participate with the group in acceptable activities whenever possible.
- Do not laugh at pranks. Praise well-disciplined children openly.
- Provide a good role model.
- Use the child's lack of fear in a constructive manner; for example, give the child a role in a scenario.
- Because the child may be seeking approval, give praise when—but only when—the child performs well.
- Let the child know that he or she is liked for himself or herself.

**Problem:** A child who is apathetic.

**Solutions:**

- Make certain that the problem is not physical. Review the child's health history by checking his or her health form or by consulting with the parents or guardian.
- Treat the child as if he or she were doing well.
- Try to determine what interests the child, and discuss those interests.

**Problem:** A child who is hostile.

**Solutions:**

- Let the child express hostility through play.
- Show that you like the child.

- Ask the child's opinion.
- Use the child's suggestions when appropriate.
- Try to get the child to laugh, as he or she is unlikely to be laughing and to be hostile at the same time.
- Ask the child to talk about his or her feelings.
- Take an interest in what the child does.
- Give the child positive feedback and praise for even the smallest accomplishments.
- Talk to the parents about what might be causing the hostility.

**Problem:** A child who is a loner.

**Solutions:**

- Ask the child to help you occasionally but not so often as to alienate him or her from the group.
- Ask for the child's response in class, and create situations in which the child can work with another child easily and cooperatively.
- If the child goes off by him- or herself, talk or tell a story to the rest of the class and refer to the child by name as you talk or tell the story.
- Give the child duties that involve others.
- Let the child know you care; it works.

# The Parent/Child Aquatic Program

**To provide effective leadership to the Parent/Child Aquatic Program, you must be able to do more than just teach swimming readiness; you also should possess the following skills, knowledge, and attitudes:**

- Technical knowledge and skill in developing appropriate water experiences for children under the age of three and in teaching water safety and rescue methods to the children's parents
- Understanding of movement education philosophy, principles, and methods
- Understanding of a parenting philosophy that will help children grow into effective adults
- Knowledge, understanding, and a developmental perspective of the whole child that will contribute to the overall development of children's lifelong health, strength, coordination, and fitness
- Ability to be a leader in class and to relate well to participants, especially in promoting the parenting and physical education philosophies of this program
- Ability to encourage parents to take responsibility for their own and their children's learning, to proceed at their own pace, and to create their own experiences

When you teach Parent/Child Aquatic Program classes, you must be committed to well-planned, individualized goals for both the parents and the children in your classes. The following are general goals for each of the levels in the Parent/Child Aquatic Program:

**Shrimps**

- To introduce babies and parents to an aquatic environment
- To encourage developmentally appropriate expectations by parents of babies enrolled in water enrichment programs
- To introduce basic aquatic safety to parents
- To provide a positive parent/child experience and an opportunity to build the parent/child relationship

### Kippers

- To provide a positive and friendly aquatic environment that will encourage babies and parents to enjoy themselves while learning about the water
- To introduce basic water skills such as kicking, breath control, and body control (or balance)
- To introduce and emphasize basic aquatic safety to parents
- To have fun in the water using toys and flotation devices and interacting with other children

### Inias

- To encourage children's limited but growing independence in the water under the watchful eyes of the parents
- To encourage children to make purposeful movements in the water and movements in response to visual or verbal cues
- To introduce or enhance basic aquatic safety for parents and children
- To provide parents and children the opportunity to share common experiences, to socialize, and to interact with one another

### Perch

- To encourage children to explore their aquatic environment and their own skills in the water with their parents' help
- To encourage children to propel themselves through the water
- To teach basic aquatic and boating safety, emphasizing parental responsibility and allowing children to accept some of the responsibility for safe practices
- To facilitate the children's transition to aquatics at the preschool levels

The next four chapters provide information on teaching the Parent/Child Aquatic Program. They begin with chapter 3, which talks about parents' involvement in the program, followed by chapter 4, which covers developmental concerns and teaching methods for children under three. Chapter 5 describes all the skills in the program and the most appropriate levels for each. The last chapter in part II, chapter 6, provides methods for organizing your parent/child sessions and classes.

CHAPTER three

# Parent Involvement in the Parent/Child Aquatic Program

**One of the most important responsibilities you will have as an instructor for the Parent/Child portion of the Parent/Child and Preschool Aquatic Program is helping parents.**

**In the Parent/Child Aquatic Program, the parents teach the children aquatic skills under your guidance. You also teach the parents directly, not only about working with young children in the water but also about parenting and about water and home safety.**

This chapter begins with ideas for helping parents have a good class experience. It lays out goals for parents and the skills you need to teach parents during the program. The chapter concludes with some defining comments about the relationship between you and the parents.

## Tips for a Successful Class Experience

Parents sometimes can better understand the Y's low-pressure approach to learning about the water if you compare it to the way a child learns to walk. Remind parents at the beginning of the session that they don't really have to teach their children how to walk but that the kids learn to walk on their own by observing and practicing over time; learning to swim can occur in the same manner. Show parents how to reinforce their child's appropriate behavior and to encourage their child whenever he or she performs close to the desired manner.

Water experience offers parents good opportunities to teach their children many important developmental skills, even language skills. Encourage parents to keep repeating the words associated with a skill the child is practicing, such as "kick, kick, kick" and "pull, pull, pull." Tell parents to name various actions, parts of the body, feelings, and experiences as the child encounters them and to keep repeating these words and phrases as the need for them arises. Parents can also ask the child to repeat the words whenever possible.

Encourage parents to have lots of eye and body contact with their children in the pool and to hold them close, especially at first. Also encourage the parents and children to play together. Be enthusiastic and share this enthusiasm by encouraging parents to feel that bringing their children to this class is one of the high points of the week.

## Goals for Parents

Both parents and children have goals in the Parent/Child Aquatic Program. Here are those goals with suggested ways to achieve them.

**Goal:** To promote enjoyable experiences between parent and child in the water.

- Let the parents know that we accept and value each parent and child in the program.
- Emphasize to parents that they should enjoy their time with their child.
- Let the parents know that they are their child's instructor within your class.
- Eliminate competition and encourage cooperation as much as possible.
- Emphasize parents discovering, observing, and participating with their children.
- Encourage parents to hug and kiss their children.

**Goal:** To encourage children to experience, explore, and test the aquatic environment by responding with body movements and emotions, with the assistance and encouragement of their parents. Working toward this goal promotes children's awareness, confidence, and physical abilities.

- Provide a good balance between instructor-initiated and parent-initiated activities. Give parents suggestions for activities and encourage them to suggest activities themselves.
- Help parents to encourage their children to explore at their own individual pace, in their own individual way.
- Encourage parents to enjoy working with their children and to be creative in exploring what they can do together with their children in the water safely.
- Help parents to understand that their children can learn without being taught directly.
- Assist parents to relax and accept each child's individual motivation and abilities. This approach includes times when a child may reject an experience because of fear or other reasons. Stress that this rejection of an activity is not a failure for either the child or the parent. It is not a failure for you as their instructor either.
- Provide a great variety of equipment and suggested activities that will stimulate safe exploration of the water.

**Goal:** To increase parents' ability to help their children enjoy the water and to use it as a medium for developing coordination, strength, fitness, and physical skills.

- Show parents how to lead their children through a series of natural steps that will prepare the children for swimming or aquatic skill instruction as they grow older.
- Work with parents to develop their understanding of the class goals and to have realistic expectations about children's development of the ability to swim. This is a water adjustment and orientation program, not one that teaches infants to swim. Demonstrate methods of helping children feel secure and relaxed in the water.
- Help parents become aware of their own emotions during class and the effect of those emotions on their children.

- Explain to parents each child's capacity for learning skills based on that child's developmental abilities.
- Encourage parents to realize that each child learns at his or her own pace and should not be compared with other children. Explain that they need to be patient if their child is taking longer than expected to learn a skill and that their child may later progress more rapidly. Help them look for the positive aspects of their child's performance.
- Support parents to learn methods of increasing children's motivation and building children's confidence by helping children to succeed and reinforcing desired behavior. Encourage them to dare to let their children try and fail—and still feel loved. This process is a natural part of learning.
- Demonstrate a great variety of appropriate ways to explore the water environment using a logical progression of experiences that can develop skills.

**Goal:** To improve the parents' parenting skills, which will enrich and strengthen family life and promote the appropriate psychosocial development of the children.

- Help parents to deal with their children as people, to become aware of and understand what their children are experiencing.
- Support parents to become aware of, acknowledge, and accept their children's expressions of emotion.
- Help parents to become aware and accepting of their own emotions and to find appropriate ways to express those feelings to their children.
- Make parents aware of the many different ways their children may try to communicate with them, even though the children are not yet speaking much. Show them how to listen and how to let children know you are listening.
- Help parents to understand how to use positive reinforcement to encourage desired behavior.
- Explain to parents that individual children develop motor and social skills on different timetables.
- Help parents to be aware of and to value the uniqueness of each child, to give each child unconditional love, and to see each child's strengths positively.
- Support parents to become aware of their role in developing children's feelings of self-worth.
- Help parents to develop an appropriate balance between controlling a child and giving the child freedom of choice.
- Help parents to see how they can develop practices that enrich and strengthen their families.

**Goal:** To enhance parents' skill in providing the conditions and experiences in early childhood that will lead to lifelong health and fitness for their children.

- Help parents see how they are role models of healthy (or unhealthy) living for their children.
- Support parents to understand how early health and fitness attitudes influence such attitudes throughout life.
- Explain health and safety hazards around the home, and provide parents with appropriate steps to take to safeguard their children.
- Help parents understand the basic exercise needs of children as they grow. Explain how they can use effective movement exploration approaches to enhance the development of strength, flexibility, and coordination while helping their children enjoy the movement experience.

**Goal:** To provide opportunities for the personal growth and physical fitness of parents.

- Help each parent to feel accepted and valued as a person.
- Accept each parent's way of relating to his or her child.
- Help parents see themselves as capable parents who can be responsible for their children's development both in and out of class.
- Encourage parents to assess their own fitness, to set fitness goals, and to adopt programs to increase their own fitness.

**Goal:** To provide parents and children with enjoyable interactions with other parents and children in the class.

- Help parents become personally acquainted with other parents.
- Provide opportunities for sharing and learning among parents.
- Encourage contacts among children and among parents and other children.

**Goal:** To increase parents' knowledge of water safety and ability to provide for the safety of their children in and around water.

- Help parents learn to identify hazardous conditions in and around water. A home water safety checklist can help them look for particular hazards in their homes.
- Make parents aware of the need for continuous adult supervision of children around water.
- Explain the importance of multiple barriers for backyard pools, such as child proof door and window latches and locks, and a self-latching and locking gate.
- Help parents learn the difference between life jackets and flotation devices and the proper uses of each.
- Explain to parents that most children in this age group probably cannot swim well consistently and most likely will not do so until they are almost school-age.
- Teach parents the elementary forms of rescue, including rescue techniques, rescue breathing, CPR, how to get help, and basic first aid.
- Help parents understand the health concerns of swimming for children under three, which include lowered body temperature, fatigue, ear and other infections, lowered resistance, and the possible spread of contagious disease because of the group setting, and help them to recognize symptoms caused by these hazards.

Because class time is limited, you can only do so much to reach the aforementioned goals in class. Good planning, however, can increase the number of opportunities you have to share information with parents. Here are some suggested methods of communicating with parents:

- Take advantage of appropriate moments during class to talk about relevant topics. For example, if one of the children appears to be cold, encourage the parent to warm the child, then make a general

comment to the class about the effect of lowered body temperature on resistance to infection (colds and the flu) and on the child's enjoyment of the class.

- Give parents handouts, starting from the day they sign up for the class. Handouts can deal with both health issues and family enrichment. For instance, you can give parents a handout that lists some of the teaching principles you will be trying to get them to use with their children.
- Hold a parent orientation before classes start. This setting gives you a chance to answer questions and to discuss any issues you may not have time for during class.
- Give parents homework assignments. You can ask them to practice something at home or to observe some particular thing in their children before the next class. One example would be to ask them to have the other parent get in the tub with the child and practice one of the activities from class. Another would be to ask them to observe their children's eating, sleeping, and playing patterns on the days when they go to the Y to see if they can notice any differences. Still another example would be asking them to count how many times in one day they can be aware of and praise their children for good behavior.
- Schedule an extra class that meets in a classroom instead of in the pool. Provide child care during this class so you can talk with the parents without distractions. Discuss what is happening in the class, things such as what parents are enjoying or finding frustrating, or questions about children's diets. Some Ys schedule such extra classes a couple times during each session, meeting for about 30 to 45 minutes before or after a regular pool lesson.
- Provide a gathering place where parents and children can get snacks and drinks before or after class. This allows for informal discussion of issues and more interaction among class members so they can get to know each other.
- Create a family resource area of books, magazines, and reprints of articles on parenting, health, family activities, and other related topics; also include information about community organizations and programs relevant for families with young children. Let parents borrow or take these resources home.

## Skills for Parents

Although teaching the children skills is an important part of the Parent/Child Aquatic Program, parents also are learning in these classes. To participate fully, they will need to develop water skills, safety skills, and skills in playing with their children in developmentally appropriate ways.

The water skills that parents should learn and be able to perform with their children during the Parent/Child Aquatic Program are these:

- Enter and exit the pool safely.
- Demonstrate the skills taught during classes.
- Help the child relax and be comfortable in the water.
- Have fun in the water with the child.
- Execute the appropriate holding techniques for various skills.
- Learn how to help the child use instructional flotation devices (IFDs).
- Participate in structured and unstructured play activities with the child in the water.
- Learn the activities that are appropriate for the infant for the next developmental phase.

Parents also should learn the following safety skills:

- Know how to prevent water emergencies for the child and family.
- Be able to handle common water emergencies by using reaching and throwing assists.
- Become familiar with basic water safety and boating safety.
- Encourage the child to use safe practices around the water.

Encourage parents to develop and play appropriate water activities and games with their babies and toddlers. Games or learning activities should meet these guidelines:

- The infant or young child should be an active participant. The response or movement should be controlled mainly by the infant or young child, not primarily by the parent's moving the infant or young child.
- The infant should be held in a stable position, preferably with the chin at water level.
- The infant's mouth and face should go under the water only if the infant submerges the mouth and face by him- or herself.

- Games and learning activities might involve a toy or another infant or adult.

Within the program, additional important information can be communicated to parents through handouts, demonstrations, and discussions. Handouts for this program are in the *YMCA Swim Lessons Administrator's Manual*. Topics covered in the handouts include the following:

### *Water Safety*

Aquatic Program Guidelines for Children Under the Age of Three

Backyard Pool Safety

Beach Safety

Pool Safety

Water Safety

Waterpark Safety

### *Boating Safety*

Boat Smart From the Start: U.S. Coast Guard-Approved Personal Flotation Devices

Boating Safety

The HELP Position: Maintaining Body Temperature

*Health Safety*

Immunization

Poisoning Prevention

Sudden Infant Death Syndrome (SIDS)

Sun Safety

*Accident Prevention*

Babysitter Tips

Home Safety

Toy Safety

*Child Development*

Shrimps

Kippers

Inias

Perch

The First Years Last Forever: Tips for Parents and Caregivers

*Character Development*

Character Development and Young Children

YMCA Parent Tips: Building Your Child's Self-Esteem

*Child Abuse Prevention*

Our Bodies Belong to Ourselves: What Is Child Sexual Abuse?

Words Can Hurt, Too: Child Emotional Abuse

"Hands-Off" Discipline: Preventing Child Physical Abuse

*Family Enrichment*

Areas for Family Enrichment

YMCA Parent Tips: Beating the Frantic Family Syndrome

YMCA Parent Tips: Putting Fun Into Your Family Life

Tips for Family Volunteering

What Could a Family Be?

*Parenting Tips*

Parenting

Parenting Principles

Look for additional material in other resources on children's aquatics, first aid, safety, and parenting.

## Relationship Between Instructor and Parents

Most parents know a good deal about their children and sometimes about child development; however, they may not have much aquatic expertise. You should attempt to maximize the knowledge that parents already have by encouraging them to share it, but do not forget that you are the aquatic expert. You are there to inform the parents and guide them in aquatic activities, especially those involving their young children. Parents should be involved in aquatic-related decisions regarding their children, but those decisions should be based on the best available information. You can encourage parents to develop their own aquatic activities with their children, but you should provide the guidelines for developing those activities.

When necessary, remind parents of pertinent child development information. Encourage them to accept individual differences in development and to involve their children in as much of the decision making as possible.

Remember that, in this program, the parents are learning as well as the children. Help them understand what they are learning, whether it is a new way to relate positively to their children or a new method for helping their children to relax in the water. Tell parents what to expect of their children, both positively and negatively. Try to build trust between you and the parents; treat them with respect and follow through on whatever you say you will do for them.

Parents may occasionally ask you questions or share with you childcare problems that are beyond your expertise. When they ask for information that is best available from a physician, social worker, or psychologist, either refer them to appropriate resources within the Y or other community organizations or suggest that they contact their family physician or a member of the clergy. If a question concerning child development or specifics about babies and swimming seems beyond your scope, saying an honest "I don't know, but I'll help you find an answer" earns more respect than a vague or incorrect response. Also, other parents in the group often have valuable experiences or helpful sources to share. Call on the parents in the class to help each other.

CHAPTER four

# Teaching the Children

**Teaching infants and young children in the Parent/Child and Preschool Aquatic Program differs from teaching older children and adults.**

**First, these young children are not as developed physically, socially, or cognitively as are older children and adults. You must work within their present abilities while preparing children under three for future growth.**

Second, in the parent/child portion of this program, you actually teach the children through the parents. You are guiding the parents to instruct their children one-on-one.

In this chapter you will find useful ideas for teaching infants and toddlers. The chapter begins with a description of relevant characteristics at various stages of development, including parenting tips for each stage that you can pass along. This is followed by a description of some techniques that should work with these young children and an explanation of the importance of following an appropriate skill progression. The next section explores the use of individual flotation devices and gadgets and toys in lessons, and the chapter ends with some notes on safety and health.

## Developmental Characteristics

Before you teach young children, you should have a good idea of what children within a general age range usually are capable of doing. This information will help you form realistic expectations for those children and allow you to choose age-appropriate activities that the children will enjoy.

Figures 4.1 through 4.4 list some of the skills that children between 6 and 36 months, on average, have at particular developmental stages, according to the four levels (Shrimps, Kippers, Inias, and Perch) used in the Parent/Child Aquatic Program. The figures also include some parenting tips that you can pass along to the parents in your class. For more detailed information on children's development, refer back to Table 2.1 in *Teaching Swimming Fundamentals*. Review this basic developmental information whenever you develop your lesson plans.

Remember that, like adults, every child is a unique individual. These descriptions are only generalizations, not rigid age norms.

**Figure 4.1 Developmental Characteristics of Shrimps**

**6-8 months**

| Motor Skills | Social Skills | Cognitive Skills | Parenting Tips |
|---|---|---|---|
| • Should be able to hold head upright when lying on stomach<br>• May attempt to roll over and may be difficult for the parent to hold<br>• May splash and kick the water spontaneously<br>• May begin crawling<br>• Plays with feet<br>• Examines hands inquisitively and demonstrates a powerful grip and grasping motion using all four fingers<br>• Has a high center of gravity because of a large head and a relatively long torso<br>• May grasp small objects using forefinger and thumb<br>• May roll from stomach to back or from back to stomach | • May show stranger anxiety<br>• Plays simple games with parents such as Peek-a-Boo and Pat-a-Cake<br>• May enjoy repeating adults' actions but does not share in the traditional sense<br>• Is self-oriented; likes to repeat actions over and over as part of mastering them<br>• Reacts positively to praise | • May be fascinated with small toys and floating objects (make sure such toys and objects do not have parts that are small enough on which to choke)<br>• Can recognize own name and words such as Ma-ma and Da-da<br>• May understand more words, such as those describing body parts<br>• Places most objects in the mouth (again, try to eliminate access to objects small enough that a child could choke on them)<br>• May visually explore the environment<br>• May search for partially hidden objects (beginning of understanding of object permanence) | • Make an effort to have fun in class.<br>• Use repetition and consistency; it makes your child feel secure.<br>• Maintain eye contact with your child.<br>• Move slowly and speak to your child in a soft and reassuring tone.<br>• Expect only a smile as a signal of acknowledgment at this age.<br>• Be gentle; your child may be injured easily by sudden or forceful actions.<br>• Create a safe yet challenging environment for your child.<br>• Provide stimulating activities at the beach, when on a trip (especially visual stimuli), or at home to keep your child happy and learning.<br>• Just as your child may imitate your actions, you should lovingly imitate your child's sounds and actions; this is a good way to share and communicate.<br>• To share sights and sounds with your child, point out what you are doing or what you are holding in your hand.<br>• Try playing Peek-a-Boo with your child to build his or her confidence that you won't disappear.<br>• Never leave your baby alone in or near water, bathtubs, toilets, buckets, baby pools, or home pools even for a second. |

## Figure 4.2 Developmental Characteristics of Kippers

### 9-12 months

#### Motor Skills

- Sits, crawls, or creeps and pulls to a stand
- Physically is growing very rapidly; may be cutting teeth
- Begins to explore, climb, and stand
- Tries to climb on anything; may begin climbing up stairs (not down, initially)
- Uses pincer motion when grasping
- May crawl onto couches and tables and into various places
- May begin to walk with assistance; walks unsteadily
- Enjoys pulling objects toward him- or herself or pulling his or her body toward objects

#### Social Skills

- Plays Peek-a-Boo or Pat-a-Cake with adults
- May imitate simple gestures
- Begins to show a unique, individual personality
- Is developing a social character; is friendly to some people and unfriendly to others
- May be anxious with strangers because of new awareness of the environment and others
- Has many new socially meaningful behaviors: laughing, waving, showing off, and so on
- May cooperate in dressing and feeding
- Enjoys imitating adult actions like opening and closing a book, playing with a toy telephone, playing with plastic keys

#### Cognitive Skills

- Responds to own name and familiar objects
- Understands the words *yes, no,* and *bye-bye*
- Looks and listens with great interest; makes eye contact constantly in a group setting
- Mouths everything
- Has a limited capacity to understand danger (such as dangers associated with water, falling, or poisoning)
- Developing cognitively, depending on ability to move around

#### Parenting Tips

- Have fun in class.
- Use repetition; it makes your child feel more secure.
- Childproof your home so that your infant can begin to move about freely and explore independently.
- Play simple games and activities using familiar words such as your child's name and the names of toys or household objects.
- Talk to your child regularly.
- Listen to your child's attempts at speech.
- Give your child lots of safe things to explore and manipulate in and out of the water.
- Expect and accept growing independence.
- Smile when your child smiles, and respond reciprocally to other actions.
- Try using imagination in play, for example, playing bye-bye or talking on a play phone.
- Establish a safe exploring space, such as a rock-free fenced yard, a big box, or a childproof room.
- Praise your child for accomplishments.
- Give your child plenty of affection and reinforcement.
- Encourage independent movement under your supervision.
- Never leave your baby alone in or near water, bathtubs, toilets, buckets, baby pools, or home pools even for a second.

**Figure 4.3** Developmental Characteristics of Inias

**13-18 months**

### Motor Skills

- Walks upright alone; climbs stairs (learns to go up first, then down) and enjoys climbing
- Rolls a ball on the floor
- Opens and closes things such as boxes, doors, or latches repeatedly

### Social Skills

- Plays slightly more complicated games with parents (may have simple rule structure)
- May start to refuse simple commands and ignore limits set by parents
- Demonstrates parallel play with other children; little interaction takes place during play
- Often is sociable only with familiar adults
- Begins to socialize a little with other children but may show aggressive and unacceptable social behavior

### Cognitive Skills

- Has developed the concept of object permanence, the awareness that objects still exist when out of sight
- Does not understand danger (such as danger from falling or poisoning)
- Can use objects functionally
- Understands simple commands
- Can identify one or two body parts on request
- Begins creative play
- Needs outlet for imagination: crayons and paper, pots and pans, wooden blocks, objects for putting in and taking out of containers
- Learns by experimenting
- Imitates and learns patterns; learns quickly if an action is repeated and reinforced each day or very often
- Tastes almost everything

### Verbal Skills

- Uses simple words to communicate; first words are names of objects
- Indicates wants by pointing, pulling, or vocalizing
- Says *no* as an expression of independence and development (which is good, even if it is frustrating to parents)
- Understands more words than he or she can say

### Parenting Tips

- Childproof your home so that your child can move about freely and explore independently.
- Supervise your child closely at all times, as the child is very active and may try dangerous activities without understanding the risk.
- Never leave your baby alone in or near water.
- Maintain eye contact with your child as much as possible.
- Try body contact, including hugging and holding close, to comfort an anxious child.
- Make instructions simple and direct.
- Say the names of objects, body parts, and actions as they are encountered.
- Use positive reinforcement.
- Set reasonable limits for child behavior but encourage autonomy.
- Try color identification games with your child.
- Because children this age enjoy pulling but often have little opportunity to pull, try some good pulling activities.
- Remember that children this age do not share but instead engage in parallel play.
- Praise independent actions.
- Ignore or redirect your child's negative behavior, and reinforce good behavior positively.
- Encourage development of manual dexterity by providing your child with such playthings as crayons or toys that need building or putting together.
- Never leave your baby alone in or near water.

## Figure 4.4 Developmental Characteristics of Perch

**19-36 months**

| Motor Skills | Social Skills | Cognitive Skills | Verbal Skills | Parenting Tips |
|---|---|---|---|---|
| • Runs, jumps, climbs up and down<br>• Kicks a stationary ball with a simple step and a punch of the leg at the ball<br>• Throws a small ball overhand or underhand a short distance, with a rudimentary arm-dominated pattern<br>• May be able to stand on one foot momentarily<br>• Jumps off the floor with both feet simultaneously, especially if supported<br>• Moves very quickly | • Can be separated from parent without undue anxiety<br>• Is interested in new games and experiences<br>• Enjoys interacting with one or two other children<br>• Is ready to share objects and ideas | • Has a vivid imagination, even imaginary friends<br>• Understands most of what is said<br>• Is beginning to form gender identity<br>• Shows interest in bladder and bowel control (after two years of age) | • Has a vocabulary of 50 words or more<br>• Can communicate many needs verbally and nonverbally<br>• Refers to self by name<br>• Can call the instructor by name<br>• Begins to use two words together<br>• Understands more words than he or she can say | • *Never* turn your back on your child, even for a second; at this age children need constant supervision to keep them safe.<br>• Childproof your house. If you have a pool, spa, hot tub, or sauna in your home, make sure sufficient barriers are present, such as locked doors, windows, or gates, to prevent your child from entering the water.<br>• Encourage verbal expression.<br>• Name actions, objects, and body parts for your child.<br>• Praise your child for good behavior.<br>• Provide opportunity for peer contact.<br>• Encourage sharing toys and belongings.<br>• Reinforce understanding of sizes, shapes, and colors.<br>• Encourage gross motor skills like running, jumping, throwing, or climbing.<br>• Use real names for body parts and functions.<br>• Remember that everyone must wear a personal flotation device (PFD) during boating activities. Give your child a simple chore, such as putting away PFDs, as a safe outlet for her or his energy and the need to be active.<br>• Encourage creative behavior; limit it only when safety is jeopardized.<br>• Recognize your child's ideas as valid; encourage independent thinking.<br>• Never leave your child alone in or near water. |

## Teaching Techniques and Procedures

In the Parent/Child Aquatic Program parents act as teachers for their children, so you must provide parents with the information necessary to handle their children in the water. Parents' use of the appropriate techniques for holding, towing, and entering and exiting the pool will allow their children to try beginning swimming skills because the children will feel secure about being in the water. You also must teach parents about accident prevention and water safety as well as some basic rescue techniques in case of a water emergency.

By using the proper techniques yourself, you can ensure that parents and their children will have an enjoyable experience. First, remember that this entire experience depends on trust—the parents' trust in you as a qualified instructor and the children's trust in their parents. One important aspect of trust is respect for the individual. The feelings and thoughts of both the child and parent must be considered at all times. When a parent or a child is uncomfortable with an activity, respect his or her feelings. Often explaining why an activity is being done (and there should be a sound educational reason for every activity you do) is enough to make a parent comfortable with that activity. Children who are treated with patience and respect usually do everything that the rest of the class is doing but on their own timetable. Allow each person, parent or child, to go through the sequence of activities and skills at his or her own pace.

Most of the activities in this manual are designed to allow individual progression; however, for activities performed as a group, such as singing, you must consider individual differences. If some children or parents do not work well in a group, give them time, space, and an opportunity for them to work through the activity on their own or to substitute another activity.

Encourage parents to accept their children's progress and to be patient and loving with their children, regardless of their children's responses to the classes, the water, the group situation, or you. It may help to explain the following guidelines to parents:

- Children have good days and bad days, just like adults. Factors such as changes in routine, the state of their health, and stress can affect how children act in class.
- Children typically dislike the same things in the water that they dislike on land (e.g., being tossed into the air or spun around in a circle).
- Moving into a new environment may cause anxiety for either the parent or the child. Children often sense the anxiety or uncertainty of their parent and react negatively. This reaction may be mistaken for fear or dislike of the water on the child's part.
- Having a routine develops trust, but breaking a routine can weaken it. Even the smallest "white lie" can reduce your child's trust, for example, telling a child you will hold his or her hand and then letting go.
- Always try to end your time in the water while the children are happy, would like to stay, and are having fun.

Three important principles to remember when teaching parent/child classes are sequential progression and skill mastery, modeling, and signaling and cuing. These principles are discussed next.

### Sequential Progression and Skill Mastery

Parent/child activities are organized so that, within each class and level, and between levels, skills build on each other. This organization is called a *teaching progression*, and it is based upon a developmental perspective. Because the skills are organized in a sequential fashion, you should allow children to master each skill before attempting more difficult ones. Their future success is based on their past success, which comes from mastering the basic skills through practice.

This mastery concept applies to all skills within a category; for example, pool entry skills move from baby wait, to climbing in, to stepping in, to jumping in. Stroking skills move from front towing to towing with arm and leg action, and backstroking moves from back cradles to a back float.

Sometimes prerequisites come from another category of skills. When this happens, those prerequisites are specified. For example, before using instructional flotation devices (IFDs), the student must master the breath control skill of putting the face in the water. Expect each student to progress and develop mastery at his or her own rate.

### Modeling (Imitating)

Just as children learn to walk by watching others walk, by practicing, and by having the prerequisite skills, they also learn to swim by watching; practicing; and, when they have the prerequisite skills, accomplishing. Working with children of differing abilities is difficult for the instructor, but it allows the children to watch each other and to model important motor skills. Children will also model their parents and other adults. If a child sees that everyone is happy and comfortable in the water during a swim lesson, the child may try to model those behaviors. Parental demonstration of aquatic skills and, when possible, demonstration by infants and young children also can be helpful.

### Signals and Cues

Modeling is more effective when it is tied to signals and cues. Tell parents that when they introduce a new skill to a child they should

- give a name to the skill,
- give a signal, and
- demonstrate the skill for the child.

Parents should allow plenty of time for the child to develop each basic skill. This is especially important for the first few classes. The child will use the parent's demonstration as a cue or signal for imitation or action. After some practice the child should be able to identify the skill by the name that the parent has given it and may execute the skill when the parent signals.

Before the child performs a skill, the parent should name the skill and give the unique signal for that skill. If the child does not respond with the appropriate action, the parent should name the skill again, give the signal, and then demonstrate the skill. The parent should then say, "your turn," name the skill, and give a signal. Both parents and instructors must be careful to consistently use the same signals and cues for each activity so children can learn what to expect.

## Skill Progression

The activities chosen for the Parent/Child Aquatic Program were designed to be enjoyable for both parent and child. These activities represent some of the natural steps that will prepare the child to be able to swim later. The way the activities are done is more important than the activities themselves. Some important principles that need to be reinforced to parents are these:

- Class activities are fun and playful—for both you and your child.
- The only failure is the failure to enjoy the experience.
- Make progress slowly and patiently at your child's natural pace.
- Do not force your child beyond what he or she is willing to try.
- Build trust and do not betray it.
- Communicate with your child constantly at his or her level:
  - Listen with care and respect and be aware of what your child is experiencing.
  - Continually let your child know what will happen next. Tell him or her what to expect by showing, touching, and tone of voice.
  - Constantly express to your child your appreciation, satisfaction, enjoyment, and love. Keep comfortably close body contact.

Motor skills develop in a predictable, orderly progression. Some skills normally are learned before other skills. Each skill itself changes and improves over time, and each individual changes at his or her own rate. A child may acquire several skills rapidly during a particular time period, while consolidating and improving the skills already learned, but then develop no new skills for a period after this time of rapid growth. These differences in a child's learning curves are normal, as are individual differences in learning among children.

All children need to feel comfortable, confident, and competent. Comfort is not established just by caring for a child's physical needs; it also requires consistency, uniformity, and routine. Children under three will be more comfortable in a situation in which there is as little change as possible. Confidence evolves in part from routine (knowing what is going to happen next), a loving and caring environment, and a sense of self-competence. Competence is a result of reaching challenging, yet attainable, goals. Although each child is allowed to progress at his or her own rate, the goals set at that rate must still be challenging and appropriate. Your task as an instructor is to establish goals with the parent and child's help, providing activities that will lead to the child's success in the water and will make the child feel positive about her or his accomplishments.

## Use of Instructional Flotation Devices (IFDs)

Using instructional flotation devices (IFDs) with infants and children under three can allow them to practice their head control, balance, and nonweight-supporting locomotion. Select the type of IFD to be used based on the primary purpose of the activity: to facilitate development of movement skills, to develop swimming skills, or to have fun. In general a device that holds the child in a vertical position with the chin at water level works well. The parent, with his or her own hands under the water, should gently hold the child's hand or wrist, or should place his or her hands under the child's armpits. When the child is comfortable with floating, he or she will let go, or the parent can gradually release the child.

Instructors and parents have varying opinions about the use of flotation devices for children under three. If you follow these three guidelines, however, you can avoid most of the problems associated with such devices:

1. Make sure that the use of IFDs does not replace other aquatic activities performed without IFDs; instead, let the use of flotation devices *supplement* and support other activities.
2. See that the use of flotation devices is not the first or last activity of the class but that this activity is always preceded and followed by other activities.
3. IFDs should be used as aids to make instruction more successful. They should not be used outside the instructional setting.

The bottom line on the use of IFDs is that they should support and assist a child in succeeding at moving in the water. They should not be used as a replacement for other appropriate instruction or for parental supervision. For more information on the appropriate use of IFDs, see chapter 4 of *Teaching Swimming Fundamentals*.

## Gadgets and Toys

Gadgets and toys make playtime fun and can help children adjust to the water. They are aids for playtime as well as for skill instruction. Parents can help provide many of these items. Here are some examples:

- Large objects such as a rubber (sealed foam) gym mat on which several youngsters can hang at a time
- Rubber rafts or inflatable boats
- Large, floating inflatable toys

- Small, floating toys with no detachable parts that can be placed in the mouth
- Nonfloating, brightly colored toys
- Hoops
- Diving rings, metal mirrors, racquet balls, dowels, pieces of rope
- Plastic stools, benches, or aquatic steps to stand on that are heavy enough to sink
- Plastic flowers attached to weighted bottoms
- Toys that squirt, spray, or make noise
- Balls of various sizes
- Soap bubbles
- Buckets and watering cans, cups

Use any objects that can be made safe and that encourage fun, playing, and exploring. Be certain that objects have no sharp edges, cannot break readily, and do not have parts that are small enough to be swallowed. Parents should supervise children's play with these objects.



## Safety

An important element of the Parent/Child Aquatic Program is keeping participants safe during class and teaching them procedures for being safe in the water away from the Y. Much of what parents and children learn in class can be transferred to other aquatic situations.

## Safety at the Y

The pool can be dangerous for babies and young children because of the water, but other areas in and around the pool can be hazardous as well. Locker rooms contain a number of dangers:

- Tile floors often are wet and may be soapy, making them slippery.
- Benches may be fairly high off the floor, presenting a danger of babies falling off and injuring themselves.
- Lockers may become attractive hiding places for toddlers, who may inadvertently lock themselves in.
- Saunas, hot tubs, and whirlpools or spas should be off limits for children in this program, as children below the age of five cannot tolerate the levels of heat these devices generate. Hot tubs and whirlpools or spas also carry the risk of drowning. Barriers should be used to prevent children from accidentally entering them.

The pool deck and the edge of the pool can present a risk of injury to infants and young children, too. They can injure the teeth, chin, and back of the head as they get into or out of the pool, so parents closely supervise while children crawl on or slide over the side of the pool.

Be sure to warn the parents in your classes about these dangers. Explain these safety concerns, and give parents suggestions on how to avoid unsafe situations.

Some special health and safety concerns arise when babies are in an aquatic environment, such as the appropriate water temperature or limits on the number of immersions per class. Appendix A, Aquatic Program Guidelines for Children Under the Age of Three, explains the Y's stance on these topics. Read this document so you know the Y's policy on these concerns.

## Safety Away From the Y

Parents should know the location of all sources of water (such as pools or lakes) near their residences and should plan ahead for their children's safety. If a child has even a remote possibility of gaining access to water—whether it involves a hot tub, a wading pool, a bathtub, or a toilet—an adult must constantly watch the child, or access must be blocked by several barriers (such as fences and self-latching and self-locking doors, windows, and gates). Any infant or child should be allowed near any water source only when accompanied by a responsible adult. When aquatic activities other than swimming are planned, such as a boating trip or a picnic by a lake or river, everyone should wear a PFD at all times.

For planned swimming away from the Y, continuing a routine similar to the one used at the Y is helpful for safety purposes as well as instructional ones. A child who only enters the water from a designated location at the request of an instructor or parent is less likely to rush into the water before adequate adult supervision is available. In addition, the parent will develop the habit of being in the water when the child enters the water.

The two main keys to aquatic safety are planning ahead and establishing a routine that diminishes the probability of a child's entering the water without direct adult supervision.

## Boating Safety

Learning to swim is just one aspect of YMCA Swim Lessons that helps children be safer around water; another is teaching them boating safety. Many people now boat, but they may not be aware of the dangers of boating and open water or what to do in case of a water emergency. By teaching boating safety to children in swim classes, we can make sure they are aware of the fundamentals. Those students also share handouts and ideas from class with their families, making family members more aware as well.

You may notice in the manual that we are using rafts to demonstrate boating safety skills. Because we are teaching mainly in swimming pools, it can be more practical to use rafts than boats. While these types of rafts may be appropriate for teaching basic boating safety skills, be sure to point out the difference between the actions of the rafts used in class (which are flexible and pliable) and actual boats (which have rigid boat hulls).

CHAPTER *five*

# Parent/Child Aquatic Program Skills

**The skills in the parent/child portion of the Parent/Child and Preschool Aquatic Program are arranged in a specific skill progression based on general developmental norms and changes.**

**This means that, if you have an older child join your class, you may need to have that child participate and move through the earlier level activities to make sure he or she acquires the appropriate levels of readiness.**

Usually the older child can accomplish this relatively quickly. For example, a child who joined a Perch-level class and was developmentally ready at the Perch level would actually participate in activities from the Shrimps, Kippers, Inias, and Perch levels.

The class components for each of the Parent/Child Aquatic Program levels are the same:

- Personal safety
- Personal growth
- Stroke development
- Water sports and games
- Rescue

The skills taught at each level are shown in Table 5.1.

The stroke development component is further broken down into the following categories:

- *Water adjustment*, including skills and tasks such as water entry and exit, getting wet, climbing out of the pool, and independent water entry
- *Breath control*, including tasks such as blowing bubbles, shipping or expelling water, holding the breath, bubbling, and submerging
- *Balance*, including buoyancy, body positions, and changing positions
- *Locomotion*, including front towing, knee balance, arm patterns, leg patterns, back cradle, back towing, launch, and the use of instructional flotation devices (IFDs)

**Table 5.1 Skills by Level by Children**

**Component:**
**Stroke Development**

| Shrimp | Kipper | Inia | Perch |
|---|---|---|---|
| • Has happy expression in the water | • Is supported by parent in the water with minimal holding by child | • Enters pool eagerly from a sitting position on the side at the parent's request | • Relaxes in both the front and back float positions |
| • Has relaxed muscles; sense of fun while being held close | • Imitates parent by putting the face in the water | • Puts face in the water and blows bubbles without swallowing water | • Allows another adult to hold in the water |
| • Blows bubbles spontaneously | • Relaxes in both the front towing and back cradle position | • Ships and expels water on cue | • Inhales and blows out independently |
| • Blows bubbles on request or signal | • Blows bubbles on cue | • Negotiates to various locations independently while wearing an IFD | • Stands without aid in shallow water |
| • Puts mouth in and out of the water without swallowing when chin is held at water level | • Ships and expels water on cue | • Climbs out of pool with assistance | • Moves body parts on request, including kicking and arm motions |
| • Remains stable while in towing position with minimal parental support | • Balances on parent's knee without support of parent's hand | • Turns from 180 to 360 degrees while wearing an IFD | • Changes positions and directions while wearing an IFD |
| • While wearing an IFD, turns 180 degrees by turning the head | • Focuses on parent's face during towing to remain stable | • Controls body position while putting face in the water and taking face out of the water | • Controls body position while putting face in the water |
| • Kicks or wiggles legs while being towed | • Maintains stable vertical position in an IFD without parental support | • Maintains stable vertical position in an IFD without parental support | • Enters and exits the pool without help by climbing |
| • Kicks on cue or signal | • Kicks while in towing position | • Kicks or moves arms on request | • Moves through water a short distance (5 to 10 feet) without help |
| • Positions in the water while being cradled (front, back, vertical) | • Lets go of the parent's arm while being towed | • Moves intentionally toward a target | • Walks 10 feet to a target in shallow water without assistance |
| • Wets face and arms | • Moves arms (waving, pulling) while being towed | • Does not enter the pool until requested to do so by parent | • Negotiates to various locations independently while wearing an IFD |
| | • Climbs out of pool with some assistance | • Does not leave parent while on the deck or in the dressing room | • Climbs into a boat or holds on to a floating safety object |
| | | • Moves cautiously on deck while entering or exiting the pool | • Floats in a PFD (Class I, II, III) |

**Table 5.1 Skills by Level by Children** (continued)

| | Shrimp | Kipper | Inia | Perch |
|---|---|---|---|---|
| **Personal Growth** | • Happy expression<br>• Relaxed muscles<br>• Imitation<br>• Hygiene<br>• Signs of being cold | • Eye control<br>• Balance<br>• Relaxation<br>• Imitation<br>• Independence | • Following directions<br>• Happy expression<br>• Independence<br>• Relaxation | • Allows another adult to hold in the water |
| **Personal Safety** | • Pool entry and exit<br>• Correct, safe holding by parents<br>• Safe temperatures<br>• Safety concepts | • Pool entry and exit<br>• PFDs<br>• Proper use of IFDs<br>• Follows pool rules | • Emergency procedures<br>• Pool entry and exit<br>• Boating safely<br>• First aid for choking<br>• PFDs | • PFDs and boating safety<br>• Tour of locker room and pool area<br>• Equipment overview<br>• PFDs<br>• Floating with PFDs |
| **Rescue (All assists are by parents)** | • Reaching assists<br>• Extension assists<br>• Throwing assists | • Reaching assists<br>• Extension assists<br>• Throwing assists | • Reaching assists<br>• Extension assists<br>• Throwing assists | • Reaching assists<br>• Extension assists<br>• Throwing assists<br>• Climbing into and out of the pool |

**Note:** No specific skills are assigned to the water sports and games component.

These skills develop aquatic readiness. At each level these categories are addressed based on the children's development and readiness (see chapter 7 of *Teaching Swimming Fundamentals* for more on stroke development). Table 5.2 shows each stroke development skill category as it is addressed in each level. This chart is meant to help you work with parents to set realistic expectations for their children. The chart is not comprehensive and should not be used as a standard for moving children from one level to another or for comparing children's progress. Organize your classes so that all the skills for your level will be attained under normal circumstances during your session.

**Table 5.2 Suggested Water Skills**

| | Shrimp<br>6-8 mo.<br>Supportive | Kipper<br>9-12 mo.<br>Imitative | Inia<br>13-18 mo.<br>Exploring | Perch<br>19-36 mo.<br>Independence |
|---|---|---|---|---|
| **Water Adjustment** | • Has happy expression in water<br>• Has relaxed muscles; has a sense of enjoyment and fun while being held close | • Is supported by parent in the water with minimal holding by child<br>• Imitates parent by putting face in the water<br>• Is relaxed in both the front towing and back cradle position | • Enters the pool eagerly from a sitting position on the side at the parent's request | • Is relaxed in both the front and back float position<br>• Allows another adult to hold in the water |
| **Breath Control** | • Blows bubbles spontaneously<br>• Blows bubbles on request or signal<br>• Puts mouth in and out of the water without swallowing when chin is held at water level | • Blows bubbles on cue<br>• Ships and expels water on cue | • Puts face in the water and blows bubbles without swallowing water<br>• Ships and expels water on cue | • Inhales and blows out independently |
| **Balance** | • Remains stable while in towing position with minimal parental support<br>• While wearing an IFD, turns 180 degrees by turning the head | • Balances on the parent's knee without the support of the parent's hand<br>• Focuses on the parent's face during towing to remain stable | • Negotiates to various locations independently while wearing an IFD<br>• Climbs out of the pool with assistance<br>• Turns from 180 to 360 degrees while wearing an IFD<br>• Controls body position while putting face in the water and taking face out of the water<br>• Maintains stable vertical position in an IFD without parental support | • Stands without aid in shallow water<br>• Moves body parts on request, including kicking and arm motions<br>• Changes positions and directions while wearing an IFD<br>• Controls body position while putting face in the water |

**Table 5.2** **Suggested Water Skills** (continued)

| | Shrimp<br>6-8 mo.<br>Supportive | Kipper<br>9-12 mo.<br>Imitative | Inia<br>13-18 mo.<br>Exploring | Perch<br>19-36 mo.<br>Independence |
|---|---|---|---|---|
| **Locomotor** | • Kicks or wiggles legs while being towed<br>• Kicks on cue or signal<br>• Positions in the water while cradling (front, back, vertical)<br>• Wets face and arms | • Maintains stable vertical position in an IFD without parental support<br>• Kicks while in the towing position<br>• Lets go of parent's arm while in the towing position<br>• Moves arms (waving, pulling) while in the towing position | • Kicks or moves arms on request<br>• Moves intentionally toward a target | • Enters and exits the pool without help by climbing<br>• Moves through water a short distance (5 to 10 feet) without help<br>• Walks 10 feet to a target in shallow water without assistance<br>• Negotiates to various locations independently while wearing an IFD |
| **Safety** |  | | • Does not enter the pool until requested to do so by parent<br>• Does not leave the parent while on deck or in the dressing room<br>• Moves cautiously on deck while entering or exiting the pool | • Climbs into a boat or holds on to a floating safety object<br>• Floats in a PFD (Class I, II, III) |

The rest of this chapter describes the activities within each skill component, including tips on how to guide the parents in helping their children perform the activities.

## Component 1: Personal Safety

In the parent/child portion of the Parent/Child and Preschool Aquatic Program, the personal safety information is presented to the parents instead of to the children. Again, this area includes a number of handouts from the *YMCA Swim Lessons Administrator's Manual* (see pages 27–28 for list of handouts in chapter three). Hold discussions on the deck during class or in separate meetings before or after class. Incorporate ideas into the At-Home section of your lesson plan and into skills presented during class. The following topics are covered under personal safety:

- Safety in and around water
- Pool tour
- Pool safety and backyard pool safety
- Health safety in the water
- Use of PFDs
- Skin and sun safety
- Heat exhaustion and heat stroke

### Safety In and Around Water

Even when children have learned some swimming skills, parents of children in the Parent/Child Aquatic Program age range need to be vigilant constantly. Topics to cover with parents include the following:

- Explain the importance of routine and repetition for developing safe practices in and around the water. Children are less likely to get into the water by themselves if parents are in the habit of carrying them or leading them in or being in the water first.
- Children must be constantly supervised, in or out of the water, by a parent or a competent adult. Children have a limited capacity to understand the dangers associated with water and boating activities.
- When an outing in the water is planned, parents must go into the water with their baby and must be within reach of the baby, even if the child is wearing a flotation device.
- Only trained lifeguards should enter the water to attempt a rescue. Throwing and reaching assists are acceptable rescue techniques for most individuals.

### Pool Tour

At the beginning of each session, show parents where to enter and exit the pool and dressing area, where to change their own clothes and dress their children, and the location of the designated waiting area on the deck. Provide them with any other information necessary to make them feel comfortable in the locker room and pool environment.

#### *Locker Room*

Discuss the use of hallways, lockers, toilets, showers, and changing tables, along with any hazards those areas might present (see the "Safety at the Y" section in chapter 4).

#### *Pool Area*

Examine the pool deck, edge, and gutter. Discuss the water depth and individual characteristics of the facility. Alert parents to the pool's features and tell them how to protect their children from potential dangers.

### Pool Safety

Due to babies' inquisitive natures, many areas of the pool are dangerous for them—even those who are just learning to walk and talk:

- Babies can fall into the pool, tub, or toilet.
- Babies can crawl and slip on a wet surface.
- Babies can topple over while sitting.

Parents also need to be aware of safe and unsafe water toys. Buckets and tubs can be pulled over a baby's head. Balloons that have deflated can be swallowed and cause choking. Big plastic inflatable balls are safer than small balls that fit into the mouth and can cause the child to choke.

### Backyard Pool Safety

Explain to parents who have a backyard pool that an emergency plan is needed as well as rescue equipment. Discuss items that could be used for rescue. Also discuss how to keep kids out of the pool when an adult is not present to supervise by using barriers such as self-latching gates, four-sided fencing, and childproof locks on all doors and windows.

### Health Safety in the Water

Explain to parents how to dress their children for the water, and discuss with them other water-related hygiene and health concerns. Hygiene concerns include vomiting, urination, or defecation in showers, toilets, or the pool; refrigeration of formula and food; and disposal of wastes. Health concerns include keeping children from becoming chilled in the water, avoiding hyponetremia, and keeping children out of class who have gastrointestinal infections or viral illnesses.

Parents also need to know that children's bodies' thermoregulatory mechanisms may not yet be mature enough to allow them to cope with the heat until at least five years of age and until that time they should not be allowed in a sauna, steam room, or whirlpool (spa).

### Use of Personal Flotation Devices

On deck show participants several types of personal flotation devices (PFDs) for adults and children and how they should be worn. Examples of children's PFDs should include a Type III ski vest in Child small and Youth, a Type II collared Infant, Child small and Youth (not a yoke-style device) a Type III zippered, slide adjustment device in Child small and Youth, and Type V Swimwear Flotation Device in small, medium, large, and X-large.

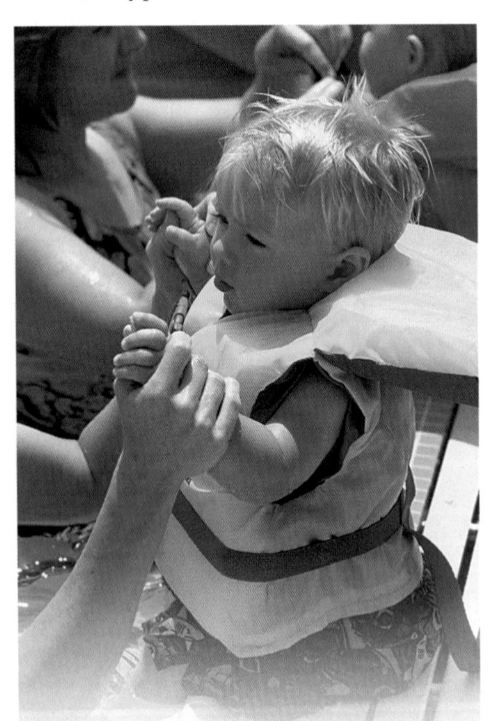

Examples of adult PFDs should include a segmented vest, a safety harness, and a four-buckle ski vest. Point out the characteristics of the various types. Emphasize reading the inside label for sizing information. Also point out the valuable information included in the "Think Safe" pamphlet.

Have everyone try on a PFD. Have parents try letting the babies float independently on their backs to find out which PFDs will hold the babies up. If possible, let the child indicate how tight the device can be adjusted before it becomes uncomfortable. Parents must stay close by and not let their babies get overly upset. This is a crucial exercise to learn how each baby will react if he or she should fall into the water wearing a PFD. For the collared devices, let the child's face be placed in the water; the device should roll the child onto his back. Also stress to parents that an improperly adjusted or incorrectly sized PFD can cause a child to be involuntarily submerged.

Once you have put PFDs on the babies, have the parents take the babies into the water. Parents should help the babies balance until the babies are settled. Bring out toys and let the babies play with them. Also have the babies kick while wearing a PFD. Parents should help the babies as little as possible. Other activities that children can try while wearing a PFD include these:

- Climbing out and clinging to the edge
- Rolling from back to front
- Rolling from front to back
- Kicking on the back

Have parents engage in these activities:

- Demonstrate a reaching assist to parents, then have them lie on the deck and do reaching assists to their babies, who are still wearing PFDs.

- Demonstrate the HELP position and have parents try it.
- Demonstrate the HUDDLE position and have parents try it.

Play with PFDs. Push them underwater and "discover" that they keep popping back up. Explain the basic local/state regulations on when to wear PFDs, and show the parents how to find the USCG stamp on PFDs to make sure they are approved. Also point out the sizing parameters (weight ranges, chest size markings) on the inside label.

Demonstrate to parents how to put on a yoke-style PFD properly. Explain that because these are oversized, they would hold a baby on his or her back, like a turtle on its shell. Emphasize the need to have the tape tied into a bow and the body strap maximally adjusted in order to secure a snug fit.

Explain to parents that everyone must wear USCG-approved PFDs during boating activities or other activities in or near water. If a child does not like wearing a PFD, let the child learn to like it by first using it as a toy, then gradually beginning to wear it around the house. Emphasize to parents that, even when wearing a PFD, a child cannot be considered safe around water or boats. Children must be supervised constantly when on or near water.

Finally, talk about the care of PFDs. A PFD in bad condition may be useless. Explain how to visually check for rips and tears. Demonstrate how to wash a PFD in warm, sudsy water. See the related handout in the *YMCA Swim Lessons Administrator's Manual* for more information.

### Skin and Sun Safety

Teach parents how to avoid sunburn and protect the skin (see the related handout in the *YMCA Swim Lessons Administrator's Manual*). They should learn these points for themselves and their children:

- Stay out of the sun in the middle of the day, usually between 10:00 A.M. and 4:00 P.M. Daylight Savings Time, and be aware of the length of time spent in the sun.
- Prevent sun damage by using a sunscreen or sunblock of at least 15 SPF.
- Sunscreen should be applied 30 minutes prior to going outside. It should be reapplied every few hours when you are in the sun or water.
- Stay covered with light-colored clothing and a hat when outdoors in the sun or wear photoprotective clothing.

### Heat Exhaustion and Heat Stroke

Teach parents the symptoms and first aid for heat exhaustion and heat stroke (see the related handout in the *YMCA Swim Lessons Administrator's Manual*).

### Safe Boating

Discuss tips for safe boating with parents:

- Talk about the proper use of PFDs.
- Discuss the regulations regarding the use of PFDs in small boats such as rowboats or canoes.
- Practice entering and exiting a small boat from a dock using a three-point entry:
  - Reach across and hold onto the far side of the boat.
  - Hold onto the side closest to you with the other hand.
  - Put first one foot then the other into the boat. Stay low.

Have participants perform the following activities:

- Help a child into the boat in the pool.
- Practice hanging on to the boat.
- Climb into and out of and play around a boat in the water.
- Have children practice swimming while wearing clothes (pants, shirt, socks).

Talk to parents about safe boating with children, covering the following:

- Remember that everyone in a boat, from the smallest baby to the oldest adult, should wear a PFD and know how to use it. Practice wearing them on a regular basis.
- Dress your baby in bright colors while boating so the baby can be spotted easily if he or she falls into the water. This includes choosing a brightly colored PFD. Neon colors seem to provide the most visual contrast to the water. Such colors are hot pink, neon green, neon orange, and neon yellow. Have the baby wear a nylon jacket and pants because nylon will help keep the body warm and won't absorb water if your child should fall into the water.
- Make sure your child responds to adult commands before taking him or her boating or near water.

Instructor Note: *You may notice in the manual that we are using rafts to demonstrate boating safety skills. Because we are teaching mainly in swimming pools, it can be more practical to use rafts than boats. While these types of rafts may be appropriate for teaching basic boating safety skills, be sure to point out the difference between the actions of the rafts used in class (which are flexible and pliable) and actual boats (which have rigid boat hulls).*

## Component 2: Personal Growth

In the parent/child portion of the Parent/Child and Preschool Aquatic Program, as in the personal safety component, the personal growth information is presented to the parents instead of to the children. Topics covered under personal growth include the following: teaching character

development, networking with other parents and learning more about oneself as a parent, movement education, parenting tips, and family enrichment. (Many of these are addressed in the parent handouts in the *YMCA Swim Lessons Administrator's Manual.*) You can hold discussions of these topics on the deck during class or in separate meetings scheduled before or after class, and you can reinforce this information through activities in the At-Home section of your lesson plan. (See chapter 6 for more on lesson planning.)

### Teaching Character Development

Character development involves teaching children to acknowledge and follow the core values of caring, respect, responsibility, and honesty. Chapter 9 provides some ideas on how to teach character development, and some of the activities described for the preschool levels in chapters 10 and 11 include elements that address character development. You can also refer to appendix B for further activities that focus on this important area of personal growth.

### Networking With Other Parents and Learning More About Oneself as a Parent

Although much of the time in a class is spent with the parent and child working and playing together, some opportunities do arise for parents to interact with other parents and their children. You can promote this interaction by doing some of the following:

- At appropriate times throughout the session, encourage parent and child teams to create ways to play with other teams. For example,

create a new water experience such as forming a four-person circle and moving around the pool.

- Do some of the water activities in groups, such as having each parent and child team go through a plastic hoop in their own way.
- Use group games and songs for fun and socializing. They help children feel at home and allow the children to try a variety of water experiences.
- Give parents and children opportunities to meet together before or after class in a special room with toys and refreshments.
- During class, when children are playing with toys, have them exchange toys from time to time to experience sharing.
- Hold special meetings just for parents on topics of interest such as CPR and first aid or home safety tips.
- Promote interaction during class by asking parents questions and having them each share their answers with the group:
  - Why are you taking this class?
  - What new accomplishments has your baby achieved since our class?
  - What discoveries and funny things have you noticed about your baby since our last class?
  - What kinds of behavior can we expect from children the age of your child? How will new skills affect the children's safety at the pool?
  - What are your current fears about raising your child?
  - Who is your pediatrician, and what do you like or dislike about him or her?
  - What other group activities are you involved in with your child? How did you get involved?
  - What places do you like to go to with your child (such as parks, restaurants, or playgrounds)?

### Movement Education

Understanding basic movement education principles will help you as you teach children to explore and discover how their bodies move in water. Teach parents the fundamentals of movement education as a way to play with a purpose at home as their children grow. Help parents and children learn to work as a team as they explore movement together in the water:

- Give parents suggestions for various simple movements to explore, such as sitting up and down, rolling over, turning around, taking steps, blowing bubbles, and expelling water.
- Pose movement problems so that the problem solving can be either entirely up to the parent or shared with the child. For example, ask parents, "How many different ways can you tow your babies across the pool that will be fun for them?" Parents with older children could share the problem with the child: "How many different ways can *we* tow that will be fun for us?"

The movements and problems to try with your class are limitless; here are some examples:

- What are some things you can do with this hoop in the water? What about with this toy? What can you do with this kickboard?
- How many ways can you and your child (hold onto the board, kick your feet, push the board)?
- How high can we jump up together? How far can we float together with a push from the side?

Actions to explore include the following:

- Splashing
- Kicking
- Pushing and pulling with the hands
- Balancing on some part of the parent (standing or sitting on the shoulder, head, leg)
- Blowing bubbles
- Going underwater to see and move
- Using toys and apparatus (balancing, tossing, going through, hiding)
- Bobbing with rhythm
- Moving along the edge of the pool (going in and going out)
- Performing paired actions with another parent/child team such as "Ring Around the Rosey"

Movements and experiences can be repeated over and over with or without changes or additions that change the movement's complexity or difficulty.

### Parenting Tips

You can help parents to better understand their roles as parents by supplying them with information on topics such as children's development, child abuse prevention, and accident prevention and home safety. Use the parent handouts in the *YMCA Swim Lessons Administrator's Manual.*

### Family Enrichment

Help parents strengthen family bonds by suggesting a variety of fun family activities they can try. Some of these can be found in the handouts in the *YMCA Swim Lessons Administrator's Manual*.

## Component 3: Stroke Development

This section lists activities for each category. The activities are arranged in the order in which they should be attempted. The component includes water adjustment, breath control, balance, and locomotion.

### Category 1: Water Adjustment

#### *Water Acclimation*

Sing songs and play games that help the babies get used to the water (see appendix B).

Have parents hold their babies in the knee balance position (facing toward or away from the parent) and get their babies wet. This activity can be accompanied by a game or a song. Remind parents to be gentle and quiet while encouraging their children to have a good time. Have parents try activities such as washing their babies' face, hair, or body; blowing bubbles; or moving their arms, legs, and shoulders in the water. Showering is another activity parents can use to help babies and children adjust to the water.

**Baby wait**

Place the baby on the side of the pool, with the parent standing in the water sideways to the baby and five to six feet away. Wait 5 to 10 seconds. If the baby begins to move into the water, the parent should say, "No, wait until I am ready." An instructor on the deck and the parent in the pool should both watch carefully to make sure the baby doesn't enter the pool prematurely. Then have the parent move to face the baby three to four feet away and ask the child to enter the pool. The parent should catch the baby under the armpits to control the level of submersion.

Instructor Note: *Take into consideration your pool's design when you teach skills such as baby wait. The height of the gutter or the availability of steps may require you to adapt how skills are performed.*

### Independence

Have an adult other than the parent hold the child. Make sure the parent is nearby so the child is not upset by the parent's brief absence.

Instructor Note: *Use this exercise to emphasize the need for parents to watch their children at all times. No babies or young children are "water safe," and the parent or another adult must be in the water if the child is in the water. Even past age seven the child must be closely watched by a parent who is nearby, vigilant, and prepared to reach or help the child if necessary. No one of any age should ever swim alone, and everyone should swim only if someone is available who is capable of providing help if necessary. This usually means a certified lifeguard or, for children, a parent trained in water safety.*

## Water Entry and Exit Techniques

Take into consideration your pool's design when you teach skills such as water entry or exit. The height of the gutter or the availability of steps may require you to adapt how skills are performed. Each of these entry techniques described next can be reversed for leaving the pool at the end of class.

The best technique is one that matches the pool design and the baby's developmental level. The partner and heartbeat entries are preferred for babies who cannot sit without support. As many pools do not have stairways, the use of the heartbeat entry is limited. The baby sits entry is preferred for babies and children who can sit without support and is appropriate for most pools.

### Partner entry

The parent has another adult hold the baby while the parent enters the pool. Then the partner hands the baby to the parent.

### Heartbeat hold entry

The parent holds the child close so child and parent are chest to chest. This entry allows the child to feel the parent's heartbeat and lets the parent hold the baby securely at the hips and head. The heartbeat hold entry requires the use of both the parent's arms, so it is appropriate only in pools with wide, nonskid stairways on which the vertical and horizontal edges of the steps are outlined in a contrasting color.

### Baby sits entry

The parent sits on the side of the pool with the baby alongside; puts his or her far hand on the baby; and, using the near hand for support, turns and slips into the pool. After the parent is stable in the water, the baby can be lifted into the water.

## Getting Wet

Anyone entering the water should take time to get acclimated to it. This can include gradually wetting the body parts, walking around the pool (especially if the pool is unfamiliar), and warming up for the activities. The process should be the same for adults and children. Establishing a routine of washing and wetting, checking the surroundings, and warming up further reduces the possibility of a baby making an accidental entry or trying to swim without a parent.

The parent and instructor should demonstrate washing by splashing water from the pool on to various body parts and wetting various parts of the body and should help the babies do the same. Encourage children to wash and wet themselves. Blowing bubbles, taking water into the mouth and spitting it out again, putting an ear in the water to listen, and walking around the pool should all be part of the daily routine. The parent should give a signal, then submerge his or her own face, lifting it out of the water after five counts with a big smile. When a baby submerges his or her face, the baby should lift the face after 5 to 10 counts. A baby never should submerge for more than 10 seconds. If the parent sees a large bubble, he or she should immediately lift the baby's face because the child has expelled most of his or her air.

**Immersing the face**

Have parents put their faces in the water and encourage their babies to imitate. Parents should give a signal ("1, 2, 3 " or "ready, set, go") before immersing their faces. When parents raise their faces they should smile, then give the same signal and say, "your turn," or some other encouraging phrase. When the children do put their faces in the water, the parents should reinforce the behavior with words of praise, a favorite toy or game, or a hug.

Instructor Note: *On the first day allow babies to immerse their faces only one time. On the second day the babies can immerse their faces two times, and on the third day, the babies can immerse their faces three times.*

*The babies should immerse their faces on a cue (with the signal "okay, it's your turn, 1, 2, 3"). They should put their faces in the water on request while being towed. Be sure to limit the number of times babies immerse their faces per class.*

Instructor Note: *If a child has put his or her face in the water 3 times without choking, is happy, and can blow bubbles, the limit should become 10 times. In other words, a baby who has reasonable breath control, who likes to put his or her face in the water, and who does so on his or her own should be allowed to immerse the face up to 10 times in 30 minutes.*

*If a baby does not imitate the parent, the parent should keep demonstrating and encouraging and should alternate this with other activities until the baby is able to imitate face immersion. Remind parents to be patient; children may not put their faces in the water for several weeks of practice.*

## *Climbing Out of the Pool*

Perhaps the single most important aquatic safety skill children can learn is to climb out of the pool. As soon as children demonstrate climbing skills on land, they should be encouraged to climb out of the swimming pool. The secret of success is for the child to keep the head close to the side on the way up and close to the deck once the head is over the top. Because the head of a baby is relatively large compared to the body, the balance point is changed. A baby also may not have sufficient arm strength to raise

him- or herself up easily. Head position, therefore, is critical in helping the young child get out of the water.

Practice having babies climb out of the pool, both with and without IFDs. Make a game of throwing toys onto the deck and having the children climb out, retrieve the toys, and get back into the pool. The children should not get back into the pool until the parents say, "Okay," or give some other signal.

### *Independent Water Entry*

Babies who can put their faces in the water and who can sit independently are ready to attempt an "independent" entry from the side. To do the entry, the parent begins by setting the child so that the child's legs are over the edge of the pool. The parent must watch carefully so the child doesn't fall backward or sideward. The parent then stands in the water directly facing the baby, with the parent's hands under the baby's arms. On the usual signal to immerse the face ("1, 2, 3" or "ready, set, go") the parent gently tilts the child forward, helping him or her slip into the water. The child and the parent's arms should be under the water. Gradually the parent will not have to tilt the child forward, so the parent can wait with the arms under the surface for the baby to catch onto the parent's arms.

Have children who are able to stand or sit on the side of the pool positioned to face their parents. On a signal have parents encourage the babies to lean or reach toward them, overbalancing into the water. The parents will hold their arms toward the babies under the water. As the babies pass

the parents' arms, the parents make contact with the babies, but they allow buoyancy to bring the children to the surface.

Have children stand on the side of the pool, facing parents. On a signal, encourage the babies to jump into the water toward their parents and overbalance into the water toward the parents. The parents will hold their arms toward the infants under the water. As the infants pass the parents' arms, the parents make contact with the infants, but allow buoyancy to bring the children to the surface.

Have the children first step into the water from a standing position on the side of the pool as parents wait in the water, then recover to the surface with parents maintaining contact.

The next step is to have the children first step into the water as parents wait for them there, then recover to the surface, turn around, and move back to the side while parents supervise closely.

Have the children first jump into the water as parents wait for them there, then recover to the surface, turn around, and move back to the side while parents supervise closely. Children jump into the water, rise to the surface, roll over to their backs, change position to their stomachs, and paddle to the side.

Instructor Note: *Limit the total number of immersions (while towing, imitating, and stepping in) to 10 or less per day. This is a maximum; it is better to allow too few submersions by babies than too many.*

## Category 2: Breath Control

This category describes the progression for breath control. This includes blowing bubbles, shipping and expelling water, learning to control breathing, and submersion.

### *Blowing Bubbles*

Have parents demonstrate blowing bubbles and encourage their babies to imitate. Have infants blow bubbles on request. Have infants blow bubbles while being towed.

### *Shipping and Expelling Water*

Have parents demonstrate to their children how to immerse the open mouth into the water and come back up, letting the water dribble out of the mouth. Then have them encourage their children to imitate this process. Warn parents to watch that their children do not swallow much water.

Once young children can take water into their mouths and let it out easily, without choking or swallowing, have the parents demonstrate how to take water in, then expel it forcefully in a stream (preferably into the gutter). They then should encourage their children to imitate this action.

When young children can easily make a stream of water, parents can demonstrate making a fountain up into the air, like a whale spouting. Again, parents should encourage children to imitate. This fountain action can be worked into various games.

Instructor Note: *Allowing water in and around the mouth is a little recognized but important basic aquatic skill. Even more than immersion, however, this skill can lead young children to swallow water, which in rare instances can lead to hyponatremia (see chapter 2). Both instructors and parents need to be alert to symptoms in children such as a protruding stomach or copious urination following lessons, which indicate that the children are swallowing the water instead of shipping and expelling it.*

### *Learning to Control Breathing*

Parents can begin to help their children control breathing by demonstrating exaggerated breathing. The parents make a display of opening the mouth, inhaling loudly, then exhaling loudly. They then encourage the children to imitate.

Have parents demonstrate a loud inhale, then a brief face submersion followed by exhaling underwater. See if the children can imitate it. Have parents demonstrate inhaling, submerging, then exhaling loudly underwater, creating copious bubbles. Then parents encourage the children to copy them, using a designated cue or signal. The parents can blow loud bubbles next to the children's bubbles, tickle them, and make blowing bubbles a game or play opportunity.

Instructor Note: *Although this skill has typically been called* ***breath holding****, the skill children actually need to learn is* ***breath control;*** *this is because in most normal aquatic activities, the breath is really only held very briefly. Unlike on land, breathing in the water requires inhaling at times when the face (or at least the mouth) is out of the water.*

*Some people have noticed that a child "automatically" gasps and holds his or her breath if someone blows in the child's face. This has led to a practice of asking parents to blow in their children's faces before submersion to condition the breath-holding reflex. This practice is not only unkind to children, but it is also unsanitary and violates the spirit of the YMCA aquatic guidelines; we suggest that you avoid this practice.*

### *Submerging*

Play games like "London Bridges" in shallow water where children can stand. Raise or lower the arm bridge so the children eager to submerge must do so to go under the bridge, and the children who do not want to submerge can go under the bridge without submerging completely.

Hang a mat over the pool edge to serve as a tunnel or cave, encouraging partial submersion.

Drop toys that sink into the water and encourage children to go get them.

Have the children paddle/swim though a submerged hoop or a floating mat.

Instructor Note: *Voluntary submersion requires the prerequisite skills of shipping and expelling water and controlling the breath before submersing the mouth. This category often requires a long time and a great deal of patience. Spend the time; it is a foundational skill.*

## Category 3: Balance

In the balance category, buoyancy and body positions are covered. With the use of a variety of IFDs and PFDs the child can learn about being in the water.

### *Knee Balance*

For the knee balance, the parent stands with the back against the wall or in a stable position in chest-deep water, with one leg bent at the knee and the thigh horizontal. The baby is seated straddled on the parent's thigh. Usually the child will face the same direction as the parent, but he or she can also face the parent. This is a good position to use for getting the child wet (pretending to wash the child's face, hair, and so on), practicing arm and leg movements, or singing songs and playing games. In water waist-deep on the parents, have the parents crouch and balance the babies on their knees without parental support. In water between midchest and chin on the parents, have the parents crouch and have children sit on their parents' knees and balance without assistance.

### *Buoyancy*

Demonstrate balancing a baby vertically and releasing your hold gently, watching to see whether the baby will remain balanced. If the baby doesn't stay upright, rebalance the baby, but do not scoop the baby up as though he or she needed saving; this type of response may startle or frighten the baby. Have parents try this activity with their children.

Next, instruct parents to balance their babies on the side of the pool, take one step back and call the babies to come to the parents' outstretched fingers. Have the babies grab the parents instead of the parents grabbing the babies when possible.

You should have enough child and adult personal flotation devices (PFDs) available so that everyone can try wearing one. Parents may have to cradle their children at first, but they should encourage the children to use

the PFDs to move around in the pool. If a child is unhappy in the PFD, limit his or her time in a PFD to one or two minutes until the child becomes more comfortable with it. Encourage parents who boat with their children to occasionally practice being in the water wearing a PFD and to check the size, fit, and condition of all PFDs on a regular basis. PFDs must be the right size and type for the individual and for the purpose intended to work properly.

Instructor Note: *This may be a good opportunity to educate parents about the five types of U.S. Coast Guard-approved PFDs and about the different uses and functions of IFDs compared with PFDs. Then try the buoyancy activities with IFDs. They tend to provide less support than PFDs.*

### *Body Positions*

Form a circle with the babies facing the center. Everyone should be wearing IFDs. Ask to see the children's toes in front, at the surface of the water. You show your toes, then children show theirs. Play in the water with the toes down, the toes behind, the toes up in front, and so on. The parents help the babies with position adjustments, using very little force. The babies should be at floating level and balancing by using the flotation device as much as possible.

Children who can put their faces in the water should try wearing an IFD and practice changing body positions semi-independently, with minimal parental assistance.

Encourage children to become more independent and to try new variations on movements while wearing IFDs.

Children who are tall enough to walk in shallow water can practice walking to a target.

Instructor Note: *Caution parents about the dangers and risks of their children's growing independence in and around the water. Parents of children who are becoming more physically active must redouble their vigilance and supervision as well as make sure that barriers are installed around water sources at home.*

### Category 4: Locomotion

This category covers forms of movement in the water. Front towing, arm and leg patterns, the back cradle, back towing, the prone launch, and the use of IFDs are included.

#### *Front Towing*

Front towing is the primary skill that acquaints babies and young children with moving through the water. In front towing the parent holds the child under the arms, either with fingers facing up (this works well for babies with particularly low centers of gravity, who ride lower in the water) or with fingers down (for older children and for those with a higher center of gravity who float almost horizontally). Both the parent's and the child's shoulders should be submerged, which often means the parent must assume a semisquat position. The parent should keep the arms straight and allow the water to provide support for the child; otherwise he or she will fatigue quickly and the child will not experience buoyancy. The child's weight should be supported by the water. When face to face with the child, the parent can maintain eye contact, talk and signal, and give instructions. In addition, the child can observe the parent blowing bubbles and immersing the face.

Have parents and children learn the holding positions for front towing and try out those positions.

Have parent/child teams perform continuous towing for 30 to 60 seconds.

Have parents blow bubbles and ship and expel water while towing and encourage babies to imitate.

Have parents immerse their faces as well as ship and expel water while towing their children and encourage the children to imitate. Children who can put their faces in the water will assume a nearly horizontal position while being towed. Parents also can verbally cue babies to kick while the babies are being towed. Have the parent/child teams do continuous towing for one to two minutes.

Have parents encourage babies to let go of the parents' arms when in the towing positions. Some ways parents can encourage their children to do this are to ask them to wave their arms, to push the water to their feet, or to show their "motors."

Encourage children to make various arm and leg movements (up and down, sideways, around in circles).

Have children blow bubbles, ship and expel water, and/or put the face in the water while being towed without using the arms for support.

Have children blow bubbles, ship and expel water, and/or put the face in the water while being towed and moving arms and legs.

Have children do five- to eight-count bubbling and breathing while moving the arms and legs (see Breath Control category). This sequence takes a great deal of practice. As the parent/child teams practice the sequence, the children will gradually need less help, support, and cueing from the parents. This skill is much easier for the child to do if the parent moves backward as rapidly as possible, as the child uses momentum and buoyancy to maintain a horizontal position. Have the parent/child teams perform continuous towing for two to three minutes.

#### *Arm Patterns*

Infants do not exhibit the same motor patterns as adults, or even older children, in skills such as walking, throwing, or jumping; and the same usually holds true for swimming. In fact, initially many babies and young children use practically no arm movements, but instead they rely on leg actions, as they do on land. Infants should never be expected to make the same stroking motions as adults. Typically babies move their arms using either a breaststroke-type pull (both arms simultaneously pushing water toward the feet) or a crawl-type pull, a rudimentary alternating paddling action underwater (one arm at a time, pushing water toward the feet).

Have parents observe the type of motion the children naturally make with their arms, if any.

Have parents model splashing motions with the hands.

Swim or have parents swim (face in the water, doing a breaststroke or crawl stroke) so the children can observe and have something to imitate.

Encourage children to continue using whichever arm motion seems to come naturally. Parents may demonstrate a more advanced arm stroking action for the children. Moving children passively through an arm motion while in a knee-balance position probably is not useful. Simply using verbal cues to remind the children to use their arms and encouraging natural motions is best.

Have children put their faces in the water and simultaneously move their arms (pushing the water toward their feet) and legs (also pushing water backward for propulsion).

### *Leg Patterns*

Infants' leg motions typically taught at this level are either a modified frog kick (both legs at the same time) or a modified flutter kick (alternate kicking). Whatever leg movement a baby exhibits should be encouraged. Many babies will change movement patterns from day to day, or even from trial to trial.

As parents sit on the side, have them move their children's legs up and down while they say, "kick, kick, kick."

Have parents tow their children, placing the children's arms up on the parents' shoulders and holding on to the children's legs just below the knee. They then say, "kick, kick, kick," as they move the children's legs up and down.

Have parents encourage their children to move their legs and/or arms while being towed. They can again say, "kick, kick, kick," or some other verbal signal. The type of kicking motion is not important.

### *Back Cradle*

In the back cradle position, the parent holds the child in a horizontal position with one arm under the child's back and the other around the child's chest. The child rests against the parent's chest, the water level remaining even with the child's ears. The parent holds the child still (no rocking), leans over so the child can look straight up into the parent's face, and talks or sings quietly. This position should be maintained briefly at first (5 to 30 seconds), then gradually extended if the child does not cry, wiggle, or try to roll over. As the length of time increases, the parent should gradually reduce the amount of arm support under the child so that the water

gradually supports the child more and more. If the child protests this activity, discontinue it for now.

### *Back Towing*

The purpose of back towing is to allow the child to experience buoyancy in a moving back floating position. Many babies automatically roll over to the back position because their heads are proportionately much larger than an adult's. They also may arch their backs, submerging their faces and ingesting water. The parent should hold the child's head still, at first by placing one hand on either side of the child's face or beneath the head and later by maintaining eye contact.

The parent begins with the child's back against the parent's chest and the chin at water level. The parent tips the child's head back so the child is looking up at the parent and holds the baby's head near the ears for control and support. Once the child's ears are submerged, the legs usually float toward the surface in a stable back float position. At this point the parent simply walks backward slowly. The child will follow behind the parent stretched out on top of the water. With practice the parent can shift to placing a finger on the child's chin, a hand under the child's shoulder blades, or making no contact at all.

For those children comfortable in the back towing position, parents can remove support briefly; a finger touching or a hand nearby is often enough to keep a stable child in the back float position on his or her own.

### *Prone Launch*

A baby may be launched in many ways, but the preferred method is to have the child do it on his or her own. From the knee-balance position, with shoulders in the water, the child can reach forward and move through the water. The child should be moving toward a target (e.g., the side of the pool, a parent, or the instructor).

Have babies launch themselves from the knee-sitting position to either the side (place a favorite toy there) or to the parent (if the baby is sitting on another adult's knee). Babies should begin with their chins at water level.

Have children lean forward from the knee balance, move off the knee, and move to a target.

### *Use of Instructional Flotation Devices*

Instructional flotation devices (IFDs) should be used only on children whose parents or caregivers are in the water with them. Use IFDs only for instructional purposes and always with in-water supervision; do not rely on them for safety when children are unsupervised in the water. The parent should put the IFD on the child. Once the IFD is securely in place, the parent should hold the child either around the rib cage or by the wrists. The child should be face to face with the parent, and the parent should talk or sing quietly to the child while attaching the IFD. The parent should gradually allow the IFD and the water to support the child, but he or she should remain in constant physical contact.

It is very important that you emphasize the proper use of IFDs when you are introducing them to the class. Parents must always be within easy reach of babies wearing IFDs, as IFDs are not lifesaving or rescue devices. IFDs are used only to supplement other activities in the water.

For infants that have not put their faces or mouths into the water, allow them to touch, push, and play with their IFDs and to observe teams using IFDs.

Activities children can do wearing IFDs include balancing, turning around, and traveling by moving the feet and/or the legs.

For those babies who can remain stable with no parental support, begin with turning around. Once babies are comfortable facing away from their parents, place them with their backs to the parents, directly in front of the parents. This positioning can be done either by you or the parents. On a signal from the parents ("1, 2, 3" or "ready, set, go") the babies are instructed to turn around and see mom or dad. The first few times children may need help in turning, but they eventually will understand that by turning their heads and trunks they can turn around easily.

Have babies practice turning around 180 degrees.

Have parents hold their children with their backs facing the parents, and give the children a signal to put their faces in the water. When the children put their faces in the water, parents should help them turn around to face the parents. The children should then lift their faces out of the water.

Young children who can remain stable while wearing IFDs can practice moving forward by moving their legs and lower bodies. Their arms may remain still and underwater or paddling gently. The parents stand behind their children and encourage them to turn around by turning the head.

Infants who can remain stable and turn around can try to follow parents' directions or demonstration and move about the pool. The movements should include changing direction (left, right, front, back), changing position (legs behind, legs in front), moving forward and backward, and stopping and starting.

Children wearing IFDs should practice moving intentionally toward a target, such as a parent or a toy. Have children launch themselves from the knee-balance position to either the side (place a favorite toy there) or to the parent (if the child is sitting on another adult's knee). Children will begin with their chins at water level.

## Component 4: Water Sports and Games

Activities, games, and songs for the Parent/Child Aquatic Program are listed in appendix B. Select games and activities that support the objectives of your class by reinforcing the skills being taught and providing additional practice. The games and songs are categorized by their stroke development category: water adjustment, water entry and exit, balance, buoyancy, and locomotion.

## Component 5: Rescue

This instructional component contains not only the crucial rescue skills for water emergencies, but it also includes procedures for emergency situations on land. Ask parents to give situational examples for each safety concept.

The topics covered under rescue include the following:

- Reaching and throwing assists
- Handling a child in deep water (If a parent is uncomfortable in deep water, this should be avoided.)
- First aid, including choking and poison prevention
- Rescue breathing and baby and child cardiopulmonary resuscitation (CPR)

### Aquatic training

Those parents with aquatic safety training should have a PFD or other flotation device on and/or have a flotation device with them to provide additional support. The flotation device should be kept between the parent and the child.

### Assists

Parents need to know how to perform reaching and throwing assists to keep their children safe in an aquatic emergency. Some activities you can try include these:

- Have one parent watch two children on the deck while another parent tries reaching assists with a pole, a towel, or a hand. You play the victim.
- Have parents lie on the deck, and help them perform reaching assists to their own babies.
- Talk about different items that can be used for extension rescues and try them.
- Talk about items that float and that would be good for throwing assists, such as rescue tubes or ring buoys, and try them.
- Have parents extend objects commonly found at a pool, such as a kickboard, barbell, or rescue tube, to a parent/child team in the pool.
- Have parents practice throwing common objects that float, such as a kickboard, barbell, or noodle, to a parent/child team in the pool.
- Teach parents how to throw a ring buoy to a swimmer properly.

### Handling a child in deep water

Parents who are comfortable in deep water and who have aquatic safety training can take their children into deep water. When a parent does this, he or she should bring a PFD or other flotation device to provide additional support for the child. The parent should keep the flotation device between him or her and the child.

### First Aid

- Provide parents with basic information on what steps to take in certain types of emergencies, such as these:
- Discuss the danger of children choking on small objects, such as marbles, balloons, or removable parts of toys. Cover emergency measures for helping a child who is choking.
- Talk about poison control and prevention (see the related handout in the *YMCA Swim Lessons Administrator's Manual*).
- Discuss where parents can take first-aid courses for certification.

### *Rescue Breathing and Infant and Child Cardiopulmonary Resuscitation (CPR)*

Discuss and demonstrate the steps for rescue breathing for babies and children and for baby and child CPR. Share with parents when your Y offers CPR classes.

**Having a set class routine is important in most classes, but it is especially critical for the Parent/Child Aquatic Program.**

**Babies and young children feel more comfortable when they know what to expect and can anticipate it.**

You also will feel more confident when you have a written plan for each lesson and know what you are going to do. A lesson plan allows you to keep track of which skills have been taught or need to be reviewed, and it encourages you to jot down ideas that can make your classes work even better. You also can use your plan to remind you of what to review with parent/child teams who were absent.

This final chapter of part II provides ideas for setting up a class routine and planning individual lessons and your overall session. Some sample lesson plans are included as a starting point. The chapter also touches on how you can help children make the transition from the Parent/Child to the Preschool Aquatic Program.

## Organizing Your Parent/Child Lessons

When you start your parent/child classes, establish a regular class routine. Design each class using this routine. You may want to do the same games, songs, or other ritual activities for opening and closing class or the same lead-up activity before you change activities.

After they change into their bathing suits and shower, the parent/child teams should enter the pool area from the same location each lesson. Designate an area for parents and children to sit and wait for you before class begins.

On your signal, the parents and children should move to the pool edge, sit, and enter the pool by one of the methods described in chapter 5. You must insist that parents enter the water before their children are allowed into the pool. No parent/child team should ever leave or reenter the pool without your knowledge. Make the parents aware of any boundaries that they need to stay within during class, such as within the shallow water or between two given points. Explain that they need to remain within those boundaries so you can keep them in view at all times.

At the end of each lesson, all teams should return to the designated waiting area. Once you have accounted for everyone and indicated the class is over, they may leave the pool area.

You may find that it's easier to discuss some topics on the deck rather than in the water. If you plan to talk about these topics before every class, let parents know that they and their children should meet on the deck without taking a shower. Once you have completed your discussion, they



can then shower before entering the water. Another option is to meet right after class in another classroom (or an area of the locker room that is dry and warm), and make snacks and toys available for the children while you talk with the parents. It's a good idea to provide child care. Providing child care during the meeting will help parents to participate more comfortably.

Sometimes children have minor mishaps in class or miss a session because of illness. When this happens call parents to ask about their children's progress and recovery. By doing so you may encourage a parent who is on the brink of dropping out to come back to the class.

## Session Planning

Chapter 5 supplied you with the skills to be taught in the Parent/Child Aquatic Program, sequenced in the order in which they should be taught. What you now need to do is to organize your teaching of those skills over the length of the session. The sample session planning form shown in figure 6.1 can guide you in doing this. It has a column for each of the five main components (personal safety, personal growth, stroke development, water sports and games, and rescue), so you can touch on each of them in every lesson. A copy of the blank form can be found in the *YMCA Swim Lessons Administrator's Manual.*

# YMCA Swimming Session Sample Planning Form

Y SWIM LESSONS.

**Level:** Parent/Child **Number of students:** 10 Teams **Session:** Spring **Instructor:** Cindy

| | Personal safety | Personal growth | Stroke development | Water sports and games | Rescue |
|---|---|---|---|---|---|
| #1 | pool tour | networking | water acclimation<br>water entry<br>water exits | Ring Around the Rosie<br>Mulberry Bush<br>Hokey Pokey | |
| #2 | pool safety | networking | climbing out of pool<br>knee balance | same as #1<br>Humpty Dumpty | reaching assists |
| #3 | health safety | parent tips | immersing face<br>breath control<br>front towing<br>use of IFDs | same as #1<br>London Bridge<br>Little Green Frog | throwing assists |
| #4 | skin and sun safety | movement educ. | buoyancy<br>leg patterns | same as #1<br>Motor Boat<br>Wheels on the Bus | handling child in deep water |
| #5 | use of PFDs | family enrichment | body positions<br>arm patterns<br>back cradle | same as #1<br>My Bonnie Lies over the Ocean<br>Open Them, Shut Them | rescue breathing |
| #6 | boating safety | character development | shipping & expelling water<br>submersion<br>backtowing | same as #1<br>Pop goes the Weasel<br>This is the Way | infant CPR |
| #7 | heat exhaustion<br>heat stroke | networking | independent water entry<br>prone launch | same as #1<br>Sailing, Sailing<br>Swim Little Fishie | first aid |
| #8 | backyard pool safety | parent tips | review | same as #1<br>favorite songs of class | |

## Lesson Planning

Once you have finished the session planning form, you need to develop lesson plans for each of the individual class days. Start by taking your session plan and the first day's topics and describing how you will actually lead the activities. Planning each day helps you to be organized when you lead your classes. Of course, situations may come up to which you will have to adapt, but having a written guide will make your classes much more effective. The lesson planning form has the following elements:

### Greeting

- When your class gathers in your designated meeting place, make announcements and tell parents relevant information. You also may want to give parents an overview of the day's lesson, listing the topics to be covered.
- If this portion of the lesson is going to take a few minutes, you may want to do the greeting while parents and children are still dry. Follow this portion of the class with a class trip to the showers before entering the pool.
- Select an opening song or activity. Use it consistently throughout the session to establish a familiar routine.

### *Warm-Up/Series Swim*

The series swim in the Parent/Child Aquatic Program is not quite the same as in classes for older children. In this program it will include a variety of songs and activities that keep the parents and children moving for a few minutes. Such activities might be circle activities or ones in which the class moves back and forth across or around the pool. Describe those activities in this section of the form. Be sure to designate activities with educational and instructional objectives in mind.

### *Review*

Whenever you present skills and experiences to a group, you should review them periodically. Each lesson should include a review of some activities from previous lessons. During this time you review any skills you introduced in earlier classes. The skills can be incorporated into songs and games (see appendix B). Setting time aside to repeat previously taught songs and activities and to discuss children's progress reinforces the learning process and promotes a smooth progression. In this section of the lesson planning form, list the skills to be reviewed.

### *Introduce New Skills*

Choose which skills you want to introduce in this day's class, and write them in this area of the planning form. This may include both water skills and discussion topics for the parents. Choose activities from each of the five components: stroke development, water sports and games, personal growth, personal safety, and rescue.

### Practice

Provide opportunities for parent/child teams to practice the skills you have taught. You may want to provide toys for children to use during this time. Describe in this space on the form how you will provide the class with opportunities for practicing.

### Conclusion

Choose a fun activity or song that you can use consistently to end the class throughout the session. This routine will signal to the children that the class is coming to a close. You also may include any business, news, general information, or an at-home activity just before this time. Having a concluding activity, such as a song that says good-bye or a quiet activity and time to let each team know they are special, is a fitting end to a class. On the form, describe what activity you will use to end the class.

### At-Home Activity

At the YMCA we hope that the information presented in class becomes an integral part of the parents' and children's lives. To achieve this aim, you should assign an at-home activity (Family Huddle, found in the *YMCA Swim Lessons Administrator's Manual*) at the end of each class so the parent/child team can continue to practice their aquatic activities at home. Such at-home experiences can help the children progress and develop skills such as recognizing colors and shapes, blowing bubbles, or using IFDs, as well as reinforcing what they have accomplished in class. Through either handouts or discussions during the class, provide parents with suggestions for activities to do at home between classes. List what you plan to do in this section of the form.

One at-home activity for parents is to have them keep a daily diary or journal of their child's aquatic activities, reactions, and development. Feelings about the class, cute or funny things the child does at home, and other bits of information can be quickly and simply recorded on the pages of a YMCA Parent/Child swim program diary. The diary is used to record the child's progress. A sample diary is in the *YMCA Swim Lessons Administrator's Manual.*

Use the teaching ideas in chapter 4 to build your lessons. You also can use the games and activities in appendix B. After each class is over, note how the class went, record suggestions for improving the flow of the class, and add any new ideas that came to mind. Figure 6.2 is a sample daily lesson plan to give you an idea of how to construct one.

# YMCA Swimming Lesson Planning Form

YSWIM LESSONS.

Instructor: Cindy
Day: Saturday
Date: 4/10 (day 5)
Class (level): Parent/Child
Session: Spring
Class time: 10:30

Today's learning objectives:
1. learn about PFDs
2. body positions
3. arm patterns 4) rescue breathing

Safety considerations:
1. Add'l help for rescue breathing demo
2.
3.

Material/equipment:
1. PFDs
2. manikin (infant)
3. toys/IFDs

| | Time | Description of activity/ method of teaching | Class organization pattern | Equipment needed | Notes or explanation |
|---|---|---|---|---|---|
| Greeting | 10:30 | welcome at pool deck<br>overview of today<br>pool entry | line | | |
| Warm-up/series swim | 10:35 | water acclimation<br>front towing | line<br>(working across the pool) | | Ring Around the Rosie<br>motor boat |
| Review | 10:40 | breath control<br>buoyancy<br>leg patterns | circle for songs | belts/logs | Little Green Frog<br>share fun family activites<br>Mulberry Bush |
| Introduce new skills | 10:45 | body positions<br>arm patterns<br>back cradle, use of PFD | circle | PFDs | demonstrate new skills<br>My Bonnie Lies Over the Ocean<br>Open Them, Shut Them<br>overview of PFDs |
| Practice | 10:50 | stations or activities | station 1: rescue breathing<br>station 2: PFDs/body positions<br>station 3: toys, Climbing in/out<br>station 4: towing/movement | toys | set up stations |
| Conclusion—fun activity | 10:55 | Hokey Pokey | circle | | Hokey Pokey |
| At-home activity | 11:00 | | | | handout: Beating Frantic Family Syndrome |

## Transition from the Parent/Child to the Preschool Aquatic Program

For the classes in which the participants soon will be three-years-old and entering the preschool section of the YMCA Swim Lessons program, you can take some of the following steps to prepare the children for being in class without a parent:

- Work with the children directly, or have the parents work with each other's children. This can be done like a relay, passing each child from one adult to another.
- If a child is ready to participate on his or her own, the parent begins by coming in with the child and working as a volunteer with other children. Then the parent just comes and observes from the deck, and finally the parent does not accompany the child at all. (This also is a great way to see if parents might be interested in becoming aquatic volunteers.)
- Gradually move to giving the children instructions instead of the adults.
- Teach some basic preschool skills in the class.
- Have the children experience water activities in all parts of the pool, including the deep end, taking appropriate precautions.

# Part III
# The Preschool Aquatic Program

**In the preschool portion of the Parent/Child and Preschool Aquatic Program, children develop fundamental swimming skills and water and boating safety awareness.**

**What they learn in these classes can be used in water recreation activities that they will enjoy when they are older and should form a foundation for swimming as a lifelong physical fitness activity.**

In addition, the physical skills preschoolers learn can help them develop an awareness of their own bodies, acquire a feeling of independence, gain a sense of success, and increase their self-esteem.

The ages of three through five are an ideal time to begin learning or expanding swimming skills. By the age of three, children usually have begun their socialization and often are old enough to attend classes without a parent or another adult caregiver. They can follow simple instructions, can communicate with adults and other children, and usually enjoy cooperating with the instructor. At this age children usually understand what they are doing and what is expected of them, and they have the ability to follow through when asked to perform appropriate skills. They are ready to begin sharing with other children and making simple, logical decisions.

A word of caution: Parents and caregivers of preschool-age children should not harbor a false sense of security just because their children are taking swim lessons. Children must always be supervised by an adult trained in water safety when they are in or near the water or could gain access to water. This is just as important in the home pool or bathtub as at the beach or the public pool. Parents often know very little about water safety; they must learn about it through this course. Safety should be emphasized to both parents as well as children.

Another important objective of the Preschool Aquatic Program, in addition to teaching swimming skills, is teaching children water and boating safety. The children learn to respect the water and to exercise caution when on or near it.

An important part of water and boating safety is to give each child an understanding of, and an ability to perform, elementary rescue skills. These basic skills include simple throwing and reaching assists with objects normally found around every pool and in most boats. Knowledge of these simple rescue skills can enable even three-year-olds to save their own or someone else's life.

The next five chapters explain the Preschool Aquatic Program. Chapter 7 introduces some of the basics of working with children three- to five-years-old and explains how parents may be involved in the program. Chapter 8 presents ideas for organizing your session and classes. Chapter 9 focuses on ways to teach preschool-age children the four core values of caring, honesty, respect, and responsibility; and the last two chapters, chapters 10 and 11, contain descriptions of sample activities for teaching the skills for the four Preschool Aquatic Program levels—Pike, Eel, Ray, and Starfish.

CHAPTER Seven

# Understanding the Preschool Aquatic Program

**The preschool portion of the Parent/Child and Preschool Aquatic Program differs from the parent/child portion in several ways.**

**The Preschool Aquatic Program is less focused on water adjustment. In addition to helping children orient to a water environment the program is working toward preparing children with some elementary swimming skills.**

It also is often the first class that the children attend on their own, without their parents, although some Ys do run preschool classes that include parents. Parents are still involved in the program but usually in a less direct way than they were in the Parent/Child Aquatic Program. The instructor works directly with the preschool-age children.

This chapter covers some of the basics of the Preschool Aquatic Program. It explains how the Preschool Aquatic Program relates to the Youth and Adult Aquatic Program and outlines the components and skills taught in the Preschool Aquatic Program. It also provides some information on the developmental characteristics of children between the ages of three and five and on discipling young children, and it reviews some of the various ways that parents can be involved in the Preschool Aquatic Program.

## Relationship to the Youth and Adult Aquatic Program

The Preschool Aquatic Program includes all the skills that are taught in the Polliwog and Guppy levels of the Youth and Adult Aquatic Program. Some modifications have been made to the levels to accommodate the developmental abilities of preschoolers. The methods of teaching those skills have been adapted to work with the younger children. The skills taught to school-age children in the Youth and Adult Aquatic Program in one level (Guppy) have been broken down into two levels (Ray and Starfish) for the preschool-age children. The Pike and Eel levels in the Preschool Aquatic Program are equivalent to the Youth and Adult Polliwog level; the Ray and Starfish levels are equivalent to the Guppy level.

Those children who successfully complete the Starfish level of the Parent/Child and Preschool Aquatic Program should be ready for the Minnow level of the Youth and Adult Aquatic Program. If you are teaching children at your Y who have completed the Starfish level but who have not yet turned six, you may want to consider offering a Minnow-level class for children under the age of six. These children have the swimming skills for the Minnow level, but they may not be ready to participate in a program with older children. Discuss the options with the children's parents, and determine the best course of action.

## Class Components and Skill Objectives

The skills taught in the preschool portion of the Parent/Child and Preschool Aquatic Program can be grouped into five main components, the same components used in the Youth and Adult Aquatic Program:

- Personal safety: Activities and information concerning safety tips and rules for behavior, health issues, pool entry and exit, water orientation and safety, boating safety, and floating
- Personal growth: Activities and discussions designed to instruct the young child in the YMCA's four core values
- Stroke development: The skills needed to develop a readiness for more advanced swimming activities
- Water sports and games: Songs, games, and activities that help children learn; also includes developmental activities related to aquatic sports, including wetball water polo, (beginning or junior) synchronized swimming, springboard diving, and underwater sports
- Rescue: Activities and discussions on how to help others or oneself in an emergency situation; activities are presented to the children in a manner appropriate to their developmental abilities

Table 7.1 provides a summary of the Preschool Aquatic Program skill objectives for the Pike and Eel levels and the Ray and Starfish levels.

The Preschool Aquatic Program for children over three has been carefully structured; however, at this age children often respond best to self-initiated activities. You can encourage children to be creative within the parameters of the program.

As an instructor you will need to provide students with a safe environment, one that encourages experimentation. Teach natural progressions, and ask children in your class to perform only those skills that they are developmentally ready to perform. Backtrack and repeat steps whenever necessary. Repetition aids the learning process, and preschoolers find repetition reassuring, not boring. You may want to review the material in *Teaching Swimming Fundamentals* on developmental progressions.

## Table 7.1 Objectives Summary Chart

**Levels:**

**Pike and Eel**

| Personal Safety | Personal Growth | Stroke Development | Water Sports and Games | Rescue |
|---|---|---|---|---|
| • Pool rules<br>• Class expectations<br>• Swim away from the wall, turn and grab the wall; take feet off the floor<br>• Front and back float<br>• Wear a PFD<br>• Jump into pool with a PFD, paddle stroke, kick on back<br>• Enter and exit a boat<br>• Step away from the side<br>• Sun safety | • Self-confidence<br>• Interpretation of core values<br>• Water fun involving a game | • Paddle on front, side, and back | • Finning and flat/stationary sculling<br>• Tub<br>• Climb down pole and swim back up to the surface<br>• Dribble a ball<br>• Pass and catch a ball | • Danger recognition<br>• Yelling for help<br>• Asking adult for assistance<br>• Dialing emergency number<br>• Performing reaching assist |

**Ray and Starfish**

| Personal Safety | Personal Growth | Stroke Development | Water Sports and Games | Rescue |
|---|---|---|---|---|
| • Diving safety rules<br>• Front and back float<br>• Tread water<br>• Wear a PFD<br>• Jump into pool wearing a PFD, paddle, back float, return<br>• HELP position<br>• Bob without an IFD<br>• Get into and out of boat safely and independently<br>• Know how to sit and change positions in boat safely | • Danger recognition and emergency procedures<br>• Demonstrate core values<br>• Safety precautions | • Front alternating paddle<br>• Front symmetrical paddle<br>• Side alternating paddle<br>• Back alternating paddle<br>• Back symmetrical paddle | • Front and back somersault<br>• Canoe sculling<br>• Jump into deep water<br>• Jump off 1-meter diving board<br>• Kneeling dive<br>• Throw, pass, catch, and dribble a ball; shoot goals | • Reaching and throwing assists<br>• Rescue breathing |

**IFD**–instructional flotation device; **PFD**–personal flotation device.

Every child should receive special, individualized attention during every class session. Try to keep class enrollment at a level that allows comfortable and appropriate interaction between you and the participants.

## Working With Three- to Five-Year-Olds

It is important that you understand the developmental abilities of three- to five-year-olds so that you can choose the appropriate games, songs, and activities for your classes. We have listed some of the common characteristics and abilities of this age group here. You also can refer to *Teaching Swimming Fundamentals* for additional information about working with children in this age range. Chapter 2 in this manual can provide you with additional helpful hints for working with children in class. Please keep in mind that age-group charts provide only a very general, approximate method of identifying children's behaviors. Many children within each age group may be either less or more developmentally advanced.

### Developmental Characteristics of the Three- to Four-Year-Old

- Has large muscle control in arms and legs, evidenced by the ability to jump down and in place and balance on one foot, walk on narrow surfaces, or play with balls (rolling and throwing them but not as successfully catching them)
- Has fine motor skills to enable basic scribbling
- Can understand and follow very specific verbal directions; accepts limits
- Uses sophisticated words like *can't* and *won't* and understands the words *cold, tired,* and *hungry*
- Speaks in full sentences but words may be only partly understandable
- Begins to have favorites—colors, foods, clothes, friends
- Classifies and names different sizes, shapes, body parts, familiar objects, and spatial concepts (e.g., on, under; bigger, smaller)
- Likes to share and play with other children
- Enjoys imaginative, imitative, and water play
- Has increased memory and understanding
- Becomes more aware of feelings and can name the simpler ones—happy, sad, angry

- Likes to find new ways to move the body through space (water play is one good way)
- May dress independently and enjoys doing things independently
- Likes to play make-believe

### Developmental Characteristics of the Five- to Six-Year-Old

- Often is happy, agile, and busy
- Asks "why" seriously, not because he or she simply likes saying the word *why*
- Jumps down, forward, and up, hops on one foot several times, and climbs ladders (up and down)
- Has fine motor skills developed well enough to allow manipulation of scissors, paste, crayons, and pencils to create rudimentary drawing or writing
- Expresses moods or needs (such as the need to go to the bathroom) to adults other than parents
- Enjoys sorting objects and classifying relationships as well as retelling stories and experiences
- Likes to inspect and collect objects (suggest the child start a "things in or for the water" collection)
- May cooperate for a while but is still very self-centered
- Can wait a short time for his or her own turn
- Plays with other children as well as parallel to other children
- Begins to understand prepositions and relationships (try using the words *to*, *from*, *over*, and *under* in the water)

- Counts to 10 or higher
- Is good at playing pretend and using drama
- Sings songs
- Commonly has imaginary playmates and tells fantasty stories
- May be quite bossy and self-assertive
- Can help around the house or in swim lessons doing simple errands and chores
- Anticipates and enjoys a consistent routine
- Follows simple rules and directions dependably

### Discipline and Young Children

Disciplining young children is a way to not only limit behavior that's inappropriate, but also teach coping skills. When you discipline, you need to look for ways to show children why their harmful or aggressive acts are not acceptable. These situations also provide opportunities for you to teach children how to solve their own problems with love and support, as well as to develop confidence and self-control.

When children are young, they may not understand why what they are doing is not appropriate. In such cases, you should direct them to more acceptable behaviors and activities. Understanding the developmental characteristics of children at this age will help you be more realistic about what you can expect to do. You will be able to tell when children are just testing the boundaries and when they are being inappropriate.

Make sure you apply consequences immediately after children misbehave. When the consequence follows right away, children are better able to understand why they are being disciplined and to relate it to their behavior. If possible, offer them positive alternatives to their inappropriate behavior.

As a last resort, you may want to use time out when a child behaves inappropriately. Remove the child from the area where the problem occurred in order to give him or her time to calm down and think about what happened, then rejoin the group. Use time out infrequently and only for short periods of time. The time out should not last longer than it takes for the child to calm down. Once the child is calm, explain what the inappropriate behavior was and what behavior would have been appropriate. Make sure the child understands this, as when he or she understands, it is more likely that he or she will not repeat the behavior.



## Role of the Parent in Preschool Classes

The Preschool Aquatic Program is structured to provide a developmentally appropriate experience for participating children. This suggests that classes can be composed of parent/child teams, children without their parents, or a mixture of both. Often parents who are involved in their children's swimming classes enjoy working in the Parent/Child and Preschool Aquatic Program as volunteer assistants, even if the class is not organized for parents and children together.

Parents should be offered an orientation meeting. This gives them an idea of the scope of the program's objectives and structure so that they understand what their children will be learning and how the classes will be conducted. They can keep abreast of what is happening in the class with the use of family huddle handouts that review class skills and suggest related activities for the whole family (see the *YMCA Swim Lessons Administrator's Manual*).

Another dimension of the parent issue is the creative use of "Parents Only" meetings. YMCA staff (instructors and/or aquatic directors) or volunteers can conduct parent discussion groups apart from the Parent/Child and Preschool Aquatic Program classes for the purpose of sharing information with parents about child development and parenting. These meetings can help the YMCA build a support group of parents who may become interested in other Y programs and community efforts. Some of the handouts in the *YMCA Swim Lessons Administrator's Manual* that lend themselves to use with parents are the following:

*Water Safety*

Aquatic Program Guidelines for Children Under the Age of Three

Backyard Pool Safety

Beach Safety

Pool Safety

Water Safety

Waterpark Safety

*Boating Safety*

Boat Smart From the Start: U.S. Coast Guard-Approved Personal Flotation Devices

Boating and Open Water Safety

The HELP Position: Maintaining Body Temperature

*Health Safety*

Immunization

Poisoning Prevention

Sudden Infant Death Syndrome (SIDS)

Sun Safety

*Accident Prevention*

Babysitter Tips

Home Safety

Toy Safety

*Child Development*

Shrimps

Kippers

Inias

Perch

The First Years Last Forever: Tips for Parents and Caregivers

*Character Development*

Character Development and Young Children

YMCA Parent Tips: Building Your Child's Self-Esteem

*Child Abuse Prevention*

Our Bodies Belong to Ourselves: What Is Child Sexual Abuse?

Words Can Hurt, Too: Child Emotional Abuse

"Hands-Off" Discipline: Preventing Child Physical Abuse

*Family Enrichment*

Areas for Family Enrichment

YMCA Parent Tips: Beating the Frantic Family Syndrome

YMCA Parent Tips: Putting Fun Into Your Family Life

Tips for Family Volunteering

What Could a Family Be?

*Parenting Tips*

Parenting

Parenting Principles

Parent sessions also provide excellent opportunities to teach parents aquatic safety skills that can help families enjoy a variety of water sports and activities safely. Meetings can focus on elementary forms of rescue, the use of personal flotation devices, boating safety, and even rescue breathing and CPR.

CHAPTER Eight

# Session and Lesson Planning

**Planning your overall session and individual classes is essential to teaching well. Planning provides you with a map to follow throughout your session, although you may need to change your plan as you see how your students progress.**

**This chapter includes hints on session and lesson planning as well as ideas for initially organizing your classes and creating special events that can add interest to your program.**

## Session Planning

Use a copy of the session planning form in figure 8.1 to plan your session of classes (A copy of the blank form can be found in the *YMCA Swim Lessons Administrator's Manual*). The form contains a column for each of the five main components, so you can touch on each of them in every lesson. After reviewing the list of skills to be included in the level that you are teaching, determine how you will organize your class and how you will cover all the skills in the number of classes you have at your Y within one session.

## Lesson Planning

Once you have finished the session planning form, develop lesson plans for each of the class days. Start by taking your session plan and the first day's topics and describing how you will actually lead the activities. Planning each day helps you to be organized when you lead your classes. Of course, things may come up to which you will have to adapt your class plan, but having a written guide will make your classes much more effective. Figure 8.2 is an example of a completed daily lesson plan. The form covers the five components of stroke development, water sports and games, personal growth, personal safety, and rescue. Use this form when planning your class greeting, warm-up and series swim, review, introduction of new skills, practice, and class conclusion.

# YMCA Swimming Session Sample Planning Form

Y SWIM LESSONS

**Level:** Pike **Number of students:** 8 **Session:** Spring **Instructor:** Jaki

| | Personal safety | Personal growth | Stroke development | Water sports and games | Rescue |
|---|---|---|---|---|---|
| #1 | pool rules<br>class exp. | self confidence<br>games | intro IFDs<br>paddling w/ w/o IFD | dribbling | |
| #2 | walk, turn, grab<br>front float | caring<br>games | paddling w/ w/o IFD | dribble pass/catch | danger recognition |
| #3 | front float | honesty<br>games | front paddling<br>w/ w/o IFD | climb down/up pole | yell for help<br>adult assist.<br>call emergency |
| #4 | PFD<br>jump/paddle PFD | honesty<br>games | back paddling<br>w/ w/o IFD | finning | reaching assists |
| #5 | back float | respect<br>games | side paddling<br>w/ w/o IFD | finning<br>pole | |
| #6 | PFD paddle f/b<br>enter/exit boat | respect<br>games | increase distance<br>w/ w/o IFD | sculling | danger recognition<br>reaching assists |
| #7 | sun safety | responsibility<br>games | increase distance<br>w/ w/o IFD | tub<br>dribble pass catch | yell for help<br>adult assist.<br>call emergency |
| #8 | review | all values<br>games | increase distance<br>w/ w/o IFD | review | review |

# YMCA Swimming Lesson Planning Form

Y SWIM LESSONS

Instructor: Jaki
Class (level): Pike
Today's learning objectives:
1. orientation
2. movement
3. comfort

Day: Saturday (1st week)
Session: Spring
Safety considerations:
1. good orientation for students
2. watch students carefully
3.

Date:
Class time: 9–9:30 AM
Material/equipment:
1. water logs/kickboards
2. belts
3. floating toys/rings

| | Time | Description of activity/ method of teaching | Class organization pattern | Equipment needed | Notes or explanation |
|---|---|---|---|---|---|
| Greeting | 9:00 am | welcome/tour pool & class rules | class group discussion | | name game |
| Warm-up/series swim | 9:05 | water entry comfort assessment walking games | corner swim | floating toys rings belts | hokey pokey head, shoulders, knees & toes |
| Review | 9:10 | | | | |
| Introduce new skills | 9:15 | intro IFDs paddling | single circle swim | water logs kickboards float belts | put on belts |
| Practice | 9:20 | paddling | circle swim | | take off belts |
| Conclusion—fun activity | 9:25 | games: simon says red light, green light | | | |
| At-home activity | 9:30 | handout family huddle | | | pool rules family huddle |

### Greeting

When your class gathers in your designated meeting place, make announcements and tell parents relevant information related to the class. You also may want to give parents an overview of the day's lesson, listing the topics to be covered, and give specific instructions regarding safety and conduct.

Select an opening song or activity. Use it consistently throughout the session to establish a familiar routine.

### Warm-Up/Series Swim

The series swim is a key method with which the YMCA Swim Lessons Program provides skill repetition and develops fitness endurance. It involves swimming widths or lengths. Children in the Preschool Aquatic Program should begin the series swim by putting on their flotation belts or getting kickboards or other instructional flotation devices (IFDs), based on their skill level. (Additional information on series swims is provided within the Preschool Aquatic Program in Component 3 of chapters 10 and 11.)

### Review

Whenever you present skills and experiences to a group, you should review them periodically. Each lesson should include a review of some activities from the previous lessons. During this time you review any skills you introduced in earlier classes. The skills can be incorporated into songs and games. Setting time aside to repeat previously taught songs and activities and to discuss progress made reinforces the learning process and promotes a smooth progression. In this section of the lesson planning form, list the skills to be reviewed.

### Introduce New Skills

Choose which skills you want to introduce in this day's class and write them in this area of the form. This may include both water skills and short discussion topics. Choose activities from each of the five components: stroke development, water sports and games, personal growth, personal safety, and rescue.

### Practice

Provide opportunities for the children to practice the skills you have taught. Describe in this space on the form how you will provide the class with opportunities for practicing, and list any IFDs or instructional equipment you will need.

### Class Conclusion

Choose a fun activity or song that you can use consistently throughout the session. This routine will signal to the children that the class is coming to a close. Having a concluding activity, such as a song that says good-bye or a quiet activity and time to let each child know that he or she is special, is

a fitting end to a class. On the form describe what activity you will use to end the class. If parents are not part of your class, you also will need to escort the children from class to the designated area where their parents are waiting to pick them up.

### At-Home Activity

At the YMCA we hope that the information presented in this class becomes an integral part of parents' and children's lives. To achieve this aim, you should assign an activity at the end of each class for the family to do at home so that the children can continue to practice their aquatic activities outside of class. Such at-home experiences can help the children progress and develop skills, reinforcing what they have accomplished in class.

Handing out family huddle handouts (found in the *YMCA Swim Lessons Administrator's Manual*) is one option. These handouts are designed to reinforce the learning in the YMCA Swim Lessons program and to encourage family activities. The front side of each family huddle handout suggests an activity for the child. The other side provides helpful information for parents, a family activity, and a Y tidbit. Children can take the handouts home to their families to complete, then talk about the at-home activity at the next class session. Use the daily lesson planning form to list the appropriate family handout or activity.

Another option is to send home parent handouts (also found in the *YMCA Swim Lessons Administrator's Manual*). These handouts provide parents with information on parenting issues. You may want to select the subject, time, and place to discuss specific issues with parents and then share the appropriate handout. Handouts may also be used in response to a question from a parent. (A list of handouts appears on pages 27 and 28 of chapter three).

Chapters 10 and 11 give you activities to help you build your lessons. You also can choose from the activities, games, and songs in appendix B. After each class is over, note how the class went, record suggestions for improving the flow of the class, and add any new ideas that came to mind.

## Class Start-Up

Assign children to the different Preschool Aquatic Program levels—Pike, Eel, Rays, and Starfish—by current skill level rather than age. Most YMCAs offer all four levels at the same time, allowing friends and siblings to participate simultaneously, although in different classes.

The first class meeting can include all the parents and children and should cover the following topics:

- Introduction of staff
- Explanation of why the YMCA conducts a preschool swimming instruction program
- Presentation of realistic program expectations
- Reasons why the YMCA advocates the use of flotation devices and the advantages of their use for the children
- Ways that parents can help prepare their children for class, such as observing rules for showering, toileting, and so on
- Explanation of who will be permitted to observe the classes, or why watching is not allowed if the policy is not to allow observers



- A tour for parents and children that follows the path they will take through the building to the swimming pool
- Screening of children to determine ability level
- A question-and-answer period

The first day of the session is exciting and scary for young children. New faces, sounds, smells, and the pool environment itself all contribute to their feelings. The sooner the children can get into their classes, the more comfortable they will feel. Follow whatever procedures your Y has developed for screening children and assigning them to the appropriate levels and instructors.

Once the group has had some time to acclimate to the class and has begun working on skills, you may find that some students need to be placed into different levels. After the children become comfortable and confident in the class situation, they may be able to demonstrate additional skills not observed on the first day. The first day tends to be scary and uncomfortable for them. Don't be surprised to find that a child who was reluctant, scared, and unhappy on the first day of class is able to perform at a higher level of skill by the second or third class. Such children can be moved to another level in the program after only one or two lessons.

## Special Events

Each of the levels of the Preschool Aquatic Program may be repeated more than once by any of the participants. In fact, often children repeat levels of the program several times, as the levels were not designed to ensure progression from one level to the next within one session. Thus, the classes should vary from session to session to give students a feeling of progress and improvement. Even if a level is repeated, performance will improve as long as the instructors provide new and different ways of doing things.

Special events can aid this process. Use such events to create new themes for classes, and in some cases you may want to invite parents to join in the fun. The following are some ideas for special events you may want to incorporate into your session:

- *An imaginary trip to the circus:* Children go through their paces, performing in a decorative circus atmosphere created with their own themes and ideas that might include a center ring, leaping tigers, diving seals, and so on.
- *A superstars competition between teams composed of kids or of parents and kids:* Events can include ball pushing or dribbling, object recovery, obstacle courses, or kickboard races. The general atmosphere should be noncompetitive, and a spirit of fun should prevail.
- *A water show for children to demonstrate their skills to their parents:* Prearranged routines can be included.
- *A Challenge Day:* Children demonstrate skills, and parents are challenged to try the skills themselves.

- *A Story Day:* The children use water skills to act out a story. This can be improvised or prepared, depending on your confidence and experience.
- *A Special Guest Day:* Invite a particular skill group (synchronized swimmers, scuba divers, etc.) to demonstrate their specialty, and let the children try some parts of the activity.
- *A Dress-Up Day:* Ask children to wear different types of swimsuit costumes (especially around Halloween).

You might also plan a special day of the session that includes the following:

- A demonstration or show and tell, with the children performing nonswimming rescues and other skills learned during the session
- A short talk, or show and tell, on safe boating and the use of PFDs
- Songs and games for everyone
- A certificate distribution ceremony
- Encouragement to join up for the next session—when, where, and how
- Discussion and refreshments as a chance for parents to ask questions and make comments about the program

CHAPTER nine

# Teaching Character Development

**Character development involves teaching students how to recognize and follow these four core values:**

***Caring:*** to love others; to be sensitive to the well-being of others

***Honesty:*** integrity; to tell the truth; to act in such a way that you are worthy of trust

***Respect:*** regard; to treat others as you would have them treat you; to value the worth of every person, including yourself

***Responsibility:*** to do what is right, what you ought to do; to do what you say you will do

The most effective and common methods of working with preschoolers on these values are simple games, stories, and praise and reinforcement. Being a positive role model for each of these values goes a long way. An important aspect of your role as a YMCA swim instructor is being aware of the YMCA core values and reinforcing the appropriate behavior. When children are between the ages of three and five, we need to help them understand what the word for a value means and how the value is expressed in behavior. Pointing out the behavior when it occurs and naming the value it demonstrates is important. Take a few moments during class and let students know when one of the values has been put into action.

This chapter provides you with general tips and some activities for teaching each of the four core values: caring, honesty, respect, and responsibility. You can find additional character development activities in appendix B.

## Caring

### General Tips

- Teach by example. Being nice, helping others, and showing manners and politeness are ways of demonstrating caring for others. Demonstrating these qualities and smiling and sharing with young children helps them understand that helping others is enjoyable and makes both the children and yourself feel good. Explain to the children that usually when you are nice and kind to people, or tell them nice things or compliment them, they are nice to you in return.

- Respond to a child's inappropriate behavior in a firm but caring manner. If a child does something wrong in class, let the child know what he or she did wrong. Give the child a chance to apologize, and help the child to understand how the inappropriate behavior affected others. Reinforce that you still care for the child, like the child, and want him or her to be in your class.

### Activities

- Tell stories that demonstrate caring. Many of the rescue and personal safety activities are ones that can be used to show how caring for others is good and helpful. Children enjoy the stories and can learn from them.
- Have children think of things they can do for others, for instance, sharing the helpful safety and rescue information they learn in class with their friends and family. This is a way the children can demonstrate how they care for their friends and family. At the next class ask the children what happened after they shared their new safety information with others.
- Play the care game. Give examples of situations, and let the children tell you whether the person in the situation was being caring or uncaring. Here are some situations you might use to describe to the class:
  - Earl was playing at his grandmother's swimming pool. After playing, he left after putting the pool toys away. Was Earl being caring or uncaring?
  - Earl and Rose were playing in the sand at the beach. Rose threw sand at Earl and ran away. Was Rose being caring or uncaring?
- Talk about examples of caring in between activities during class or whenever an appropriate moment occurs among students in class.
- Provide children with an opportunity to serve others. Even young children can be given things to do to help others. They can get equipment for their classmates or help one another with activities. Ask them to help, and tell them how happy it makes you when they help. Tasks such as these can help young children experience the joy of caring for others.

## Honesty

### General Tips

- Be honest. This shows your commitment to the importance of the value of being honest. Avoid "convenient lies," and, if you cannot answer a child's question, tell them why you will not answer their question.
- Praise children for telling the truth. "Catch them doing something right" when they tell the truth and praise them for it. Give them a chance to have a "do-over" if you believe they are not telling the truth by reminding them it is important to tell the truth.
- Point out consequences. Find examples in real life, books, or television shows that demonstrate being honest and not being honest, the consequences to the person being dishonest, and the effect dishonesty has on others. Show the positives of being honest as well as the negative effects of being dishonest.

### Activities

- To help preschoolers understand what honesty means, ask them if they know the difference between something that is true and something that is not true. Then say, "Let's see how good we are." Share with them examples of things that you say that may be true or not true, and have the children tell you which each one is. Start with physical facts; then move to things relating to behavior. The following examples relate to physical facts. You can make this a fun and silly game.
  - The pool water is red. [Not true]
  - (Point to your nose.) This is my foot. [Not true]
  - We walk on our feet. [True]
  - We breathe through our elbows. [Not true]
  - (Take a cookie and eat it.) I did not eat the cookie. [Not true]
  - (Put a towel on your head.) The towel is on my head. [True]

Next, move on to issues of behavior. Ask the class, "If you say something that is not true, what is it called?" [A lie] Then suggest, "Let's play another game, Truth or Lie. Say 'truth' if what I'm saying is true, and say 'lie' if it is not true."

  - (Take a toy from one of the lockers.) I didn't find any toy. [Lie]
  - Instruct the children to give a kickboard to one of their classmates. Then have them say, " I gave a kickboard to ___________." [Truth.]

Ask children why they think it would be better to tell the truth instead of telling lies.

- Preschoolers tend to repeat behavior for which they receive attention. For this reason you must frequently point out behavior within your classes that demonstrates honesty. Preschoolers thrive on positive attention and praise rather than negative attention, but they would rather have negative attention than no attention at all.
- Help children realize that feelings are caused by what happens to a person and that it is okay to feel things and to tell others how we honestly feel. You can help them to do this by asking questions about how they think someone feels in a sample situation and why. Help children to identify their feelings and the probable causes of those feelings. Tell them that it is okay to feel that way and to tell other people about what they feel.

## Respect

### General Tips

- Create an environment that promotes mutual respect. If you respect the children, you can expect respect in return. Say "please" and "thank you." Avoid explaining yourself by saying, "because I said so." Ask for children's advice, ideas, and opinions, and respect them. Ask the children to do things, instead of telling them to do so; this helps set a respectful tone. Make it clear that respect includes tone of voice as well as actions. Be consistently respectful.
- Encourage respectful behavior by noticing when children demonstrate it and praising their behavior. Praise courtesy and politeness. Give the children a chance to have a "do-over" if they fail to show respect by reminding them that it is important to be nice and courteous.
- Be a good role model for respect. Show your commitment to being respectful of others, yourself, property, and nature, and to being polite in all situations.
- Encourage children to be good listeners, and model it by being a good listener to the children yourself.

### Activities

- Help preschoolers learn about respect by helping them to understand what it means. Use the term often in your class, and point out situations that involve respectfulness, such as taking turns. To a young child, respect can be understood more easily as "acting nice," "talking nice," or "minding others."
- A simple way to incorporate the concept of respect into your classes is to use a character, a puppet, or a name of some other imaginary child as an individual about whose actions you will ask questions. Have the children tell you whether this individual is being respectful or not. Here are some examples:
  - Earl the eel was asked to put his float belt and water log in the box after class. He said, "No! I don't want to." [Not respectful]
  - Earl the eel took the only ball to play with and would not let others play with him. [Not respectful]
  - Earl the eel had to go to the bathroom during class. He said to the teacher, "I need to go to the bathroom. May I go?" [Respectful]
  - Earl the eel sat in his wet swimsuit on the car seat. [Not respectful]
  - Earl could not paddle all the way across the pool. He said, "I'm not good at swimming. I'm stupid." [Not respectful]
- Another activity that can help young children to understand why respect should be shown is letting the children play adults and you play the child. Think of short scenarios, and let each child get a

chance to be an adult. After the scenario ask the child, "How did it make you feel?" Here are some examples:
- Children are not paying attention to the teacher while the teacher is trying to lead an activity.
- A child pushes in front of another adult to take his or her turn first.
- A child gives a toy to the teacher.

→ Play a modified tag game. You start by being "It." If you catch them, they have to make up and say a long, silly word to be released. After a few examples, ask them if they want easier words. Let them know that using words like "please" will often cause people to do things you want them to do; "thank you" is a word that makes others feel good.

## Responsibility

### General Tips

→ Be a role model. Let the children know how you are trying to improve and be better. Let them know what you think you do well and on what things you want to work to improve. If you make a mistake, let the children know you have made a mistake. Say, "It's my fault. Here's what I could have done differently." Let the children know you can accept responsibility and blame and that you take pride in who you are and that you are working to be better.

→ Give praise. By praising children you are helping to build their self-image and confidence in themselves, which is important for building self-reliance. Catch them doing something responsible and let them know it. When they make a mistake, help them accept responsibility for it, and then praise them for accepting their mistake and for showing that their pride in their self-reliance outshines the concern over their mistake. Look for things that each child does to improve him- or herself, and praise the effort he or she is making. Helping children to like and to become capable of relying on themselves allows them to accept responsibility and to reach their full potential.

### Activities

→ Use time out. If two children get into a dispute, have both children sit in time-out for a short period until they can tell you what they both (not the other child) did wrong. This helps build self-reliance and gives practice in accepting responsibility instead of blaming others. (see "Discipline and Young Children" in chapter seven).

- Give each child a job to do for the day during class. It could be getting toys, kickboards, or flotation belts; giving the "listen" signal; checking that everyone's flotation belt is on properly; and so on. At the end of class, praise the children for being responsible and for their ability to do things for themselves.
- Discuss children's responsibilities or chores at home. Are they required to pick up their clothes and put them away? When they get ready for bed, where do they put their dirty clothes? Do their parents have them brush their teeth at night? Explain that these are all responsibilities.

CHAPTER Ten

# Pike and Eel Levels

**This chapter contains sample instructional steps for specific activities to teach the skills of the Pike and Eel levels.**

**The activities are grouped by the five components in this order: personal safety, personal growth, stroke development, water sports and games, and rescue.**

Under each component you will find the following:

- *Objectives:* Several objectives are given for each component. Each objective is immediately followed by discussion guidelines and performance criteria.
- *Skill description:* Occasionally a skill description precedes the sample teaching instructions. When one or more new skills are to be introduced, a description of each of those skills can be found here. This information is provided to help you in guiding students to discover the best way to perform each skill.
- *Discussion guidelines for instructors:* A sample of steps is given for you to use in teaching the skill being presented. Each skill can be presented in many different ways, however, and you need to develop alternative methods as part of your development as an instructor.
- *Materials Needed:* If specific equipment or materials are needed to carry out the teaching steps, those materials are listed here.
- *Performance criteria:* This section describes the minimum performance that students should be able to achieve for each objective.
- *Summary of performance criteria:* At the end of this and the next chapter is a list of the criteria to be met for each activity described in the chapter. The Pike and Eel levels in the Preschool Aquatic Program are equivalent to the Polliwog level in the Youth and Adult Aquatic Program. Students move toward meeting the criteria in smaller steps in the Preschool Aquatic Program, so in some activities we have presented two different criteria, one for each level.

Also scattered throughout this and the following chapter are *Instructor Notes.* These are cautions,

recommendations, or suggestions for instructors to follow regarding specific activities.

While enrolled in the Pike and Eel levels, the student is

- Introduced to pool rules
- Acquainted with class expectations
- Oriented to the pool surroundings and water as well as to the use of instructional flotation devices (IFDs)
- Helped to learn the front float, how to take a breath, and to recover to a stand from a glide
- Helped to learn the back float and the resting float
- Given an explanation of the correct use of U.S. Coast Guard-approved personal flotation devices (PFDs) and allowed to practice wearing them
- Helped to learn how to get into and out of a boat safely
- Helped to learn to step or jump away from the pool wall, turn around, and reach for the wall without assistance
- Involved in a discussion of sun safety
- Helped to gain self-confidence
- Involved in a discussion of the core values at the YMCA
- Helped to relax and have fun in the water through a game
- Helped to learn the front paddle stroke
- Helped to learn the side and back paddle
- Introduced to finning and sculling
- Introduced to the tub, a synchronized swimming skill
- Allowed to experience going underwater
- Helped to learn to pass and catch a ball (push pass) and to dribble a ball across the pool
- Introduced to victim and danger recognition and reaching assists
- Given practice in calling for help or going for or phoning for adult assistance

Prerequisite: Child must be at least three years old.

## Component 1: Personal Safety

**Objective:** To learn the pool rules and the importance of pool safety

*Discussion Guidelines for Instructors*

### YMCA Cool Pool Rules

**It Takes Two to Enjoy the Pool!**
*Always swim with a friend or where a lifeguard or parent is present.*

**Enjoy the Pool Safely!**
*No running in or near the pool area.*

**Swimmers Use Their Mouths for Breathing!**
*No food, drink, or gum is permitted in the pool area.*

**Help Keep the Water Clear!**
*Always use the restroom and take a soap shower before entering the pool.*

**Be Prepared!**
*Learn safety, rescue, and first aid.*

1. Talk about why we need rules when we are around water.
2. Ask students what rules they think would be important.
3. Let the students decide why these rules will help keep them safe.
4. Have the students put the rules into their own words.
5. Let students create their own additional rules.
6. Ask the students if they can think of any other good ways to be safe in the pool, at the beach, at home, and at the Y.
7. Talk about how rules relate to values.

Here is a sample of the questions you might use to discuss pool rules:

"How can we keep the water clean (or respect the water and others in the water)?" Look for answers such as *Always shower before entering the pool* or *Wash our hands with soap and water after using the restroom.*

"Why don't swimmers chew gum in the pool?" Look for answers such as *Swimmers need to breathe through their mouths.*

"Why is it your responsibility to throw away your gum before getting in the pool?" Look for answers such as *So I won't choke* or *So another swimmer doesn't step on it.*

"Why should you wait for your instructor before you get in the pool?" Look for answers such as *It's safer to wait until the instructor is there, so he or she can help you.*

"How do we move around when on the deck in the pool area?" Look for answers such as *We always walk* or *We watch where we're going.*

"Do we splash other swimmers? Why or why not?" Look for answers such as *We don't splash because we respect others' likes or dislikes* or *We don't splash because we care about how others feel, and they might not like getting splashed.*

"What can we do to get ourselves ready for swim lessons?" Look for answers such as *We bring our towels, We put on our flotation belts,* or *We go to the bathroom and take a shower first.*

"How do we care for the swim equipment?" Look for answers such as *We pick it up and put it away, We don't break it,* or *We always use it the way it should be used.*

The rules become an important part of the pool environment when the students tell each other about infractions and become self-disciplined.

Instructor Note: *Also be aware of the following important safe teaching guidelines for yourself:*

- *Keep all students in view at all times. Never turn your back.*
- *Never ever leave your class unattended, even for a few seconds.*
- *Comply with your local YMCA lifeguard policy.*
- *Be aware of each student's limitations.*
- *Make sure the pool is clear at the end of each class.*
- *Establish a quick method of communication for class control, class organization, and pool evacuation.*
- *Know your emergency procedures so well they are almost automatic.*
- *Be sure the pool rules are posted in a visible place.*
- *Take and record attendance for each class.*

## Performance Criteria

The student should

**Pike and Eel**

→ participate actively in the discussion,

→ be able to repeat the rules, and

→ be able to discuss the rules.

**Objective:** To learn expectations that help make class fun and enjoyable for all

## Discussion Guidelines for Instructors

Instructor Note: *Introduce some basic class expectations for conduct so students immediately learn what is acceptable and unacceptable behavior in class. The following expectations can help you get started. You can use these as they are, adapt them, or add to them. Remember, however, to keep them simple.*

- ***Take turns talking****...let everyone have a chance.*
- ***Be a polite listener****...then others may listen to you.*
- ***Don't call people names****...be friendly instead.*
- ***Share toys and take turns****...that way everyone gets to play.*
- ***Take charge of yourself****...you are responsible for you.*
- ***Show respect****...every person is important.*

1. Discuss the importance of each expectation with your group.
2. Let the students decide why these expectations will help make class more pleasant.
3. Have the students put the expectations into their own words.
4. Let students create their own additional reasonable expectations if they like.

## Performance Criteria

The student should

***Pike and Eel***

→ participate in the discussion,

→ be able to repeat the class expectations, and

→ be able to discuss them.

**Objective:** To learn to walk away from the wall, turn around, and reach and grab onto the wall without assistance; to be comfortable in the water; and to take the feet off the floor while wearing an individual flotation device (IFD)

Materials Needed: IFDs

## Discussion Guidelines for Instructors

1. Have students walk around and explore the pool area on deck as a group.
2. Ask, "Do you know where the shallow water is? Where are the steps? Where is the ladder? Where is the deep water? Are you ready to get in?"
3. Have the students sit on the pool edge as you stand in the water facing them. Ask a series of exploratory, problem-solving questions such as the following to help guide the children to enter the water safely:
   - "Can you put one body part in the water while staying on the deck?" If they are successful, move on by asking, "Can you put a different body part in the water?" Have children try moving their feet, legs, hands, arms, and so on.
   - "Safely, can you put two body parts in at once?" Repeat, looking for unique combinations.
   - "Safely, can you get all the way into the water feet first? Safely, can you do it another way?"
4. Begin to ask a series of questions such as the following to work toward floating and buoyancy:
   - "While you are in the water, what body parts can you get or keep out of the water?" Repeat the question, looking for other options.
   - "Can you get two body parts out of the water and only touch bottom with one body part?" Repeat, asking for different solutions.

5. "Can you make air bubbles in the water?" Possible solutions may be splashing with the hands or feet or blowing bubbles through the mouth or nose.
6. "Can you make bubbles with your ears? No, I guess not. How about with your elbow? What body part works best in making bubbles?" (Note: Hands and feet can make "splash" air bubbles.)
7. "Can you make bubbles with just your nose? How about just with your mouth? How about both?"
8. "Has anyone ever seen a fish underwater? Has anyone ever tried to talk to a fish? Must be pretty silly, isn't it? What would it be like if you tried to talk to a fish—show me."
9. "Can anyone hum? What songs can you hum? How about 'Pop Goes the Weasel'? Does anyone know 'Row, Row, Row Your Boat'? Try humming one of those songs underwater. What happens?" Can anyone hum 'Row, Row, Row Your Boat' underwater?"
10. Ask students who can step out to you (you are about two feet away from the wall) to give you a celebration signal after they step. It could be a high five, or clapping, or cheers to celebrate success. Students probably can suggest alternative celebration techniques. After they step out, help them turn around and reach for the wall. (Being able to step out and turn around to reach for the wall is an important safety skill.)

Instructor Note: *If your pool is too deep for students to stand in, encourage them to give you a high five while holding on to the side with one hand or to try to swim or paddle a few feet while wearing an IFD.*

These steps may be done with or without students wearing flotation (or float) belts, depending upon the students' comfort in the water. Flotation belts are used to help students participate with more confidence and to allow the entire class to spend more time in the water instead of just taking turns one-on-one with you. Explain to children how and why IFDs are used, and as you strap them on the children, tell them to only let you take them off.

You can gradually alter the body position toward the horizontal of a student by moving the flotation belt from the child's hips to the chest. For each individual child, put the belt in the most helpful place that still allows him or her to balance safely.

Students who are reluctant to put their faces in the water can paddle in the water with float belts or kickboards. This allows them time to get used to the water and to learn basic paddling skills without the fear of putting their faces underwater until they are ready.

To encourage students to get their faces wet, ask them to pretend they are washing their faces at home in the bathtub. Alternatively, you can ask them a progressive series of questions such as the following. First ask them, "What can you use to wash your face? Show me how." They may use washcloths, sponges, or just their hands. Then continue by asking,

"Can you wash your nose with one hand? What about with two hands? Can you wash your chin with one hand? With two hands?" Last, follow up with "Can you wash behind your ears? Can you wash your cheeks? Can you wash your whole face? Can you wash your hair?"

Additionally, while holding on to the pool edge in the water, students can go through another movement exploration series using "Who can?" questions to help them get used to being in the pool. Examples are "Who can see the bottom?" and "Who can hold their breath and put their face in the water?" Never force students to do anything that frightens them. You can achieve more by using humor, exploration, and fun than by pushing, urging, or coercing.

### *Performance Criteria*

The student should

***Pike***

- be able to walk away from the pool wall, turn around, and reach and grab onto the wall with assistance, *or*
- if the child can't stand in the water, be able to let go of the pool wall while wearing an IFD, swim or paddle a few feet, turn around and grab the wall with assistance, and
- be comfortable being in the water, and
- take the feet off the floor while wearing an IFD.

***Eel***

- be able to walk away from the pool wall, turn around, and reach and grab onto the wall without assistance, *or*
- if the child can't stand, be able to let go of the pool wall while wearing an IFD, swim or paddle a few feet, turn around and grab the wall without assistance, and
- be comfortable being in the water, and
- take the feet off the floor while wearing an IFD.



**Objective:** To learn how to back or front float, with or without support, and to be able to take a breath and to recover to a standing position

### Materials Needed:

various flotation devices and kickboards, one for each student

### *Skill Description*

The student does the front (prone) float with the front of the body down in the water, usually with the face in the water. The position may vary in the angle of the body in the water, the position of the arms, the degree of symmetry, and the amount of bend at the elbows, shoulders, hips, and knees. To do a front float, the student must be able to hold the breath, must not be afraid to put the face into the water or to float, and must be able to right him- or herself from the prone position to standing.

The student does the back (supine) float with the back of the body down in the water. The position may vary in the same ways as in the front float; however, the student does not have to be able to hold the breath or put the face into the water as in the front float. He or she still must not be afraid to float and must be able to right him- or herself from the supine position to standing.

Keep in mind that because all body types are different (depending on the amount of muscle mass and bone density vs. fat), students will float at different levels and positions in the water. Some might not float at all without using their arms or legs for stability and support. Consider this factor when evaluating students' floating skill performance.

### *Discussion Guidelines for Instructors*

Have students sit in a circle on the deck or stand in the shallow end of the pool. Say, "Let's play a game. We're at the beach. It's warm, and the water is beautiful. Show me or tell me some safe things we might be doing at the beach." (Answers include sunbathing, building sand castles, and swimming.) Continue, "Okay, if we were in the water swimming, we might get tired. What could we do if we were tired?" (Answers might be get out of the water, rest, stand up, have Mom or Dad hold me up.) "What if we got tired and were in too deep to stand up? How could we rest?" Have them tell you their ideas; then have them actually try to stand up, float on the back, and roll over.

Instructor Note: *Give students the opportunity to experiment, first verbally, then physically, with different methods of staying afloat. Guiding questions asking them to focus on what they do with their hands and arms, legs, and buttocks may help. It is best to ask and help them explore rather than tell them. Make this a game by having students time each other, by letting them vote on the most enjoyable way to stay afloat, or by having a friendly contest of showing how many different variations of floating they can do. Talk about various types of flotation devices, such as inner tubes, water logs, and barbells, and floating objects, such as beach balls. Place several such devices around the pool so students can have fun choosing which one they like the best.*

**Buoyancy**

Ask the following series of questions:

1. "With your shoulders underwater, who can balance on the big toe? Can you do this on land? It would hurt, wouldn't it?"
2. "Why is it easier to balance in the water than on land?" (Answer: The water holds you up.)
3. "What does this mean?" (Answer: That we can float in the water.)
4. "Why does the water hold us up?" (Answer: The pressure of the water.) For a more detailed answer, use the flotation lesson from The Physics of Swimming section of chapter 7 in *Teaching Swimming Fundamentals.*
5. "Why do we use a float belt, kickboard, or water log? (Answer: It helps the water 'hold us up' even more because it floats so well.)

**Front float**

Ask the following progressive series of questions:

1. "Can you get your feet off the bottom? Show me."
2. "How many different ways can you get your feet off the bottom?" (Examples: jump up, with the feet off momentarily; lift one foot; hold on to the side; hold on to someone else; hold on to the instructor; use a flotation belt.)
3. "Who can keep both feet off the bottom for one second? How about two seconds? Three seconds?"
4. "How many ways can you keep your feet off the bottom for three seconds?"
5. "What position is best?"
6. "What happens when I pull you? This is like going for a ride."
7. "What does your body feel like?"
8. "Where did your feet go?"

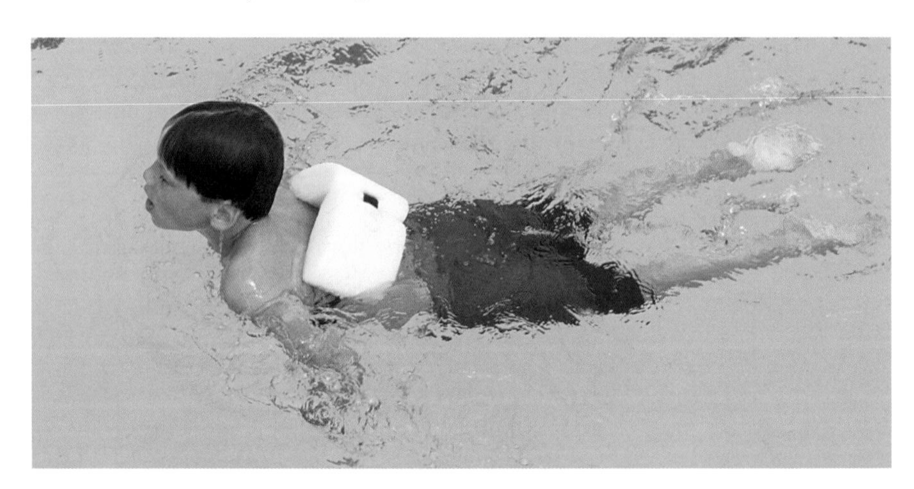

Instructor Note: *As you move through this process, students should become more familiar with being in the water and letting the flotation belt support them. As students relax while you pull them, see if they can try to put their faces in the water while being pulled. Then try to see if they will let you release their hands for a few seconds. Ask them what it feels like when they are floating by themselves. See if they can recover to vertical, standing position by themselves. Then*

*ask them how else they could float if you weren't holding on to them. What else could they use to help them? (Answers: flotation belts, water logs, kickboards, holding on to the side, kicking their feet, paddling their arms.) Next, have students try going for a ride with the belt on and a kickboard under each arm.*

**Recovery to a standing position**

1. Say, "Now that we can float, how can we stop?" Have them try their ideas while they are being pulled. (Examples: putting feet down, pushing back against the water, grabbing the wall.)
2. After a few attempts, ask them which way was easier or better for them. Point out those who drew their knees to their chest, pressed down with their hands, and lifted their heads. This helps position the feet and legs under the hips and makes it easier to stand.

**Getting a breath**

1. Ask, "If you had your face in the water and you wanted to be able to float longer on your stomach without standing up again, what could you do? Show me." (Examples: roll over, lift head to vertical, then float on back.) Continue with guiding questions until they try to press their arms down and lift their heads.

**Back float**

Ask the following series of questions:

1. "Who can get both feet off the bottom and still keep your face dry? How would you do this?" (Examples: side or back positions, hanging on to the side, using an IFD, using another person.) If they need a hint, say, "Use a different body position."
2. "What seems to work best for your body—being straight or bent?"
3. "Where can you put your arms when you are on your side? How about when you are on your back? Does it make a difference where you put them?"
4. Distribute one kickboard to each student. Then ask, "Can we pretend this kickboard is a pillow?" (Wait for responses.) "What could you do with it if it were a pillow? Cuddle it? Put it under your head? Sit on it?"

5. "What if the kickboard were a piece of bread—a big piece of bread? Let's spread peanut butter and jelly all over your body and make a sandwich using the kickboard!"
6. "Can you be a peanut butter and jelly sandwich with the bread down?"
7. "Can you be a peanut butter and jelly sandwich with the bread up?"
8. "Can you be a peanut butter and jelly sandwich with the bread facing some other direction?"

9. "How can you float on your back using a kickboard? On your side?"

Instructor Note: *Start by supporting the students' heads while taking them for a ride. As the students become comfortable, tell them that you are going to release their heads, but you will stay right by them if they need anything. You also can try this using a water log.*

10. "Now that you can float, how can you stand back up? Let's see." (Examples: drop hips and sit, push with arms, roll over, sink down and stand, thrash around a lot.)
11. "Which methods of trying to stand up kept your face dry?"
12. "Which methods of trying to stand up do you like best?"

Instructor Note: *To stand up from the back float, students should look toward their feet and drop their hips down (like sitting in a chair) as they circle their arms forward and then backward.*

## *Performance Criteria*

The student should

***Pike***

- be able to support him- or herself in the water for 30 seconds with a flotation belt,
- be able to demonstrate the front and back float with a flotation belt for 20 seconds,
- be able to take a breath on the front float with a flotation belt, and
- be able to recover to standing from both the front and back float with assistance.

***Eel***

- be able to support him- or herself in the water for 30 seconds with a flotation belt,
- be able to demonstrate the front and back float without a flotation belt for 10 seconds,
- be able to take a breath on the front float without flotation support, and
- be able to recover to standing from both the front and back float without assistance.

 Objective: To learn about the U.S. Coast Guard (USCG)-approved personal flotation devices (PFDs) and to be able to select an appropriately sized one, put it on, secure it, and take it off; to understand the differences between a PFD and an instructional flotation device (IFD)

Materials Needed: PFDs, one for each student and various classes of PFDs

## *Discussion Guidelines for Instructors*

Instructor Note: *PFDs are personal flotation devices that have been determined to be in compliance with USCG specifications and regulations related to performance, construction, or materials. Look for the USCG stamp of approval on the device to confirm that it is certified.*

*IFDs are used for specific teaching purposes during swimming. They may help students float, but they are not designed to hold the students up in the water for a long period of time in the absence of an adult. They also are not certified. These are important and critical differences that both students and parents need to know and take into account.*

1. Show students a PFD and ask them, "What is this called?" (Answers: a lifejacket or a PFD.)
2. Ask, "What is it used for?" (Answer: to help you float.)
3. Ask, "When should you wear it?" (Answer: whenever you are in a boat or in other water-related activities.)
4. Show students examples of IFDs such as a kickboard, belt, and water log. Ask, "What are these used for?" (Answer: to help you while you are learning to swim.)
5. Ask, "How is one of these different from a PFD?" (Answer: PFDs are designed to be worn for safety in water; IFDs are worn for play or instructional use only when an adult is in the water.)
6. Discuss the available types of PFDs and why we wear them, explaining at a level suitable for the cognitive abilities of your students. Make the following points:
   - PFDs are made in high-visibility colors. Ask students why this is important. (Answer: So you can be seen easier in the water).
   - A PFD has proven and tested buoyancy. Show where this is stamped on the PFD and let everyone see it. Ask students why this would be important. (Answer: To know it's a real PFD).
   - PFDs may have different kinds of fasteners. Have students practice fastening all the various types.
   - PFDs keep you warmer in cold water, which can help prevent hypothermia. Explain to students that, if they should fall into cold water and have to stay there for a while, their body temperature could be cooled down to where it is dangerous. A PFD could help hold their heat in.
   - PFDs come in many sizes and styles so people can select the one that fits most comfortably and for the right purpose. Ask students questions such as the following: "How can you tell if a PFD fits properly? Could you wear an adult PFD? Why or why not? Could you wear one that your little brother or sister would wear? Why or why not? Who should wear PFDs? " (Answer: Everyone who is boating or engaged in whitewater activities.)
7. Have students practice putting lifejackets on and securing them. Allow students to check each other to see if the lifejackets are on correctly.

8. Help students take off their lifejackets and store the lifejackets in their proper place.

### *Performance Criteria*

The student should

| | |
|---|---|
| ***Pike and Eel*** | → be able to secure and take off and put away a PFD and |
| | → be able to explain the differences between a PFD and an IFD. |

**Objective:** To learn how to jump into a pool wearing a PFD (giving the PFD a hug), perform a front paddle stroke for 10 yards, then turn onto the back, paddle, and perform a back kick for 10 yards

**Materials Needed:**

PFDs, one for each student; a large plastic hoop. Place a mark on the pool indicating to which point students should swim.

### *Discussion Guidelines for Instructors*

1. Distribute a PFD to each student, and have the students put the PFDs on. Tell them that you will check each one to see if it was fastened properly and if it fits right.

Instructor Note: *According to the National Safe Boating Council and the U.S. Coast Guard (1997), to test for proper fit, lifejackets should fit properly with all zippers, straps, ties, and snaps correctly secured. Instruct students to enter the water and walk into water up to their necks. Have them lift their legs and tilt their heads back, in a relaxed back floating position. Their mouths should be out of the water, and they should be floating without any physical effort. If a student's lifejacket rides up, try securing it tighter to the body. If it still rides up, the student may need a smaller lifejacket or a different style. Students should be comfortable and able to float with very little effort.*

2. Now have students try paddling while wearing PFDs. Ask if it's easier or harder to paddle while wearing a PFD.
3. Say, "Let's see how many ways you can paddle with your lifejacket on. Can you paddle on your front? How? Can you paddle on your back? In what ways? Can you paddle lying on your side? How?"
4. Ask, "Who can turn around in circles?"
5. Ask, "Can you roll onto your back? Now can you roll back on your stomach? Can you roll onto your side? Can you change from front to back without rolling? How about from back to front?"
6. Ask, "Which of you can paddle out to me?" Gradually increase the distance between you and the students until you are on the other side of the pool. "Can you come back without touching the other wall? Can you paddle on your front? How about on your side? Can you paddle on your back?"
7. Say, "Let's try to jump into the pool. Do you need to do anything different with your PFD?" (Answer: Cross the arms on top of the jacket to keep from riding up.)
8. Say, "Let's see if you can jump in and paddle out to me. Give yourself a big hug and say, 'Oh, I'm so cute.' Say that when you jump in."
9. Place a mark on the side of the pool at the distance to which you want them to swim. Ask, "Can you jump in, paddle to the mark, roll over to your back, and then paddle back while on your back?" Gradually increase the distance until students can perform this for 10 yards.

A

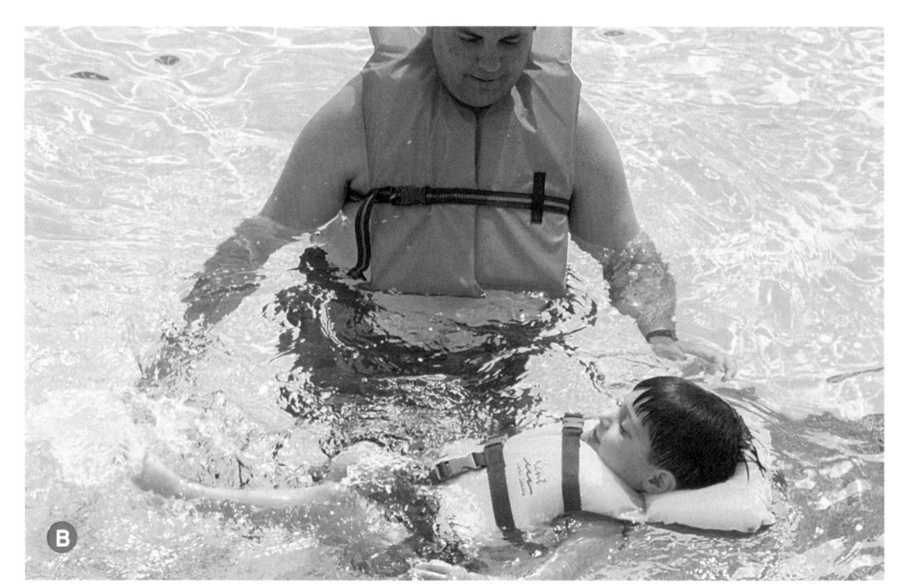
B

10. Have all the students line up on deck as you stand in the water holding a large plastic hoop on the water's surface. Tell the students to, one at a time, call out the name of someone they respect and why, then jump into the middle of the hoop.

### *Performance Criteria*

The student should

***Pike*** → while wearing a PFD, be able to paddle stroke five yards on the front, then turn on the back and paddle and kick for five yards.

***Eel*** → be able to jump into a pool wearing a PFD (giving the PFD a hug), paddle stroke 10 yards on the front, then turn on the back and paddle and kick for 10 yards.

---

## Objective: To learn how to get into and out of a boat safely with assistance

### Materials Needed:

PFDs, one for each student; a boat (canoe, rowboat, dinghy, inflatable raft)

### *Discussion Guidelines for Instructors*

1. Have a boat on the deck, such as a canoe, rowboat, dinghy, or small inflatable raft.
2. Have the students select and put on PFDs (you should wear one, too).
3. Ask students what safety rules should be followed in and around boats. Discuss some of the basic boating safety rules such as the following:
   - Never enter a boat without an adult.
   - Always wear a PFD whenever you are in a boat.
   - Always stay seated when in a small boat.
   - Maintain three points of contact when getting in and out.
   - Step in the center to keep the boat balanced.

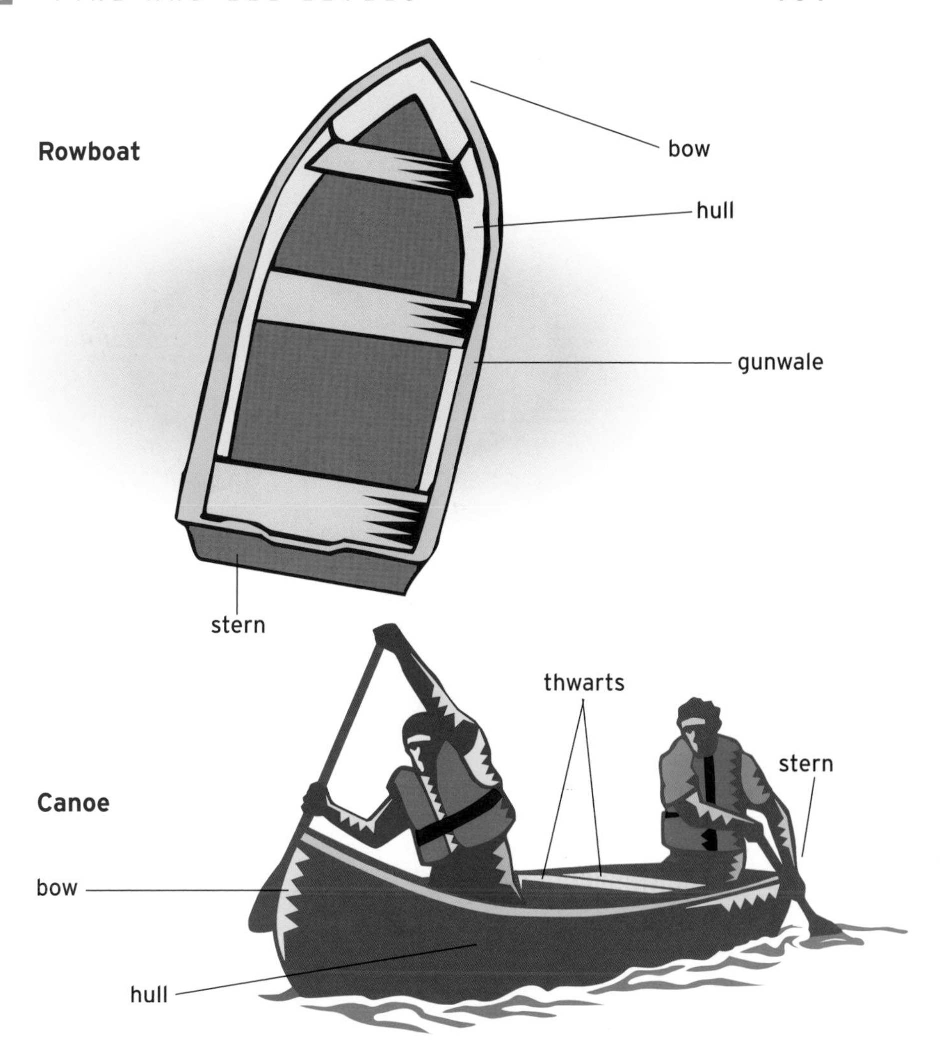


4. Explain the names of the different parts of the boat.
5. Explain how to safely get into and out of a boat:
   - Climb into the boat by stepping in the middle, keeping your weight low by crouching or bending over (which keeps your center of gravity low). Stabilize yourself by placing your hands on the edges or gunwales of the boat.
   - Exit by doing the reverse.
6. Practice with the boat on the deck and provide assistance.

*Instructor Note: You may notice in the manual that we are using rafts to demonstrate safety skills. Because we are teaching mainly in swimming pools, it can be more practical to use rafts than boats. While these types of rafts may be appropriate for teaching basic boating safety skills, be sure to point out the difference between the actions of the rafts used in class (which are flexible and pliable) and actual boats (which have rigid boat hulls).*

### Performance Criteria

The student should

**Pike and Eel** → be able to enter and exit from a boat with assistance while wearing a PFD.

---

**Objective:** To learn how to step out as well as jump away from the side and into the pool, paddle to the surface, turn, and return to the side without assistance

Materials Needed: IFDs

### Discussion Guidelines for Instructors

1. In shallow water ask students who can to step out away from the side and into the pool and get back to the wall with assistance or wearing an IFD.
2. Next ask the student to step away from the side and into the pool and get back to the wall without any assistance or an IFD.
3. In deep water ask the students to try to jump out away from the side and into the pool, paddle and kick up to the surface, and turn around and return to the side.

*Instructor Note: Be there in the water to make sure they jump out into the pool and to assist if necessary. Have a kickboard, rescue tube, or water log with you, and keep it between you and the students. Students may or may not wear IFDs at first, depending on their comfort level.*

### Performance Criteria

The student should

**Pike** → be able to step out away from the pool side into the water, turn, and return to the side with assistance or flotation support.

**Eel** → be able to jump into deep water out away from the pool side, paddle to the surface, turn, and return to the side without assistance or flotation support.

## Objective: To learn about sun safety

### Discussion Guidelines for Instructors

1. Ask, "What happens if you stay in the sun too long? What can you put on to protect yourself from the sun? What is something else you can put on? Anything else?" Continue asking until you get the following items:
   - Sunscreen (minimum 15 SPF)
   - Hat
   - Sunglasses
   - T-shirt or other clothing
2. Ask, "What else can we do to protect ourselves from the sun?" Continue asking until you get the following:
   - Drink lots of water.

Stay in the shade and limit time in the sun, especially when the sun is hottest (usually between 10 A.M. and 4 P.M. during Daylight Savings Time).

- Reapply sunscreen every couple of hours.

### Performance Criteria

The student should

| | |
|---|---|
| ***Pike and Eel*** | → participate in the discussion and |
| | → know at least one way to protect him- or herself from the sun. |

## Component 2: Personal Growth

## Objective: To gain self-confidence

### Teaching Instructions

Use the following discussion activities to orient students to the YMCA philosophy throughout the Pike and Eel levels. Begin each class with some of these ideas:

- Welcome students and encourage them to get to know each other.
- Introduce yourself to students in new ways each time the class

meets by sharing something new about yourself and asking them to share something new about themselves.

- Reassure students that they will never be asked to do anything they cannot do or that is dangerous. Ask them, "If you were really scared to do something I asked you to do in the water, what would you do?" (Answer: I would tell you I am scared.)
- Have students share their favorite pastimes and other things that are going on in their lives. Do this in different ways each session.
- Discuss the YMCA Pool Rules—why we need them and whose responsibility it is to follow them (see earlier pool rules objective under the Personal Safety component).
- Try relaxation exercises. Have students back float and ask, "What would a rock do in the water? What would a feather do? What would Jell-O look like or feel like in the water?"
- Talk about goal setting. Discuss completion guidelines for Pike or Eel and how each student learns at an individual pace. As the program progresses, encourage individuals to identify their own progress. Celebrate successes at each class meeting. Teach students that you want them to do their best and that you are proud of their efforts.

### *Performance Criteria*

The student should

***Pike and Eel*** → participate in the discussion and activities.

---

## Objective: To describe what the terms caring, honesty, respect, and responsibility mean

### *Discussion Guidelines for Instructors*

1. Say, "In swimming, as in everything else we do, we must learn to get along with others."
2. Ask, "Does anyone know what caring is?" (Answers: to love others, to be sensitive to the well-being of others, to help others.) "Have you seen anyone being caring? Tell me about it."

You may want to try the following activity. If a student is having trouble completing a skill, ask the other students for ideas to help him or her. Share those ideas with the student and have the class encourage the student to keep trying. Explain to the class that it's a good idea to help others who are having trouble if you already know how to perform a skill. Tell them that this is a way to demonstrate caring for others.

3. Ask, "Does anyone know what honesty is?" (Answer: to tell the truth; to act in such a way that you are worthy of trust; to have integrity, making sure your actions match your values.) "Have you seen anyone being honest?"
4. Ask, "Does anyone know what respect is?" (Answer: to treat others as you would have them treat you; to value the worth of every person, including yourself.) "Have you seen anyone being respectful?"
5. Ask, "Does anyone know what responsibility is?" (Answer: to do what you ought to do; to be accountable for your behavior and obligations.) "Have you seen anyone being responsible?"
6. Say, "These are very important ideas because they help us get along with others. We see and watch other people all the time. We need to learn to do what is right so that we do it all the time, even if no one is watching."

Instructor Note: *Refer to chapter 2 of* **Teaching Swimming Fundamentals** *and chapter seven in this book if you need to know more about the socioemotional development of the age group in your class. Knowledge in this area will help you to modify your discussion of values so students can better understand it.*

*Pay attention to "teachable moments" as opportunities to talk about values. Take a moment during class when a student demonstrates one of the values and share it with the other students. Recognize the student and celebrate the action. Also confront any student who is not demonstrating one of the core values and bring those actions to his or her attention. Reinforce the idea of following the core values.*

For additional character development ideas, see chapter 9.

*Performance Criteria*

The student should

***Pike and Eel***
- → participate in the discussion and
- → give an interpretation of what caring, honesty, respect, and responsibility mean to him or her.

## Objective: To have fun in the water through a game

*Discussion Guidelines for Instructors*

1. Here is one example of a game to play. Let students wear flotation belts if they wish.

   **Heads, Shoulders, Knees, and Toes**

   The leader faces a line of swimmers standing in the shallow end or sitting on the side. When the leader calls out the word *head,* the swimmers should touch their heads with both hands. The leader then calls out the words *shoulders, knees,* and *toes,* one at a time, and the swimmers touch the corresponding part. Make the game



   splashy so that everyone gets wet. To make it exciting, move from one to another body part as quickly as possible.

Many other games are appropriate. See appendix A in *Teaching Swimming Fundamentals* or appendix B of this manual for more game ideas, or make up your own.

*Performance Criteria*

The student should

***Pike and Eel***
- → actively participate and
- → show enjoyment by smiles, laughter, or other signs.

# Component 3: Stroke Development

## Objective: To learn and improve the front paddle stroke

Materials Needed:

flotation belts, one for each student; kickboards, one for each student; IFDs

*Discussion Guidelines for Instructors*

Instructor Note: *Have students wear flotation belts while working on these skills. Allow some time in class for them to attempt the same skills while not wearing a belt. Discuss with the students what the belt is doing when they wear it and why they should take it off to try the same skills.*

Use the following series of questions to help students explore front paddling:

1. "When you are on your front in the water, what do you do to make yourself move?" (Answers: move arms, kick legs or feet.) "What can you do with your arms that helps make you move forward? Can you move forward? What about your legs? Can you move backward? Can you make yourself move sideways? Which is easiest?"
2. "When you are paddling on your front, what are your legs doing? How many ways can you make your legs move that help you move in the water? Which ways make you move forward best? Which ways seem easier to you?"

Instructor Note: *After asking each question, have the students try their ideas. Recognize and praise those students who are performing appropriate or creative movements. Emphasize that there is more than one good way to move the arms and legs in the water. At this point students can move their arms and legs either symmetrically (like a rudimentary circle or dolphin kick) or in alternation (like a flutter or scissors kick); either is acceptable. Refer to chapter 7 of* **Teaching Swimming Fundamentals** *to remind yourself of the standard progression for learning the crawl stroke. Move the flotation blocks on the flotation belts to the back to make it easier for students to swim on the front (paddle stroke), and adjust the location of the blocks on the trunk to help with body positioning. Work with students until they are able to move a few feet without your assistance.*

3. "Is there a way to make paddling easier or better for you?" Give each student a kickboard. Ask "Can you walk the kickboard to me? Is there another way to hold the kickboard and walk to me? Can you think of any other ways? When was it easier? Was it easier laying on top of the water, flat, or was it vertical, up and down? It goes pretty easily when it is flat, right?" Then ask, "When you are swimming, which way do you think you swim—flat or up and down? Maybe a little bit of both right now. But what can you do to make yourself flatter on the water?" (Answers: putting the face in the water, kicking the feet harder, keeping the toes near the surface.) "Let's try some of those things. How about kicking harder first?"
4. "If you wanted to swim longer than you can in one breath, what could you do?" (Answer: Get a breath of air.) "How many different ways can you try to get a breath? Let's try a few. Can you lift your face up? Can you roll over onto your back? Can you turn your head or face to the side? Which was easier?" Have students try to get a breath. Once they can swim and get two or three breaths, move on to the next activity.
5. "How can we get across the pool more quickly? Is there something different we could do with our arms or legs to help make that happen? Let's try some of your ideas."

Instructor Note: *Work on getting the class to reach out as far as they can with their arms. Also see if you can get them to kick their legs over a smaller range and slightly faster, maybe with less knee bend. Gradually lengthen the distance so students move from paddling a few feet to going across the pool.*

6. "How many ways can you get across the pool to the other side now? Show me!" (Examples: Walk on deck, walk in shallow water, hold onto the gutter and move hand over hand.)
7. "How many ways can you get across the pool without touching the bottom or the side of the pool? Let's see."
8. "Can you go across with your head up and feet down? How about with your head up and your feet up? How about with your head in the water and your feet up? Which way was easiest and fastest?"

*Performance Criteria*

The student should

***Pike***

- be able to paddle on the front for 10 yards while wearing a flotation belt. The student can move the arms and legs in whatever way is effective for him or her.
- be able to paddle on the front for five feet without wearing a flotation belt. The student can move the arms and legs in whatever way is effective for him or her.

***Eel***

- be able to paddle on the front for 25 yards while wearing a flotation belt. The student can move the arms and legs in whatever way is effective for him or her.
- be able to paddle on the front for 15 feet without wearing a flotation belt. The student can move the arms and legs in whatever way is effective for him or her.

## Objective: To learn the back paddle

**Materials Needed:** flotation belts, one for each student

*Discussion Guidelines for Instructors*

Use the following series of questions to help students explore front paddling:

1. Say, "Who can show me another way to get across the pool with your face out of the water but not laying on your side?"
2. Ask, "Can you float in the pool looking up at the ceiling? Let's see. What can you look at to guide you? How should your body be at the hips—straight or bent?"
3. Ask, "When you are on your back in the water, how can you make yourself move? Can you move forward? Can you move backward? What can you do with your arms that helps make you move to the other side of the pool?"

Back paddle stroke

4. Ask, "When you are paddling on your back, what can you do with your legs? How many ways can you make your legs move? Which ways make you move best? Which ways are easier?"

**Instructor Note:** *After asking each of these questions, have the students try their ideas. Recognize all students. At this point students can move their arms and legs either symmetrically or alternately; both are acceptable. Arm recovery can be in or out of the water, although in-water recovery may be best for most Pike- and Eel-level swimmers. Work with students until they are able to move a few feet without your assistance. Make it easier for the students by moving the flotation blocks on their belts so the blocks are on their stomachs instead of their backs. This helps students float with their heads back and stomachs up.*

*Performance Criteria*

The student should

***Pike***

- be able to paddle on the back for 10 yards while wearing a flotation belt. The student can move the arms and legs in whatever way is effective for him or her.
- be able to paddle on the back for five feet without wearing a flotation belt. The student can move the arms and legs in whatever way is effective for him or her.

***Eel***

- be able to paddle on the back for 25 yards while wearing a flotation belt. The student can move the arms and legs in whatever way is effective for him or her.
- be able to paddle on the back for 15 feet without wearing a flotation belt. The student can move the arms and legs in whatever way is effective for him or her.

## Objective: To learn the side paddle

Materials Needed: flotation belts, one for each student

### *Discussion Guidelines for Instructors*

Use the following series of questions to help students explore the side paddle stroke:

1. "Show me three positions you use to move in the water. How about holding on to the side? Holding on to a partner or me? Using a float belt? Without support?"
2. "Can you try it on your side? Show me how many ways you can move on your side."

Side paddle stroke

3. "Can you get across the pool with one shoulder pointing upward out of the water and your feet off the bottom? Let's see."

Instructor Note: *At this stage students may find the side paddle difficult to achieve. They may be able to perform only a modified front paddle stroke turned slightly on the side, which is acceptable. The exploration of trying to find an efficient way to move on the side is what is important right now. A specific arm and leg movement is not necessary at this time, and they can use either symmetrical or alternating arms and legs. When they are wearing flotation belts, twist the flotation blocks so that the blocks are on the side of the trunk nearest to the surface to assist with students' movement and position.*

### *Performance Criteria*

The student should

***Pike***

- be able to paddle on the side for 10 yards while wearing a flotation belt. The student can move the arms and legs in whatever way is effective for him or her.
- be able to paddle on the side for five feet without wearing a flotation belt. The student can move the arms and legs in whatever way is effective for him or her.

***Eel***

- be able to paddle on the side for 25 yards while wearing a flotation belt. The student can move the arms and legs in whatever way is effective for him or her.
- be able to paddle on the side for 15 feet without wearing a flotation belt. The student can move the arms and legs in whatever way is effective for him or her.

### Pike and Eel Series Swim Information

Have students stretch before beginning their series swim. Use static stretching only, no bouncing or ballistic movements.

The YMCA recommends that preschool-age students wear flotation belts (regardless of whether other IFDs are used) and swim along the pool wall. They can begin by walking across the width of the pool. Then they can paddle part way across the width, going only as far as an endpoint marked by a safety cone before they get out. Finally, they can paddle across, exit, and walk back to the starting point. When students can paddle lengths, they should begin in the deep end and move toward the shallow end.

During early series swims, you should be in the water with the class for safety reasons as well as to give students the security of having you face-to-face with them. If more than one class is swimming together, some instructors should be in the water and some should be on deck. Instructors in the water should have an IFD or rescue tube with them. Lifeguards should be stationed on deck, at waterside or in a chair, at all times. If possible, they should be located near the series swimming.

## Component 4: Water Games and Sports

### Objective: To learn how to fin and scull

Materials Needed:
kickboards, one for each student; IFDs

### *Finning*

**Skill Description**

To fin, the student starts by doing a back float with the arms at the side and hands relaxed. He or she then bends the elbows and draws the hands up, scooping the water. The student then flexes the wrists and pushes the water with the palms toward the feet. The scooping movement is a short stroke, with the hands about a foot from the sides of the body.

**Discussion Guidelines for Instructors**

Ask the following series of questions:

1. "Can you move through the water without using your legs? How? How many ways? Which way is better? Can you try it on your back?"
2. "What happens when you move your hands up? Down? Flat? Side to side? Back and forth?"
3. "What do your hands move like?" (Answer: fish fins.)
4. "Have you ever watched a fish swim? Can you use your 'fins' and swim while watching the sky? Can you move your 'fins' while on your side?"

Finning

5. "Can you fin real fast? Real slow? What's the difference? Which one is easier to help you float and move?"
6. "What happens if you move your hands down by your hips? By your waist? Where else can you move your hands? Which way are your thumbs pointing—are they up, then down?"
7. "Which hand position is easier?"

### *Sculling*

**Skill Description**

Sculling is a method for supporting the body and, if desired, moving it through the water using only the hands. The angle of the palm determines movement and direction. Sculling is a rapid "figure-eight" action.

The student holds the hands straight (not cupped), fingers together, and wrists loose and flexible to allow sideward action. The wrist should not bend up or down but should rotate around the forearm unless directed. Pressure is constant, down and/or against the water. The arms are straight or bent slightly and rotated in a figure-eight action.

Flat or stationary sculling, in which the body does not move, is done in the back float position. The student stretches the body, toes at the surface and ears in the water. He or she performs the sculling action near the hips, with hands flat (straight). The arms swing away from the body about 10 inches. The student applies downward pressure as the hands scull away from each other, thumbs angled. Hands sweep down and out about 10 inches, turned so that the little finger is angled down, and then return to the starting point. The pressure should be constant and even, not stopping as the palms are angled.

Sculling relates to all stroke mechanics. The "S" or "heart" pattern used in strokes is the same as sculling: When the hands move out, the hands are pitched out; when the hands move in, they are pitched in.

**Discussion Guidelines for Instructors**

1. Say, "With sculling, we can stay in one place. Now, if you wanted to move with your 'fins,' what do you think you could do? Let's see you try."

**Kickboard Drill**

1. Have students stand in shallow water, and give each student a kickboard. Say, "Place your arm and hand on the kickboard. Move the board back and forth on the surface of the water. Pitch your hand out when you move the board outward. Pitch your hand in when you move the board inward. See how fast you can move the board back and forth without losing the kickboard."
2. Ask, "Why does the board stay in place? Can you feel the pressure of the board against your hand?"

Instructor Note: *Hand pitch is an important concept to learn. It is essential in creating lift force for an efficient scull and eventual arm stroke (Bernoulli's Theorem). You should begin teaching the concept at this level because it will take students some time to learn it.*

**Practice**

1. Have students stand in the water with their hands on the deck. Say, "Pretend you are smoothing sand on the deck."
2. Next, have students stand in the water with their hands on the surface of the water and try the same motion.
3. Now have students drop their hands below the surface of the water and perform the motion.

*Performance Criteria*

The student should

***Pike***

- → be able to do flat or stationary sculling for 30 seconds wearing an IFD.

***Eel***

- → be able to perform a finning action by pushing or straightening the hands and arms from the elbows and
- → be able to do flat or stationary sculling for one minute wearing or not wearing an IFD.

---

## Objective: To learn about going underwater

**Materials Needed:**

toys or objects heavy enough to sink; a pole long enough to extend from the water's surface to the bottom of the pool. Mark the pole with plastic, colored tape in one-foot increments so students can see the water depth.

*Discussion Guidelines for Instructors*

1. Start in shallow water. Drop toys or other objects into the pool. Say, "There's treasure on the bottom of the pool. All we have is this pole. How can we bring the treasure up?"
2. Hold the pole steady vertically, and let the students try to get down to the treasure. To reach the bottom of the pool, the students pull themselves under the water by going hand over hand down the pole. They return to the surface by climbing up the pole.
3. Ask, "Would it be easier to get down to the bottom of the pole if the treasure were on land or in the swimming pool?" (Answer: on land.) "Why do you think so? (Answer: The water supports you, making you buoyant.)
4. Say, "Now we are going to try something else. Can you hold on to the pole going down, pick up the treasure, and climb back up?"
5. Ask, "Can you climb down, pick up the treasure, and let go and swim up? How many ways can you swim up?"

*Performance Criteria*

The student should

| | |
|---|---|
| ***Pike*** | → be able to climb down and climb up a pole in shallow water. |
| ***Eel*** | → be able to climb down a pole, let go, and swim up in shallow water. |

## Objective: To learn how to dribble a ball across the pool

**Materials Needed:**

8" foam balls, beach balls, or small playground balls, one for each student

*Skill Description*

Dribbling the ball involves moving the ball across the pool without passing. The student can do this by walking, running, or swimming to move the ball forward, without holding it, using crawl or breaststroke arm movements. The ball should move on the wave created by the body moving forward. Controlling the ball in this fashion takes a lot of practice.

Instructor Note: *For the children to do this successfully, the water needs to be shallow enough for them (armpit level). If the water is not that shallow, modify by using a tot dock or postpone this activity until later.*

### *Discussion Guidelines for Instructors*

Ask the following series of questions:

1. "How many ways can you get the ball across the pool?"
2. "How can you get the ball across the pool without touching the ball with your hands? Let's see you try." Start with going only 5 to10 feet, and gradually increase the distance.
3. "What are some things you can do to keep the ball from getting away from you?
4. "Is it easier if you go faster or slower?"
5. "Is it easier moving your arms underwater or above the water?"

### *Performance Criteria*

The student should

| | |
|---|---|
| ***Pike*** | → be able to dribble the ball 15 to 20 feet with or without an IFD while walking. |
| ***Eel*** | → be able to dribble the ball 30 to 40 feet with or without an IFD while walking. |

## Objective: To learn how to do the push pass

Instructor Note: *For the children to do this successfully, the water needs to be shallow enough for them (armpit level). If the water is not that shallow, modify by using a tot dock or postpone this activity until later.*

**Materials needed:**
foam balls, beach balls, or small playground balls, one for each pair of students. Each child should be able to hold the ball in one hand.

### *Skill Description*

The push pass is an easy way to shoot or pass the ball. The student picks the ball up with one hand and holds it at shoulder height. He or she then throws the ball in a shot put motion.

Instructor Note: *At this level the students will be using both hands; students this age are usually unable to use just one hand.*

### *Discussion Guidelines for Instructors*

1. Have students stand in a circle. Hold up the ball and ask, "How can you get the ball to someone in the circle? How many different ways can we get the ball to others?" (Answers: one hand, two hands, over the head, walk it to them, bunny hop it to them.)
2. After they have exhausted all their ideas, have them move one step back, making a bigger circle. Now ask, "How can we get the ball to someone across the circle without moving away from our own spot?"
3. Say, "Let's try again. Let's see if we can get the ball to someone else faster."
4. Say, "This time name the person you want the ball to go to before you throw it."
5. Have the students get into two lines, facing each other. Now each student has a partner. Give a ball to each pair and say, "Now see how many times you can pass the ball back and forth with your partner." Once they have done this successfully 10 times, have them take a step farther apart and try it again.

### *Performance Criteria*

The student should

***Pike***

***Eel*** → be able to pass and catch the ball with one or two hands.

## Component 5: Rescue

**Objective:** To learn how to recognize a victim in danger

### Teaching Instructions

1. Tell the following trigger story to your students:

   You and a friend are playing on a hot summer day. Your friend tells you she wants to play in a backyard swimming pool in your neighbor's yard. The family is not home, but your friend says she is going to swim in their pool anyway. You follow and watch her jump into the pool. You see she jumped into the deep end but is not swimming. She can't seem to reach the side of the pool either.
2. Ask the following questions for discussion:

   *Question 1:* Now, let's deal with the problem of your friend. How can you tell your friend is in trouble?

   *Discussion:*

   - Look of fear and panic
   - Inability to yell or speak
   - Upright position in the water
   - Hands waving or thrashing
   - Bobbing motion of head and body

   *Question 2:* Can people in trouble in the water always yell for help? Why or why not?

   *Discussion:* Usually not; they are simply concerned with trying to breathe.

   *Question 3:* What are some situations that might be dangerous?

   *Discussion:* Ask students to describe some potentially dangerous situations. Their replies might include playing with matches, crossing the street, riding a bike without a helmet, or running on a slippery hill; try to include water-related situations, such as a nonswimmer floating into deep water or being pushed into the water from the deck.

   *Question 4:* When you recognize danger, how do you call for help?

   *Discussion:*

   - Stay calm.
   - Call for help.
   - If no one is available to help, look for something to throw that floats or something to reach out to the person in trouble. Stay on deck and do not enter the water to help.
   - If you have to call for help,
     - dial the emergency number (such as 911, if your city has it) or dial 0;

- give your name, location, and the nature of the emergency; and
- wait for instructions.

*Question 5:* What are the dangers to you in trying to help someone?

*Discussion:* Issues students should consider include these:

- What might happen if I get in the water to help?
- What is in or under the water?
- How big is the victim? Am I strong enough to bring the victim in without getting in trouble myself?
- Can I do what it takes to help the victim?

*Question 6:* What is not good about this story? What did you or your friend do right? What did you or your friend do wrong?

*Discussion:* It was wrong not to respect other people's property. It was right to be caring and help a friend.

### *Performance Criteria*

The student should

***Pike and Eel*** → be present for the trigger story and discussion and

→ be able to describe two examples of a dangerous situation.

---

## Objective: To learn how to get help when needed

### *Discussion Guidelines for Instructors*

1. Ask, "If a problem came up, how could you get an adult's attention? Show me."
2. Ask, "When should you yell for help? Is it okay to yell for help as a joke?"

Instructor Note: *Always teach students to yell "Help!" instead of "Lifeguard!" They will be more likely to get help right away.*

3. Say, "Let's see how you can yell for help."

### *Performance Criteria*

The student should

***Pike and Eel*** → know when to yell for help.

---

## Objective: To learn how to go for adult assistance

### *Discussion Guidelines for Instructors*

1. Say, "Sometimes if someone needs help, yelling may not be enough. You may have to go get an adult to help. What can you do? What would you need to tell the adult?" (Answers: Stay calm. Look for an adult or lifeguard. Tell him or her what you saw and say, "Help! Call 911.")

### *Performance Criteria*

The student should

***Pike and Eel*** → be able to go to an adult for assistance.

---

## Objective: To learn how to call on the telephone for help

Materials Needed: a toy telephone

### *Discussion Guidelines for Instructors*

1. In the class prior to this activity, ask students to make sure they know their home phone number and address for the next class.
2. Ask, "What number do you call to get help?" (Answer: 911 or the local emergency number.) "What would you need to tell them?" (Answer: your first and last name, the phone number and address of where you are, and what happened.) The student should not hang up until the person on the phone tells him or her to do so.
3. Using the toy phone, have the students practice dialing the emergency number. One student pretends to be the one calling the emergency number, and the other pretends to be the dispatcher on the other end of the line.

*Performance Criteria*

The student should

***Pike and Eel***

- participate in the activity and
- be able to say his or her own phone number and address out loud.

---

## Objective: To learn about and practice reaching assists

Materials Needed:

child-sized items that could be used in a reaching assist

*Skill Description*

Reaching assists are used to help distressed or near drowning swimmers without endangering the rescuer. Many items can be used to perform a reaching assist: a light aluminum pole, a towel, a piece of clothing, or a piece of light lumber (watch for splinters). A rescuer also can extend an arm or leg. At this level, however, because of the size and age of the students, we concentrate on extending objects rather than an arm or leg.

To perform an assist the student first establishes a wide base of support by lying down, crouching, and spreading the legs, keeping the weight low and away from the victim. He or she extends the object within reach of the victim and either slides it under the victim's armpit or presses it against the victim's side. Once the victim has grasped the object, the student maintains the position and, with weight shifted away from the victim, pulls the victim in slowly, hand over hand. The student should communicate with the victim, reassuring the victim as he or she is brought to safety.

At this level you must emphasize that students should never get into the water to perform a rescue. Teach students how to grab and hold onto an extended item from a rescuer.

Instructor Note: *The reaching assist is introduced before the throwing assist because throwing requires more cognitive and motor skills than does reaching.*

Doing a reaching assist to instructor

### *Discussion Guidelines for Instructors*

1. Share the following trigger story with your students:

   Two boys, Bob and Jamie, were fishing at the end of a dock. Bob reached out with a fishing net to scoop up the fish he had just caught. But he leaned over too far and fell off the dock into the water. Jamie called, "Are you okay?" Bob didn't answer and just kept thrashing around in the water. He was trying to reach the dock, but he wasn't close enough to hang on.

2. Ask the following questions for discussion:

   *Question 1:* What would Jamie see Bob doing in the water that would tell him Bob needs help?

   *Discussion:* The look of panic, thrashing the arms up and down while upright in the water, an inability to speak clearly, and bobbing under the water

   *Question 2:* What are some of the things Jamie could do to help Bob?

   *Discussion:* Call for help, look for something to extend to him or something to throw to him that floats.

   *Question 3:* What should Jamie not do?

   *Discussion:* He should not go into the water. He also should not simply do nothing or run away.

   *Question 4:* What if Jamie had nothing to throw to Bob?

*Discussion:* Look for something to extend. Something is always available, even if it's just clothing.

*Question 5:* Because the boys were fishing, what kinds of things could Jamie use to help?

*Discussion:* An oar, pole, stick, towel, shirt, and so on.

*Question 6:* If Jamie used the fishing pole to help Bob, where should he place the end so that Bob could reach it most easily?

*Discussion:* He should extend the pole to Bob's side under the armpit to avoid injuring Bob's face or chest.

*Question 7:* What should Jamie say to Bob to get him to hold onto the pole?

*Discussion:* "Stay calm, grab the pole, and let me pull you to the side."

*Question 8:* If Bob were really scared when he grabbed the pole and pulled hard, what might happen to Jamie?

*Discussion:* Jamie could be pulled into the water.

*Question 9:* What could Jamie do so he would not fall in so easily?

*Discussion:* He could lie down or stand crouched on the deck with his legs spread and knees bent so his center of gravity would be low. He then could slowly pull Bob to the side.

3. Have students take turns pretending to rescue you, using extension items. Have them tell you, as you role play the victim, what to do: Look at me, keep your head up, kick your feet, grab and hold on to the item extended.

## *Performance Criteria*

The student should

***Pike and Eel*** → be able to perform a reaching assist.

**Reference**

National Safety Boating Council and the U.S. Coast Guard. 1997. *Wear your life jacket! Boat smart from the start.* Washington, DC: Authors.

# Summary

## Pike

### Component 1: Personal Safety

- Participate actively in the discussion and be able to repeat and discuss the pool rules.
- Participate in the discussion and be able to repeat and discuss the class expectations.
- Walk away from the pool wall, turn around, and reach and grab onto the wall with assistance, or if the student can't stand, be able to let go of the pool wall while wearing an IFD, swim or paddle a few feet, turn around, and grab the wall with assistance, and be comfortable being in the water, and take the feet off the floor while wearing an IFD.
- Support him- or herself in the water for 30 seconds with a flotation belt, demonstrate the front and back float with a flotation belt for 20 seconds, take a breath on the front float with a flotation belt, and recover to standing from both the front and back float with assistance.
- Secure, take off, and put away a PFD and explain the differences between a PFD and an IFD. ▲
- Wearing a PFD, paddle stroke 5 yards on the front, then turn on the back and paddle and kick 5 yards. ▲
- Enter and exit from a boat with assistance while wearing a PFD. ▲
- Step out away from the pool side, turn, and return to the side with assistance or flotation support.
- Participate in the discussion and know at least one way to protect him- or herself from the sun.

### Component 2: Personal Growth

- Participate in the discussion and activities that promote self-confidence.
- Participate in the discussion of core values and give an interpretation of what the core values mean to him or her.
- Actively participate in a game and show enjoyment by smiles, laughter, or other signs.

### Component 3: Stroke Development

- Paddle on the front for 10 yards while wearing a flotation belt. The student can move the arms and legs in whatever way is effective for him or her.
- Paddle on the front for 5 feet without wearing a flotation belt. The student can move the arms and legs in whatever way is effective for him or her.
- Paddle on the back for 10 yards while wearing a flotation belt. The student can move the arms and legs in whatever way is effective for him or her.
- Paddle on the back for 5 feet without wearing a flotation belt. The student can move the arms and legs in whatever way is effective for him or her.
- Paddle on the side for 10 yards while wearing a flotation belt. The student can move the arms and legs in whatever way is effective for him or her.
- Paddle on the side for 5 feet without wearing a flotation belt. The student can move the arms and legs in whatever way is effective for him or her.

### Component 4: Water Games and Sports

- Do flat or stationary sculling for 30 seconds while wearing an IFD.
- Climb down and climb up a pole in shallow water.
- Dribble the ball 15 to 20 feet with or without an IFD while walking.
- Pass and catch the ball with one or two hands.

### Component 5: Rescue

- Be present for the trigger story and discussion and be able to describe two examples of a dangerous situation.
- Know when to yell for help.
- Be able to go to an adult for assistance.
- Participate in the practice for dialing the emergency number, and say his or her own phone number and address out loud.
- Perform a reaching assist.

# Summary

## Eel

### Component 1: Personal Safety

- Participate actively in the discussion and be able to repeat and discuss the pool rules.
- Participate in the discussion and be able to repeat and discuss the class expectations.
- Walk away from the pool wall, turn around, and reach and grab onto the wall without assistance, or if he or she can't stand, be able to let go of the pool wall while wearing an IFD, swim or paddle a few feet, turn around, and grab the wall without assistance, and be comfortable being in the water, and take the feet off the floor while wearing an IFD.
- Support him- or herself in the water for 30 seconds with a flotation belt, demonstrate the front and back float without a flotation belt for 10 seconds, take a breath on the front float without flotation support, and recover to standing from both the front and back float without assistance.
- Secure and take off and put away a PFD and explain the differences between a PFD and an IFD. ⛵
- Jump into a pool wearing a PFD (giving the PFD a hug), paddle stroke 10 yards on the front, then turn on the backand paddle and kick 10 yards. ⛵
- Enter and exit a boat with assistance while wearing a PFD. ⛵
- Jump out into deep water away from the pool side, paddle to the surface, turn, and return to the side without assistance or flotation support.
- Participate in the discussion and know at least one way to protect him- or herself from the sun.

### Component 2: Personal growth

- Participate in the discussion and activities that promote self-confidence.
- Participate in the discussion of core values and give an interpretation of what the core values mean to him or her.
- Actively participate in a game and show enjoyment by smiles, laughter, or other signs.

### Component 3: Stroke Development

- Paddle on the back for 25 yards while wearing a flotation belt. The student can move the arms and legs in whatever way is effective for him or her.
- Paddle on the front for 15 feet without wearing a flotation belt. The student can move the arms and legs in whatever way is effective for him or her.
- Paddle on the back for 25 yards while wearing a flotation belt. The student can move the arms and legs in whatever way is effective for him or her.
- Paddle on the back for 15 feet without wearing a flotation belt. The student can move the arms and legs in whatever way is effective for him or her.
- Paddle on the side for 25 yards while wearing a flotation belt. The student can move the arms and legs in whatever way is effective for him or her.
- Paddle on the side for 15 feet without wearing a flotation belt. The student can move the arms and legs in whatever way is effective for him or her.

### Component 4: Water Sports and Games

- Perform a "finning" action by pushing or straightening the hands and arms from the elbows, and do flat or stationary sculling for 1 minute wearing or not wearing an IFD.
- Climb down a pole, let go, and swim up in shallow water.
- Dribble the ball 30 to 40 feet with or without an IFD while walking.
- Pass and catch the ball with one or two hands.

### Component 5: Rescue

- Be present for the trigger story and discussion and be able to describe two examples of a dangerous situation.
- Know when to yell for help.
- Be able to go to an adult for assistance.
- Participate in the practice for dialing the emergency number, and say his or her own phone number and address out loud.
- Perform a reaching assist.

CHAPTER eleven

# Ray and Starfish Levels

**In this chapter we provide the sample instructional steps for specific activities to teach the skills of the Ray and Starfish levels.**

**As in chapter 10, the activities are again grouped by the five components: personal safety, personal growth, stroke development, water sports and games, and rescue.**

The Ray and Starfish levels in the Preschool program are similar to the Guppy level in the Youth and Adult program. Because students move toward the criteria in smaller steps in the Preschool program, some activities again have two different criteria, depending upon the level.

While enrolled in the Ray and Starfish levels, the student is

- Helped to learn the safety swim
- Helped to learn diving safety
- Helped to learn the front and back float performed without an IFD
- Helped to develop treading skills without an IFD
- Helped to learn the correct use of PFDs and allowed to try performing a safety swim while wearing a PFD
- Given an explanation of the heat escape lessening posture (HELP)
- Helped to learn bobbing
- Helped to learn how to get into and out of a boat and how to sit and change position in a boat properly
- Involved in a discussion of safety precautions around water
- Involved in a discussion of the meaning of the core values in everyday life
- Helped to develop caution and patience around water environments
- Helped to learn the following strokes: front alternating paddle (with rudimentary rhythmic breathing), front symmetrical paddle, side alternating paddle, back alternating paddle, and back symmetrical paddle

- Helped to learn synchronized swimming skills, including the tub, the front and back somersault, and canoe sculling (these are for Starfish only)
- Helped to learn diving skills, including swimming up to the surface, jumping off a one-meter board, and performing a kneeling dive
- Helped to learn wetball lead-up skills, including throwing and catching a ball, passing the ball to a partner, and shooting toward large targets (goals) (this is for Starfish only)
- Helped to learn more about rescue skills such as reaching and throwing assists and rescue breathing

Prerequisites:

- Successful completion of the Eel requirements for the Ray level
- Successful completion of the Ray requirements for the Starfish level

## Component 1: Personal Safety

**Objective:** To learn about diving safety

### *Discussion Guidelines for Instructors*

1. Ask, "Who knows what diving into the pool means? How is it different from climbing in or jumping in?" (Answer: Diving is going in headfirst.)
2. Ask, "What are some things we should know before we ever dive into the pool?" Discuss the following general diving safety rules:
   - Follow posted diving rules.
   - Dive only in water that is at least nine-feet deep, and dive from a one-meter diving board only in water that is at least 11 1/2 feet deep.
   - Dive with arms extended and hands grabbed.
   - Dive only when you know the water and the bottom is clear of obstructions and other swimmers.
   - Swim directly to the nearest side of the pool after going off the diving board (follow local pool rules).
   - Use the diving board one at a time.

   - Don't dive off the board until the person in front of you has swum to the side or has cleared the area.

**Instructor Note:** *It's dangerous to use starting blocks as diving boards, especially if they are not in nine-feet or deeper water. Starting blocks are intended for competitive swimming purposes only and are to be used only under the supervision of a swim coach. Check the document, "Risk Management Involving Starting Blocks or Platforms, Water Depth, Deep Diving Starts, and Supervision," in Principles of YMCA Aquatics for more specific guidelines.*

Do not allow children to slide off a mat on the side of the pool or slide down a water slide headfirst. Sliding like this runs the risk of causing head and neck injury.

Lead the discussion by asking a series of linked questions. Here's an example for the rule, "Dive only in water that is at least nine-feet deep."

"How can we find out how deep the water is?" (Answers: Look at the pool-depth markers; try to touch the bottom and see how far the water is above your head; ask the lifeguard; place a pole in the water that is a known height or is marked by feet.)

"How deep should the water be before you dive from the deck, pool side, or dock?" (Answer: The water should be at least nine-feet deep.)

"Why should it be nine-feet deep?" (Answer: That provides enough water to cushion the diver and slow the diver's body down, like high-jump or pole-vault cushions.)

"How much of the pool should be that depth?" (Answer: Wherever a diver might dive in and start coming up; the diving envelope.)

For the rule, "Follow posted diving rules," walk the class around the pool deck and point out "No Diving" signs and depth markers. For the rule, "Dive with arms extended and hands grabbed," have each child demonstrate the correct position.

3. Ask if they can think of any other diving rules that should be followed, such as listening to the lifeguard, looking before diving, or taking turns on the board.

### *Performance Criteria*

The student should

***Ray and Starfish***

- participate in the discussion and
- be able to name the four most important diving safety rules:
  - Follow posted diving rules.
  - Dive only in water that is at least nine-feet deep, and dive from a one-meter diving board only in water that is at least 11½ feet deep.
  - Dive with arms extended and hands grabbed.
  - Dive only when you know the water and the bottom is clear of obstructions and other swimmers.

## Objective: To learn to do a front and back float without wearing an IFD

Instructor Note: *This is the first of a series of activities in this section that interrelate and build upon one another. These activities offer multiple opportunities to practice and reinforce skills.*

Materials Needed: flotation belts, one for each student

### *Discussion Guidelines for Instructors*

1. Ask, "How could you stay afloat for a minute without an IFD? Show me some ways you could stay afloat." (Examples: doing a front, back, or side float; treading water; or performing a survival/safety swim.)

Front float without IFD

Back float without IFD

Instructor Note: *Allow the class to try to stay afloat for a minute while wearing a flotation belt the first couple times. Then have them try floating without an IFD.*

The first time you use IFDs in class, explain to children how and why IFDs are used. Each time you strap IFDs on the children, tell them to only let you take them off.

2. Ask, "How many different ways can you float?"
3. Ask, "When you float, do you move a lot or a little? See if you can float without moving much."
4. Ask, "Is it easier to float if you take a big breath of air? Try it."

### *Performance Criteria*

The student should

**Ray** → be able to float for 30 seconds on the front and 30 seconds on the back without wearing an IFD.

**Starfish** → be able to float for one minute or longer on the front and one minute or longer on the back without wearing an IFD.

## Objective: To learn how to tread water

### Materials Needed

IFDs, one for each student (flotation belt, kickboard, waterlog, etc.)

### *Skill Description*

Treading water is a survival skill that helps keep the head out of the water in deep water. The student essentially swims in place with the mouth or face out of the water for breathing. Arm actions that can be used while treading include downward finning, wide sculling symmetrically or alternately, and downward short paddling. Leg actions that can be used during treading include a scissors kick, double scissors kick, a circle (whip) kick, and a rotary (egg-beater) kick; a flutter kick is not effective. The body may be positioned vertical to slightly inclined forward or back.

To tread water the student should have little fear of deep water, have relatively effective arm and leg actions, have some buoyancy (either internal or from an IFD or PFD), and have the ability to turn around and change positions, performing this all smoothly and comfortably.

### *Discussion Guidelines for Instructors*

1. Have all students put on IFDs. Then ask, "Who can do a 'dog paddle' or 'human stroke' [whatever you have called it] without moving anywhere?"
2. Ask, "How are your hands moving? Can you move them in a different way and still stay in place? Another way?" Continue having students try different hand movements.

3. Ask, "How are your feet moving? Can you move them another way and still stay in place? Another way?" Continue having students try different feet movements.
4. Ask, "Is it easier to be up and down in the water to stay in place? Why? What happens if you lean forward? Backward? Which position is easier?"
5. Ask, "What hand movements seem to go best with which leg movements? Show me."

Continue having students try different hand movements.

Instructor Note: *The most effective stroke to use at this level is an exaggerated scull in the upright position. Emphasize that the hand action helps to stabilize the body and that the leg action is basically a big, slow kick. The more space the body takes up (with bigger motions), the easier it will be to keep the head out of the water.*

It doesn't matter what kick the students use at this level; it's more important that they feel comfortable in the water. Some students may choose to use a scissors, whip, egg-beater, or bicycle kick, or even a flutter kick. (The flutter kick will not work very well, so you might encourage students who use it to kick wider, changing it to a scissors kick.) They may wear flotation belts to build their confidence and to enable them to spend more time practicing in the pool.

1. Explain the purpose of treading water.
2. Ask, "Why is it important to know how to tread water?" (Answers: for rescue, to rest from swimming, for sports and games.)

### *Performance Criteria*

The student should

***Ray*** → be able to tread water for 20 to 30 seconds with an IFD.

***Starfish*** → be able to tread water for 20 to 30 seconds without an IFD.

---

## Objective: To learn more about PFDs and their correct use

Materials Needed: PFDs, one for each student

### *Discussion Guidelines for Instructors*

1. Help students select the type and size of PFD most appropriate for them.
2. Have students put on and secure the PFD properly. Watch to be sure they perform this correctly.
3. Have students practice entering and exiting the pool from a sitting and standing position, wearing a secured PFD.
4. Have students practice balance and swimming skills in the water wearing secured PFDs. Ask them, "Can you lean forward? Backward? Sideward? Can you go from forward to backward quickly?"

5. Ask, "Can you roll over or turn around? How do you do it? With your hands? With your legs? Which leg kicks work well? What hand actions work well?"
6. Remind students that new swimmers or children on or near water must always have competent adult supervision from someone trained in water safety; they should not rely solely on a PFD.
6. Discuss when and where PFDs are necessary; for instance, they always should be worn while boating or engaging in whitewater activities.
7. Say, "We are on a camping trip and going canoeing. The canoe tips over and goes downriver. You are in the river and start to paddle, then get tired. What can you do to keep going and rest some?" (Answer: Keep your PFD on and float feet first down the river so you can protect yourself from oncoming rocks or other hazards.)

### *Performance Criteria*

The student should

***Ray and Starfish*** → be able to select, put on, secure, and take off a PFD.

## Objective: To learn how to do a safety swim

### *Skill Description*

The safety swim consists of jumping into deep water, doing a paddle stroke for 15 feet, rolling to a back float for 10 seconds, then returning to the side using a paddle stroke. This is done without wearing an IFD.

### *Discussion Guidelines for Instructors*

1. Say, "To do a safety swim, we need to be able to swim in deep water and paddle on our front and back, showing how we can change directions. Who thinks he or she can do that?" Start students wearing PFDs, then have them move to using IFDs, and finally to performing without an IFD.

### *Performance Criteria*

The student should

***Ray*** → be able to jump in wearing a PFD, paddle stroke 15 yards, turn on the back, return to the pool side, and get out of the pool.

- be able to jump into deep water, paddle stroke 5 feet, roll to a back float for 10 seconds, then return to the pool side using a paddle stroke while wearing an IFD.

*Starfish*

- be able to jump in with or without an IFD, paddle stroke 15 yards, turn on the back, return to the pool side, and get out of the pool.
- be able to jump into deep water, paddle stroke 15 feet, roll to a back float for 10 seconds, then return to the pool side using a paddle stroke without wearing an IFD.

## Objective: To learn about the heat escape lessening posture (HELP)

Materials Needed: PFDs, one for each student. Students wear clean cotton shirts and pants to class over their swimsuits and bring large plastic bags with their names on them to hold wet clothing.

### *Skill Description*

The HELP (heat escape lessening posture) position was developed to help people preserve body heat when they are immersed in cold water. To get into this position, the student floats in a tuck position with legs squeezed together and crossed at the ankles. He or she presses the arms against the sides of the body and holds the PFD across the chest, keeping the head above water.

### *Discussion Guidelines for Instructors*

1. At the previous class meeting, tell students to wear over their swimsuits clothing that they can get wet and to bring plastic bags with their names on them to hold the wet clothing after the activity. The clothes should be a clean shirt and pants. Send home a note with students explaining what the students need to bring to the next class and why.
2. Ask, "If you are cold, what can you do? If you go outside in the winter time, what do you usually put on? Is there anything on your head? What type of clothing do you have on? Why do you think you wear these things?"

3. Ask, "Now, if you were in cold water, what could you do to stay warmer? Anybody have any ideas?"
4. Have students select a PFD and put it on. Tell them to jump into the water with their clothes on and try a few of their ideas.
5. Say, "Let's think for a second. Should your head be in the water or out if the water is cold?"

6. Ask, "What do you do in bed at night if it's cold?" (Answer: Tuck the sheets around me.) "Would you be warmer if you spread yourself apart or pulled yourself together?" (Continue until students are doing the HELP position).
7. Ask, "Do you want to keep your clothes on or take them off when you're in the water? Why?"
8. Let's see if you can.
9. Have students get out of the pool and take off their PFDs and outer clothing, wring out the excess water from the clothing, then put the wet clothing into plastic bags.

### *Performance Criteria*

The student should

| | |
|---|---|
| ***Ray*** | → be able to maintain the HELP position continuously for one minute. |
| ***Starfish*** | → be able to maintain the HELP position continuously for two minutes. |
| ***Ray and Starfish*** | → have an understanding of the purpose of the HELP position. |

---

## Objective: To learn how to bob as part of breath control

**Materials Needed:** IFDs

### *Skill Description*

Bobbing consists of repeated controlled inhalations and exhalations in a series, with the body mostly submerged. Bobbing helps students learn how to breathe in with the face above water, then exhale under the water. The student breathes in through the mouth and exhales through the nose and mouth with the lips pursed to force more air out through the nose; doing this helps keep water out of the nose. With arms at the sides, the student inhales and brings the hands up with palms together over the head and submerges. He or she then surfaces by exhaling and then returning the arms back to the sides.

### *Discussion Guidelines for Instructors*

1. Ask, "Who can blow bubbles underwater? Show me. Who can do this without holding on to the side? How far down can you go?"
2. Ask, "What can you do to make it easier to go under the water? Show me."
3. Then ask, "What can you do to come to the surface?"
4. Ask, "Can you do all this faster? Slower? Can you do this while moving across the pool? How about with partners?" Make it a see-saw game.
5. Say, "This is what we call bobbing. Let's talk about what we've been doing."
6. Ask, "What happens when we breathe air in? What happens to the air? Where does it go?" (Answer: The air goes into our lungs, bringing oxygen for our brain and muscles.)
7. Ask, "When we swim, how can we breathe and swim if our faces are in the water?" (Answer: We have to lift or turn our heads to breathe air in, then let the air out into the water.) "What does the air coming out underwater cause to happen?" (Answer: Bubbles.) "We already know how to blow bubbles. Tell me where the air comes out?" (Answer: The nose and mouth.)
8. Say, "Bobbing like we've been doing helps us get better at controlling our breathing while we are swimming. It is also good to know how to bob if we get tired while swimming in medium-depth water. We can rest a bit by bobbing."

**Instructor Note:** *When you first begin working on this skill, have students try it in shallow water, then move them into an intermediate depth, then into deeper water. Some students may be more comfortable wearing an IFD, especially while initially practicing in the medium-depth water, even though the IFD will make it difficult for them to go underwater very far. If you have smaller IFDs the size of pull buoys, you might use them, as they provide some support but allow students to go under more easily. As the students progress, have them try the skill in deep water without IFDs.*

Give students a specific number of bobs to do. Caution students not to do too many bobs because it could cause them to hyperventilate.

### *Performance Criteria*

The student should

**Ray** → be able to perform 10 bobs in shallow water without an IFD, getting a breath each time.

**Starfish** → be able to perform 10 bobs in deep water without an IFD, getting a breath each time.

---

 **Objective:** To learn how to get into and out of a boat safely and independently while wearing a PFD

### Materials Needed

PFDs, one for each student; one or more boats (canoe, rowboat, dinghy, inflatable raft)

### *Discussion Guidelines for Instructors*

1. Say, "We are going to learn more about boating today. What should we always do first before we get near or into a boat?" (Answer: Select, put on, and secure an appropriately sized PFD.)
2. Say, "We're going to talk about how to get into and out of a boat, then try it by ourselves. To get into a boat, where do you think you should step in—at the front, the back, or the center of the boat? Near the side or in the middle? Can you just step in, or do you think you should do something else?" (Answers: You should enter in the center and middle of the boat. You also should reach over and hold on to the sides of the boat [the gunwales], stay low, and try to maintain at least three points of contact with the boat at all times.) "When you get out of the boat, you do the same things—stay low, hold on to the side of the boat using three points of contact, and get out in the center of the boat."
3. Put the boat in the water at the side of the pool, then have each student practice getting into and out of the boat properly.

**Instructor Note:** *Steady the boat and be sure to spot the students as they enter so that they do not fall or slip. If possible, have aides or parents assist as well, and have more than one boat available so students do not have a long wait in line.*

*You may notice in the manual that we are using rafts to demonstrate boating safety skills. Because we are teaching mainly in swimming pools, it can be more practical to use rafts than boats. While these types of rafts may be appropriate for teaching basic boating skills, be sure to point out the difference between the actions of the rafts used in class (which are flexible and pliable) and actual boats (which have rigid boat hulls).*

### *Performance Criteria*

The student should

**Ray and Starfish** → be able to get into and out of a boat safely and independently from the side of the pool using a three-point contact while wearing a PFD.

 Objective: To learn how to sit properly and change position safely in a boat

### Materials Needed

PFDs, one for each student; one or more boats (canoe, rowboat, dinghy, inflatable raft)

### *Discussion Guidelines for Instructors*

1. Say, "Now we know how to get into and out of a boat safely all by ourselves. What did you notice when you got into the boat? Were you steady like standing on the pool deck, or did you feel different? The way you balance in the boat is different from the way you balance on deck, isn't it? The boat rocks a bit, doesn't it?"

2. Ask, "How do you think you can keep balanced in the boat?" (Answers: Stay low in the boat, hold on to both sides of the boat, if possible [three points of contact], and stay seated near the center. Don't sit on the side of the boat. Keep the weight balanced between the front and back of the boat, and keep the knees bent.)
3. Ask, "How can you change position safely in a boat, without capsizing it?" (Answers: Stay low and near the center of the boat. Keep the weight balanced between the front and back of the boat and from side to side. Only one person in the boat should move at a time.)

4. Have students put on their PFDs and take turns sitting and changing position properly in the boat at the side of the pool.

Instructor Note: *Steady the boat and be sure to spot the students as they enter so that they do not fall or slip. If possible, have aides or parents assist as well, and have more than one boat available so students do not have a long wait in line.*

*Performance Criteria*

The student should

***Ray*** → be able to demonstrate the proper way to sit in and to change position in a boat safely.

***Starfish*** → be able to demonstrate the proper way to sit in and change position in a boat safely, using a three-point contact balance.

***Ray and Starfish*** → actively participate in the discussion.

## Component 2: Personal Growth

### Objective: To become aware of safety precautions

*Discussion Guidelines for Instructors*

1. Ask, "What do you think causes many accidents in water?" (Answer: Accidents can be caused by the way my friends and I behave; they can result from not thinking before doing something.)
2. Ask, "What are some things you should remember when playing with friends around the water?"
3. Say, "Know where there are water dangers. What are some danger areas around the water?" Answers should include the following:
   - Stay away from water if no adult is present.
   - Avoid playing around water, where you may trip or fall in.
   - Stay away from hills or banks above water; they may be slippery.
   - Keep away from canals, rivers, streams, and gravel pits; the water tends to be deep.
   - Avoid playing around locks, dams, and streams, where water can flow very fast.
   - Only swim in open water when a lifeguard is around.
   - Don't dive into water if you can't see the bottom or don't know how deep the water is.
4. Ask, "Around water, what are some things that would signal that it is not safe to get into the water?"

   Answers should include these:
   - Having no lifeguard or adults around
   - A broken telephone
   - Missing rescue equipment
   - A damaged warning sign or fence
   - Big waves
   - Not being able to see the bottom
5. Ask, "What are some things you can do to check whether it is safe to get into the water?" Answers should include the following:
   - Listen to a weather forecast.
   - Ask a lifeguard or an adult where it is safe to swim.
   - Look for warning signs and flags that tell you what you should or should not do.
6. Ask, "What are some things you should always do when you plan to go into the water?"

   Include the following answers:
   - Never swim alone or without an adult supervising you. If you do, no one will be there to help you if you get into trouble—and it's not as much fun.
   - At all times stay with your parents or adults that you know.
   - Only swim where there is a lifeguard.
7. Say, "In class, we will be talking about ways you can help if someone gets in trouble in the water. We've learned some already. Does anybody remember what they are?" (Answer: Recognizing when someone is in danger, calling for help, getting adult assistance, using a reaching or throwing assist.)

*Performance Criteria*

The student should

***Ray and Starfish*** → actively participate in the discussion and

→ be able to discuss where dangers are in and around water, follow safety advice, and know how to help in case of a water emergency.

**Objective:** To learn how to demonstrate caring, honesty, respect, and responsibility

### Discussion Guidelines for Instructors

1. Ask, "What do each of the core values—caring, honesty, respect, and responsibility—mean to you? Who can give an example of when he or she demonstrated caring, honesty, respect, or responsibility?"
2. As an example you might discuss students' responsibilities before going swimming, such as showering, applying sunscreen, knowing the pool rules, or knowing the pool depth before diving. Have students explain why these responsibilities are important.
3. Mention that one way of showing respect is to wait for one's turn. Discuss other ways that students can show respect in class.
4. Take a moment during class when a student demonstrates one of the values and share it with the other students. Recognize the student and celebrate the action. Also confront any student who is not demonstrating one of the core values, and bring those actions to his or her attention. Reinforce the idea of following the core values.

**Instructor Note:** *See chapter 9 for more ideas on teaching the core values.*

### Performance Criteria

The student should

***Ray and Starfish*** → be able to share a situation that demonstrates caring, honesty, respect, or responsibility.

**Objective:** To learn about caution and patience

#### Materials Needed

tape; pieces of paper with brightly colored "smiley" faces

### Discussion Guidelines for Instructors

**Instructor Note:** *Every student participating in the YMCA Swim Lessons program should become safety conscious around water. The practices learned now can be carried throughout life. As aquatic skills begin to come more easily, students may become impatient and want to undertake skills and tests that may prove not only difficult but also dangerous. Offer your firm but kind restraint and assurance that readiness for the tougher strokes and dives is not far away.*

1. Before class begins, tape a smiley face on each piece of safety equipment around the pool. When class starts, tell everyone in the class to go and find two smiley faces and bring them back. When everyone returns, have each student explain where he or she found the smiley faces and how to use the equipment on which the faces were found. Discuss why it's their responsibility to learn to help save lives and prevent accidents.
2. Discuss the following questions, encouraging students to respond. For each question, ask students whether their responses demonstrate caring, honesty, respect, or responsibility.

   *Question 1:* You and your best friend have been taking swim lessons. You are visiting a new swimming pool and your friend says, "Race you to the deep end." What should you do to be safe and still have fun?

   *Discussion:* Discuss the pool rules and suggest games for the shallow end to get used to the water. (This relates to the values of respect and responsibility.)

   *Question 2:* You and your sister are going to the beach with an older neighbor. The neighbor falls asleep or is not paying attention because he or she is absorbed in a book. Your sister wants to go off and explore because you've never been to this beach before. What should you do?

*Discussion:* Remember the rule that an adult trained in water safety must be present when you are around water. Wake or interrupt your neighbor, and ask him or her to come along exploring. (This relates to the value of responsibility.)

*Question 3:* You and a new boy in class go to the swimming pool in his building. You both know how to float and do a few strokes. He wants to race you in the water from the shallow end to the deep end. There is a lifeguard on duty. What should you do?

*Discussion:* Encourage your friend to stay in the shallow end. If you race use IFDs and ask the lifeguard where it would be safe for you to race. Maybe you can race across the pool width instead. (This relates to the values of honesty and caring.)

*Question 4:* You are at a motel with your parents and friends. Everyone decides to stay in the room and watch a movie, but you are restless. Your parents let you go to the game room. You're wearing your bathing suit and want very much to go to the motel pool. What should you do?

*Discussion:* Ask your parents if you can go to the pool, and have an adult come with you when you swim. (This relates to the values of honesty and respect.)

3. Say, "As your skills grow, remember that even the best swimmers need to be careful." Give them some safety tips for the pool:
   - Watch out for slippery decks. Be careful when walking, and never run near the pool.
   - Check the water depth of the pool. If it isn't deep enough, 9 feet or more if diving from the deck and 11½ feet if diving from a one-meter diving board, do not dive. (Caution students against diving into residential pools if the pools are not at least nine-feet deep.) Never dive from a diving board in a backyard pool unless the pool is deep enough.
4. Tell students that, although swimming pools (especially backyard and motel pools) can be dangerous, waterways such as rivers, lakes, streams, farm ponds, and quarries are much more hazardous. Explain that they need to ask themselves the following questions before using an inland waterway:
   - Are there currents, and are they too strong?
   - Is the water polluted?
   - What kind of fish or other aquatic animals live in the water?
   - Is there junk such as broken glass or metal laying on the bottom that is dangerous?
   - Do boats use this waterway?
   - Is a lifeguard present?
   - Am I with my parents or an adult I know?
   - Do I feel very safe?
5. Talk to students about beach precautions. Discuss ocean currents, wave action, undertows, riptides, and changing water conditions during the day. Look for posted warnings of dangerous beach conditions or other signs of danger. Provide students with the following rules that help the lifeguard keep the beach safe:
   - Never call for help just for fun.
   - Respect what the lifeguard tells you. Do not talk to him or her unnecessarily.
   - Avoid unsafe areas.
   - Swim long distances along the shore, not away from it.
   - Dive only when you know the water is at least nine-feet deep and the bottom is clear.
   - Stay away from boats and surfboards.
   - Remember to always swim with a buddy who can help you if you need it.

### *Performance Criteria*

The student should

***Ray and Starfish***

→ participate in the discussion and

→ show awareness of safety precautions through discussion in class.

## Component 3: Stroke Development

**Objective:** To learn and practice the front alternating paddle stroke with rudimentary rhythmic breathing

Instructor Note: *Previously learned skills for floating, treading, safety swimming, and bobbing all connect to stroke development in a variety of ways for practice and improvement. Help students build those connections.*

### Materials Needed

toy fish that sink or other heavy objects; water logs, one for each student; kickboards, one for each student; flotation belts, one for each student

### *Discussion Guidelines for Instructors*

Instructor Note: *The following are key motor development principles to change progressively as a way to help your students improve:*

- *Whether the legs or arms move*
- *How the legs or arms move, simultaneously (at the same time) or alternating (taking turns)*
- *Whether the legs and arms move fast or slow or with bigger or smaller motions*
- *Whether the face is in the water or out*
- *Whether the students are using an IFD (e.g., water log, kickboard)*
- *How far the students can swim, from the side out, out and back to the side, or across the pool*
- *Whether the arms come out of the water for recovery*

1. Ask, "Without letting your feet touch the bottom, can you push off toward me from the wall with your legs and paddling on your front? How far can you go?"
2. Ask, "Can you do it without moving your arms and legs? How far can you go now? Can you do it more easily by moving your arms and legs?"
3. Say, "Let's see if you can get here letting only one hand pull at a time. Can you move both of your arms at the same time?"
4. Ask, "How about moving faster? Moving slower?"

Front alternating paddle without an IFD

Taking a breath while doing front alternating paddle

5. Ask, "Can you make your movements bigger? Smaller?"
6. Say, "Show me the way that you think works best."
7. Ask, "Can you get here making long movements with your hands and arms? Who can get here making the least number of hand and arm movements?"
8. Say, "Let's see who can swim making the hands pull so far back that they touch the legs."

9. Drop into the water near the sides a few toy fish or other heavy objects that can sink into the pool. Then say, "Let's see who can look for fish [or the other objects] in the pool. Can you lift your head and tell me when you see one?"
10. Ask, "Who can swim holding their hands in different ways?" Guide students to try swimming with a closed fist, then with the hand flat, and then with the fingers spread wide. Ask, "Which of these ways was easiest? Which way do you think would move you fastest?"
11. Hand out kickboards, one to each student. Then say, "This time we are going to use a kickboard. Let's see if you can move the kick-board toward me with one hand on the board at a time."
12. Have students return the kickboards, then hand out water logs, one to each student. Say, "This time we are going to try using the water log the same way. How did that work? Was it easier or harder?"
13. Have students return the water logs, then say, "Try paddling out to me without the board or log." After they do this ask, "How did that work?"

Instructor Note: *Students should wear flotation belts and a water log for additional support when they begin to learn this skill. As they become stronger and more secure and their stroke becomes more effective, use just the belts, then no IFDs at all. Recovering the arms out of the water is probably one of the last things you need to encourage, if at all, for Rays and Starfish.*

### *Performance Criteria*

The student should

***Ray*** → be able to swim a front alternating paddle stroke for 15 yards with an IFD and 20 feet without one, using rudimentary rhythmic breathing. He or she should be able to swim with the face in the water and get a breath and return the face to the water. Arms alternate and can stay underwater on recovery.

***Starfish*** → be able to swim a front alternating paddle for 25 yards with an IFD and 40 feet without one, using rudimentary rhythmic breathing. He or she should be able to swim with the face in the water and get a breath and return the face to the water. Arms alternate and can stay underwater or rudimentarily come out on recovery.

---

## Objective: To learn and practice the front symmetrical paddle stroke (lead up to breaststroke)

Materials Needed: IFDs, one for each student

### *Discussion Guidelines for Instructors*

1. Give each student an IFD. Then ask, "Can you paddle moving both hands the same way at the same time? Show me."
2. Say, "Let's try it again another way."
3. Ask, "Can you go farther?"
4. Ask, "Can you paddle moving both legs in a circle instead of up and down?"
5. Say, "Let's try it going faster. Then try going slower."
6. Say, "Try using big movements, then small ones."
7. Ask, "Who can go all the way across the pool using both arms at the same time?" Have them try this first using IFDs and later without them.

Front symmetrical paddle with a water log

*Performance Criteria*

The student should

| | |
|---|---|
| ***Ray*** | → be able to swim a front symmetrical paddle stroke for 25 yards with an IFD and 20 feet without one. The arms and legs should move roughly symmetrically and simultaneously and should remain underwater. |
| ***Starfish*** | → be able to swim a front symmetrical paddle stroke for 25 yards with an IFD and 40 feet without one. The arms and legs should move roughly symmetrically and simultaneously and should remain underwater. |

## Objective: To learn and practice the side alternating paddle stroke

Materials Needed: IFDs

*Discussion Guidelines for Instructors*

1. Ask, "Who can swim with only one shoulder out of the water? Can you swim another way? Let's try swimming with the other shoulder out of the water. Are you on your side, sort of?"
2. Say, "Try again, going slow. Try with long pulls."
3. Say, "Try again, going fast. Try with short pulls."
4. Say, "This time, try moving one leg and one arm at a time. What can you do?"
5. Ask, "Can you make the movements really small? Now try with movements that are big and slow."
6. Ask, "Which way works best?"
7. Ask, "When you swim with your shoulder out (on your side), is your face in or out of the water? Can you try it with your face in? How about out?"
8. Ask, "Which way is easier? Why? Which way is it easier to get a breath?"
9. Say, "We are going to play a new kind of hide-and-seek. In this game the person who is 'It' cannot see your face, but you also cannot swim underwater. I'll be 'It' the first time. How can you swim past me without me being able to see your face? Let's try it."
10. Ask, "Is it easier to move your arms faster or slower? Use bigger or smaller movements?"
11. Ask, "Is it easier to move your legs faster or slower? Use big kicks or smaller ones?"

Side alternating paddle stroke

Instructor Note: *Be sure to provide students with opportunities to swim on both sides. For students who are wearing flotation belts, move the flotation blocks to one side under the arm, rather than to the front or back. The side paddle will probably look like a dog paddle or finning on the side.*

### *Performance Criteria*

The student should

***Ray*** → be able to swim a side alternating paddle stroke for 15 yards with an IFD and 20 feet without one. The arms and legs should make alternating motions and remain underwater.

***Starfish*** → be able to swim a side alternating paddle stroke for 25 yards with an IFD and 40 feet without one. The arms and legs should make alternating motions and remain underwater.

## Objective: To learn the back alternating paddle stroke

**Materials Needed:** IFDs

### *Discussion Guidelines for Instructors*

1. Say, "Remember the back float? Show me how you back float. Where should your head and face be? What about your feet and legs? What shape is your body in?"
2. Say, "Great! What do you remember to do when you want to stand up? Show me how you do it."
3. Say, "Suppose we want to move around—even go across the pool—on our backs. Show me what might make you move." Students may use arms, legs, or both.
4. Ask, "I see some of you are moving your arms—can that help you swim on your back? Sure it can! Show me one way to move your arms without having them come out of the water. Show me another way." Continue having students show you different ways.
5. Ask, "Can you try making your arms move bigger? What about making the arms move smaller? Which way makes you go farther more easily? Can you make your arms move any other ways? How high can you get an arm out of the water? How far can you reach over your head?"

Back alternating paddle stroke

6. Ask, "Can you make your arms take turns? Can you make them work at the same time?"
7. Ask, "Can you show me ways to move your arms and let them come out of the water? Can you show me ways to pull them, taking turns and coming out of the water?" Having students move their arms out of the water for recovery may make their faces go underwater, so don't rush this step.
8. "What about your legs? How can you move your legs? Can you show me any other ways? Is it easier to do a big kick or a smaller one? Is it easier to go farther with soldier legs [stiff] or boiling spaghetti legs [loose]? Is it easier to have the legs take turns or to move together at the same time?"

Instructor Note: *For students wearing flotation belts, move the flotation blocks to the stomach while they are working on this stroke. As students progress, have them practice without the belts.*

### *Performance Criteria*

The student should

***Ray*** → be able to swim a back alternating paddle stroke for 15 yards with an IFD and 20 feet without one. The student's arms and legs should make alternating motions that are effective enough to move him or her 15 yards, with arms recovering in the water.

**Starfish** → be able to swim a back alternating paddlestroke for 25 yards with an IFD and 40 feet without one. The student's arms and legs should make alternating motions that are effective enough to move him or her 25 yards, with arms recovering in or out of the water.

## Objective: To learn and practice the back symmetrical paddle stroke (leads up to elementary backstroke)

**Materials Needed:** IFDs

### *Discussion Guidelines for Instructors*

1. Say, "Let's see if you can move on your back moving your arms the same way at the same time."
2. Say, "Let's see how many ways you can swim on your back without letting your arms get out of the water. Are there any other ways you can do this?"
3. Say, "This time, let's see if you can move your arms the same way at the same time and swim on your back. What happens when you bring your arms back to push again? How can you make it easier?" (Answer: Keep the arms closer to the sides, staying streamlined.)
4. Ask, "How about your legs? Can you make them move the same way at the same time, too? What ways can they move at the same time? How about up and down? Try it. How about going outward? How about in a circle?" Continue exploring other ways the legs can move. Students may need to take time to sit on the side and perform the circle kick to learn how to do it.
5. Say, "Let's try doing this really slow. How did that work? How about trying it fast?"
6. Say, "Now try to make your movements really small. Can you make them really big? Which way works best?"



7. Say, "This is a good stroke to help you rest when you get tired. Why do you think it helps you rest?" (Answer: You can glide with your face out of the water.)

Instructor Note: *For students wearing flotation belts, move the flotation blocks to the stomach while they are working on this stroke. As students progress, have them practice without the belts.*

### *Performance Criteria*

The student should

**Ray** → be able to swim a back symmetrical paddle stroke (lead up for elementary backstroke) for 25 yards with an IFD or 20 feet without one. The arms and legs should move symmetrically and simultaneously and should remain underwater.

**Starfish** → be able to swim a back symmetrical paddle stroke (lead up for elementary backstroke) for 25 yards with an IFD or 40 feet without one. The arms and legs should move symmetrically and simultaneously. Legs should remain underwater with arms recovering in or out of the water.

### Ray and Starfish Series Swim Information

Have students stretch before beginning their series swim. Use static stretching only, no bouncing or ballistic movements.

Students at this level should wear a flotation belt until they have gained the confidence and strength to be able to complete lengths easily. They should swim by the wall or in the first lane, always starting at the deep end, and they should exit the pool at the end of the length and walk back to the deep end. Walking back allows them to rest between lengths and to enjoy their accomplishment of completing an entire length. Instructors may accompany children in the water for support and encouragement. Lifeguards should be stationed on deck, at the waterside or in a chair at all times. If possible, they should be located near the series swimming.

## Component 4: Water Games and Sports

### Objective: To learn how to do the tub

*Skill Description*

To do the tub, the student begins with a stationary scull, drawing the knees toward the chest as the hips sink. The shins remain at (not above) the surface of the water. The sculling is performed at the hips to support the position. To turn, the student sculls by cupping the hand on the side to which he or she wants to turn and pulling in short pulls.

The tub

Materials Needed: kickboards, one for each student

*Discussion Guidelines for Instructors*

Ask the following series of questions:

1. "Can you float on your back? Now, can you make yourself really small without coming out of your float?"
2. Distribute one kickboard to each student. Then ask, "Do you think you could balance a kickboard on your shins? Let's see you try."
3. "Is there any other way you can hold the kickboard on your shins?"
4. "How many different ways can you move in this position [forward, backward, circle left, circle right]? Are there any other ways?"
5. "Who can move the kickboard in this position toward the other side of the pool? Can you come back without turning around? See how far you can go."

*Performance Criteria*

The student should

***Ray*** → be able to do the tub with the hands only with an IFD.

***Starfish*** → be able to do the tub with the hands only, move forward and backward, and circle left and right, with or without an IFD.

### Objective: To learn how to do a front and back somersault in the water (for Starfish only).

Materials Needed: gym mats (optional)

*Front Somersault in the Water*

Instructor Note: *Before giving students directions for the front somersault, make sure they are comfortable with the face in the water and are able to hold their breath for at least 15 seconds. (Exhaling through the nose during the somersault helps keep water from going up the nose. Discourage students from holding the nose because it makes it difficult to perform the stunt evenly.) Because this is a new water experience, expect students to experience some initial disorientation. Wearing a flotation belt will hamper this movement, so encourage only those who are comfortable without a flotation belt to try it. Have them try this in water in which they can stand up easily. You may want them to work together with buddies.*

*Skill Description*

To perform the front somersault, the student gets into a front float or glide, then pulls the knees into a tight tuck position. The student reaches down with the arms, tucks the chin, and circles the arms in a big motion to finish the circle. He or she completes the move by extending the legs backward and returning to the front float.

### Discussion Guidelines for Instructors

1. Ask, "Want to try something fun? Who can do a forward roll?" If mats are available, have students try this on deck first. "Show me—I'll help!"
2. After they have tried doing a forward roll, say, "Great! Can anyone do this in the water? Do you suppose it's harder or easier in the water? That's right, a little of both. Why?" (Answer: It's easier because the water supports you, but it's harder because you have to hold your breath and keep water out of your nose.)
3. Say, "Let's get into the water and try. What do we have to do first? Do we have to get upside down? Do we have to roll forward?" Continue asking questions and letting them try the somersault.

### Back Somersault in the Water

Instructor Note: *Again, before giving students directions for the back somersault, make sure they are comfortable with the face in the water and are able to hold their breath for at least 15 seconds.*

### Skill Description

To perform the back somersault, the student gets into a back float and assumes the tub position. He or she then takes a breath and drops the head and shoulders back below the water. The student circles the arms backward and around in a circular motion (like swinging a jump rope) as the body finishes the rotation in the original tub position. He or she completes the figure by extending the legs and returning to the back float. The body should be tightly tucked throughout the somersault.

### Discussion Guidelines for Instructors

1. Say, "This time, see if you can make your circle starting from a back float. Let's see you try. Are there any other ways to do this?"
2. Ask, "Would it be easier if you were smaller or bigger? Let's try it both ways."
3. Ask, "What can you do with your hands to make it easier to turn over? Do you make them big or small?"

### Somersault Skill Exercise

Once students can do both the front and back somersaults, have them attempt this exercise:

1. Say, "Do a tub."
2. Say, "Do a tub to a back somersault."
3. Say, "Choose a partner. Now, side by side, do a back float, a tub, and then a back somersault."
4. Say, "Again, with a partner, start with your toes touching, repeat what you just did, and finish with your toes touching."
5. Say, "Find another pair of partners to work with. Then repeat what you just did, starting and finishing with all your toes touching."
6. Say, "Now, with your partner, side by side, do a front somersault."
7. Say, "Get back together with the other pair of partners. Form a line, then do a front somersault."
8. Repeat the previous skills and combinations to music.

### Performance Criteria

The student should

***Starfish*** → be able to do a front and back somersault in the water without assistance.

## Objective: To learn about canoe sculling (for Starfish only)

Materials Needed: IFDs

### *Skill Description*

The canoe scull keeps the body stationary or moving headfirst. In the canoe scull the student extends the body in a front layout and places the arms beside the body in a comfortable position between the hips and shoulders. He or she arches the lower back slightly by pressing up with the heels and slightly down with the shoulders. The student hyperextends the wrists sharply and turns the palms out, away from the body. The elbows are bent and the hands almost touch underneath the body.

The student leads with the wrists, sweeping the hands out about a foot from the body by extending the elbows. Without stopping, the student then rotates the hands so the palms face inward and sweeps the hands back toward each other by bending the elbows. The movement of the hands resembles a figure eight. The fingers and thumb should be held close together to exert maximum pressure on the water, but the wrists and elbows should be relaxed.

To remain stationary, the student should keep the palms facing down; to travel, the student should have the fingertips facing down.

### *Discussion Guidelines for Instructors*

1. Ask, "If you wanted to move on your front without moving your legs and not showing me your arms or hands, how could you move?"
2. Ask, "Where is the heaviest part of your body? (Answer: near your legs and hips.)
3. Ask, "Do you think if you tried placing your hands near your legs and hips it might help? Give it a try." After they have tried, ask them, "Where is it easier to put your hands? Right at your hips, or farther down toward your feet?"

### *Performance Criteria*

The student should

***Starfish*** → be able to demonstrate canoe sculling for 15 seconds with or without an IFD.

Canoe scull

## Objective: To learn how to swim up to the surface

Materials Needed

a kickboard, rescue tube, or water log; a shepherd's crook; a pole long enough to extend from the water's surface to the bottom of the pool. Mark the pole in one-foot increments so students can see how deep the water is.

### *Teaching Instruction*

1. In shallow water, review climbing down to the pool bottom and up using a pole.

Swimming up to the surface

2. Say, "Now let's try climbing down and then letting go and swimming up to the surface." Hold the pole vertically in the water while students try climbing down it, then swimming up.
3. Ask, "If you wanted to come up faster, what could you do?"
4. Ask, "Did you notice anything when you went underwater? Did you feel any pressure or tightness in your ears? To make it feel better, we can equalize the pressure. Try either wiggling your jaw or swallowing." Have students practice equalizing the pressure. Then tell them, "If your ears hurt when you go under or they won't 'pop,' come back to the surface."
5. Move students to the deep water. Ask, "Who can jump into the water and touch the bottom of the pool with their feet?"
6. Ask, "What can you do to go deeper into the water? Try your ideas."
7. Ask, "Does it work better if you spread out your arms and legs or if you keep them together? Try it both ways."
8. After the students surface, have them paddle to the ladder and climb out of the pool.

Instructor Note: *Have students jump out at least five feet. Mark five feet with a kickboard, rescue tube, or water log to provide students with a visual cue (you also can use these items for rescue purposes). Once students can perform this skill successfully, they can then try going off the diving board. Always have a shepherd's crook available as a safety pole to grab on to.*

### *Performance Criteria*

The student should

***Ray and Starfish*** → be able to jump into deep water and swim up from at least five to seven feet.

---

## Objective: To learn how to jump into the water from a one-meter diving board

Instructor Note: *Try this activity only if your students can strongly grip the stair or pool ladder railing when they get out of the pool. If they cannot do this, they will not have the hand strength to hold the railing for the diving board stairs.*

### Materials Needed

a kickboard or water log, a one-meter diving board, flotation belts

*Discussion Guidelines for Instructors*

1. In the deep end of the pool, have students jump out to a kickboard or water log at least five feet away from the side. Then ask them to swim to the other side of the pool.

Instructor Note: *When you want students to practice jumping into water from the side, check the water depth. Because of differing body size and height, a rule of thumb is that the water should be at least five-feet deep for children and nine-feet deep for adults.*

2. Ask, "When you jump in from the side or from a height, why do you want to jump out a few feet?"
3. Ask, "Is it easier to jump in with your feet together or apart? How would you keep water from going up your nose?"
4. Say, "We are going to try this off the diving board. What are a few things you need to remember when you use a diving board?" Review the diving safety rules covered in Component 1 of this level:
   - Follow posted diving rules.
   - Dive only in water that is at least nine-feet deep, and dive from a one-meter diving board only in water that is at least 11½ feet deep.
   - Dive with arms extended and hands grabbed.
   - Dive only when you know the water and the bottom is clear of obstructions and other swimmers.
   - Swim directly to the nearest side of the pool after going off the diving board.
   - Use the diving board one person at a time.
   - Don't dive off the board until the person in front of you has swum to the side or has cleared the area.
5. Ask, "When you climb up the ladder, what should you do?" Answers include the following:
   - Grab the hand rails tightly with both hands, or, if the rails are too big for your hands, hold on to the rungs.
   - Only release one hand at a time as you climb.
   - Step slowly up the ladder.
   - Don't start up the ladder until the person in front of you is out of the diving area and on his or her way to the side.

Instructor Note: *When you are teaching small children, stand behind them while they climb up the ladder.*

6. Say, "Let's practice climbing up and down the ladder before we try going off the board."
7. Ask, "When you're up on the diving board, what should you do? Why?" Answers include the following:
   - Hold on to the guard rails.

- Walk slowly to the end of the board.
- Always go straight off the board, never to the side.
- Curl your toes over the edge of the board so you don't slip.
- When your toes are at the end of the board, take a big step off the board and jump forward like we did off the side.

8. Ask, "After you jump, what do you do?" Answers include the following:
   - Swim up to the surface.
   - Swim directly to the closest side of the pool.
   - Climb out at the ladder.
9. Say, "Let's give it a try." Reinforce the diving safety rules before allowing students to try jumping off the board.

Instructor Note: *While they jump off the board, you should be in the water with a rescue tube off to the side.*

### *Performance Criteria*

The student should

| | |
|---|---|
| ***Ray and Starfish*** | → be able to jump into the pool from a one-meter board and swim to the side with or without a flotation belt. |

## Objective: To learn how to perform a kneeling dive

Materials Needed: several sinkable objects

### *Surface Glide and Recover*

This is the first of a series of skills that progresses to performing a kneeling dive.

### *Skill Description*

To perform a surface glide, the student pushes off the side with both feet, in shallow water. He or she glides on the surface with arms extended and hands grabbed, and with legs straight. The eyes should be open. When the student is ready to stop, he or she pulls the hands down and brings the knees forward, raises the head, and places the feet beneath him or her to stand up.

### *Discussion Guidelines for Instructors*

1. Ask, "Who can pretend to be an arrow or a rocket [hold your hands over your head to show an arrow or a rocket] that has been shot and then hits the target?"

### *Surface Glide to the Bottom*

**Skill Description**

To do the surface glide to the bottom, the student glides downward with arms extended and hands grabbed and touches the bottom with the hands. The student then brings the knees to the chest, puts the feet on the bottom, and pushes off to glide to the surface.

**Discussion Guidelines for Instructors**

1. Ask, "How many different ways can you touch the bottom of the pool with your hands over your head?"
2. Say, "This time, touch the bottom, but don't put your feet on the bottom until after you touch it with your hands."

## *Flying Porpoise*

Instructor Note: *The pool must be shallow enough for preschoolers to stand up in if they are to succeed at this activity.*

### *Skill Description*

The flying porpoise is performed in three to four feet of water. The student starts by standing on the bottom, with arms extended and hands grabbed. He or she then bends the knees and jumps up, reaches out, and then glides to the bottom. After the student touches bottom, he or she places the feet on the bottom and stands up.

Instructor Note: *If the water is too deep for the child, continue to practice the surface glide to the bottom.*

### *Discussion Guidelines for Instructors*

1. Say, "With your hands over your head, let's see if you can look like a porpoise swimming in the ocean."
2. Say, "Now let's see if you can go all the way to the bottom and jump way out of the water."
3. Ask, "Can you do it faster? Can you make your jumps longer? How many times does it take to get across the pool? Let's see if you can do it one less time."

## *Headfirst Surface Dive*

**Skill Description**

The headfirst surface dive is done in deep water. The student starts with a surface glide with arms overhead. He or she then takes a breath, tucks the chin, and reaches toward the bottom, lifting the legs and gliding. The student exhales slowly and gently during the descent and ascent.

**Discussion Guidelines for Instructors**

1. Put some sinkable objects on the bottom of the pool. Then say, "Let's see you try to get the objects on the bottom of the pool." After they try ask them, " Are there any other ways you can get the objects?"
2. Say, "Let's see if you can get near the items going head first with arms overhead. Let's see how many different ways you can get close to the objects."

3. Say, "This time when you are swimming, don't stop, but try to go and get an object."

### *Kneeling Dive*

#### Skill Description

The kneeling dive is performed in water at least nine-feet deep. The student kneels with arms extended and hands grabbed. The head is between the arms with the eyes focused on the entry point. The lead foot is positioned so the toes are over the edge of the pool. The student leans forward and touches the water before pushing with the feet. He or she glides toward the bottom, then swims up to return to the surface.

Instructor Note: *This skill should be taught in water at least nine-feet deep.*

#### Discussion Guidelines for Instructors

1. Have students get into the kneeling position with the arms extended and hands grabbed and the head between the arms.
2. Say, "Let's see if you can get into the water with your hands first. When you surface, begin paddling across the pool."
3. Say, "This time when you try it, after your arms and hands are underwater, stretch yourself as far as you can."
4. Say, "Let's try again and see if you can get to the surface faster."
5. Ask, "Would it help if, once your hands were underwater, you reached them up toward the surface? See if you can dive, surface, and paddle 15 feet."

### *Performance Criteria*

The student should

| | |
|---|---|
| ***Ray and Starfish*** | → be able to perform a surface glide, a surface glide to the bottom, and to equalize pressure. |
| ***Starfish*** | → be able to perform a flying porpoise and a head-first surface dive, and<br>→ be able to perform a kneeling dive with assistance, glide, then paddle 15 feet without wearing an IFD. |

---

**Objective:** To learn how to, in the water, throw and catch a ball, dribble the ball while paddling, pass the ball to a partner, and shoot the ball into a goal (for Starfish only)

Instructor Note: *Four lead-up skills for water polo are introduced at the Ray and Starfish levels:*

- Making a forceful throw (as in making a goal);
- Making a soft, accurate throw (as in passing to a teammate);
- Catching a pass from a teammate; and
- Dribbling the ball out in front while swimming.

Each skill requires different practice situations, and the two throws and catch require a ball small enough for the swimmer to grip with one hand.

### *Skill Description*

To pass the ball while swimming, the student grasps the ball from underneath with a relaxed hand, fingers spread wide. He or she then brings the ball behind the head, with the elbow bent at 90 degrees, to make a good pass. The student can use the opposite hand to assist with balance.

### Materials Needed

two cones; flotation belts; For throwing balls of various sizes, choose a ball that students can grasp comfortably with one hand (a racquetball, a foam ball, a small playground ball, a water polo ball, a mini-basketball), one for each pair; For catching, use larger balls.

### *Discussion Guidelines for Instructors*

1. Say, "Let's see how many different ways you can pick up the ball with one hand. Okay, is there any other way?"
2. Say, "Let's try it with your other hand. Is there any other way you can pick up the ball?"
3. Have students match up with partners. Then say, "Now let's try to pick up the ball with one hand and throw the ball to a partner. Let's try it another way."
4. Ask, "Is it easier to throw the ball from in front of your body or by bringing your arm behind your head? Try both ways."
5. Ask, "Is it easier throwing the ball with your arm straight or bent?" (The arm should be bent during the backswing and straighten at release only.)
6. Say, "Now let's try to throw the ball faster. Which way is faster?"
7. Say, "Let's see who can throw the ball out of the pool and onto the deck from five feet away." Have them try it one at a time at this distance, then move them back a little.
8. When they have succeeded in throwing the ball onto the deck from 10 feet away, have them try it with increasingly larger balls until they are using a ball the same size as a junior water polo ball.
9. Now place cones on the deck 10 feet apart. Say, "Now see if you can throw the ball between the cones." Have them try it, then decrease the distance between the cones.
10. Say, "Now let's see if you can dribble the ball and then pick it up with one hand and throw it." Once they are successful, see if they can dribble the ball faster and then throw the ball.
11. Say, "Okay, let's see if you can paddle and dribble at the same time."

Instructor Note: *Students may wear flotation belts when they begin working on this skill, then take them off as they become comfortable performing the skill.*

12. Have students pair off again. Then ask, "Can you dribble the ball while paddling and pass the ball to a partner? Let's try it a few times." After they try, say, "Now let's try dribbling and passing to your partner, then taking turns throwing it into the goal." Have students take turns being the goalie. The goalie tries to stop the ball from going into the goal, either by blocking the ball with the hands or by catching the ball.

*Performance Criteria*

The student should, while in the water,

***Starfish***

- be able to throw the ball with one hand at least five feet and catch a tossed ball with two hands,
- be able to pass a ball to a partner so the partner can catch it,
- be able to throw the ball at least 10 feet between cones that are 10 feet apart, 50 percent of the time, and
- be able to dribble the ball in front while paddling(with or without an IFD) for at least 75 feet.

## Component 5: Rescue

**Objective:** To learn more about reaching and throwing assists

### Materials Needed

IFDs; objects that can be used for a reaching assist that are light enough for students to lift and an appropriate size for the students; objects that will float, such as PFDs, kickboards, rubber balls, empty plastic bottles (soft objects are best)

### *Skill Description*

Reaching assists are used to help distressed or near drowning swimmers without endangering the rescuer. Many items can be used to perform a reaching assist: a light aluminum pole, a towel, a piece of clothing, or a piece of light lumber (watch for splinters). A rescuer also can extend an arm or leg. At this level, because of the size and age of the students, we concentrate on extending objects rather than an arm or leg. To perform an assist, the student first establishes a wide base of support by lying down, or crouching, keeping the weight low and away from the victim. He or she extends the object within reach of the victim and either slides it under the victim's armpit or presses it against the victim's side. Once the victim has grasped the object, the student maintains position and, with weight shifted away from the victim, pulls him or her in slowly, hand over hand. The student should communicate with the victim, reassuring the victim as he or she is brought to safety.

Reaching assist

At this level, emphasize that students should not get into the water to perform a rescue. Teach students how to grab and hold onto an extended item from a rescuer.

Throwing assist

A throwing assist is performed at this level by tossing a buoyant object out to a distressed swimmer to help him or her stay afloat. (Lifeguards perform assists with a rescue bag, ring buoy, or heaving line or jug, all of which have attached ropes for pulling in the victim.) The student throws the object so it lands close to the swimmer, slightly in front and near the hands.

### *Discussion Guidelines for Instructors*

1. Review with the students what they learned in the Pike and Eel levels about getting assistance for someone who needs help and about reaching assists. Emphasize that the first thing they should do is to yell for help. Say, "Try extending something to me. What could you use? What could you do to make sure you didn't get pulled into the water?" Finally, ask, "If you needed help, how would you grab the extended object?"
2. Have pairs of students take turns rescuing each other. They can wear IFDs if they like. When students play victims, check that they grab with two hands, try to kick, and do not pull on the object that is extended.
3. Explain, "If you need help, remember these things:
   - Keep calm—don't panic.
   - Listen to what the rescuer tells you.
   - Keep your head above water by kicking your feet and moving your hands underwater.
   - Let the rescuer grab you to help you in. If the rescuer reaches something toward you, grab it with both hands and kick your feet.
4. Say, "Let's look around the pool area. Tell me which things you think will float." After the students respond, say, "Now go get something you think will float." After they have retrieved the objects, have them toss the objects in the water. (If a student's object doesn't float, have him or her pick another object and try again.) Then have them retrieve the objects.
5. Say, "If you wanted to help a friend who was in trouble in the water, you could throw a floating object to him or her. How would you throw the object?" Let them try tossing their objects.
6. Ask, "What do you think you should try to do when throwing an object to someone in trouble?" (Answers: Get it close to the victim and slightly in front of him or her, near the hands.) Say, "Let's try throwing the objects again. I'll pretend to be a victim." Have them practice throwing their objects to you from no more than five feet away.
7. Ask, "Do you think you might need to talk to the person in trouble? What should you say?" (Answer: Say things such as "I'm going to help you," "Grab the object," or "Kick your feet.")

### *Performance Criteria*

The student should

***Ray***

- be present for the activity,
- be able to grasp an extended object,
- be able to extend an object to someone,
- be able to identify objects that can be used in a throwing rescue, and
- be able to perform a throwing rescue to a victim no more than two to four feet away with two hands.

***Starfish***

- be present for the activity,
- be able to grasp an extended object,
- be able to extend an object to someone,
- be able to identify objects that can be used in a throwing rescue, and
- be able to perform a throwing rescue to a victim no more than three to five feet away with one hand.

## Objective: To learn about rescue breathing

Materials Needed: a CPR mannequin (optional), a pocket mask

### *Discussion Guidelines for Instructors*

1. If possible, demonstrate rescue breathing on a CPR mannequin, using a pocket mask.
2. Discuss the following topics:
   - How to know when someone needs rescue breathing
   - What to say when you call an emergency medical service
   - Why we do rescue breathing
   - How to do rescue breathing
   - How to protect yourself during rescue breathing by using a pocket mask
   - How to become certified in CPR and rescue breathing
3. Show students the following method of remembering the important points of rescue breathing using the fingers of one hand:
   - Thumb is shake and shout. (Touch the person and ask if he or she is okay.)
   - Pointer (index finger) is call the emergency number.
   - Tallman (middle finger) is look, listen, and feel. (Look for chest movement, listen for breath, and feel for air coming from the mouth.)
   - Ringman (ring finger) is two long, full breaths.
   - Pinky (little finger) is one breath every five seconds.

   Demonstrate rescue breathing as you go through the last three phrases, then repeat all the phrases.
4. Tell students that the rescuer must have a barrier between his or her mouth and the victim's mouth. Mention that the number of breaths is different for adults than for children and infants (1:5 ratio for adults; 1:3 for children and infants). Emphasize that they would need to have more training to do rescue breathing properly on their own.

Instructor demonstrating rescue breathing on mannequin with pocket mask

### *Performance Criteria*

The student should

***Ray and Starfish*** → be present for and observe the demonstration.

# Summary

## Ray

### Component 1: Personal Safety

- Participate in the discussion of general diving safety rules and be able to name the four most important ones.
- Float for 30 seconds on the front and 30 seconds on the back without wearing an IFD.
- Tread water for 20 to 30 seconds with an IFD.
- Select, put on, secure, and take off a PFD.
- Jump in wearing a PFD, paddle stroke 15 yards, turn on the back, return to the pool side, and get out of the pool, and jump into deep water, paddle stroke 5 feet, roll to a back float for 10 seconds, then return to the pool side using a paddle stroke while wearing an IFD.
- Maintain the HELP position continuously for 1 minute, and understand the purpose of the HELP position.
- Perform 10 bobs in shallow water without an IFD, getting a breath each time.
- Get into and out of a boat safely and independently from the side of the pool using a three-point contact while wearing a PFD.
- Actively participate in the discussion and demonstrate the proper way to sit in and change position in a boat safely.

### Component 2: Personal Growth

- Actively participate in the discussion and be able to discuss where dangers are in and around water, follow safety advice, and know how to help in case of a water emergency.
- Share a situation that demonstrates caring, honesty, respect, or responsibility.
- Participate in the discussion and show awareness of safety precautions through discussion in class.

### Component 3: Stroke Development

- Swim a front alternating paddle stroke for 15 yards with an IFD and 20 feet without one, using rudimentary rhythmic breathing. He or she should be able to swim with the face in the water and get a breath and return the face to the water. Arms alternate and can stay underwater on recovery.
- Swim a front symmetrical paddle stroke for 25 yards with an IFD and 20 feet without one. The arms and legs should move roughly symmetrically and simultaneously and should remain underwater.
- Swim a side alternating paddle stroke for 15 yards with an IFD and 20 feet without one. The arms and legs should make alternating motions and remain underwater.
- Swim a back alternating paddle stroke for 15 yards with an IFD and 20 feet without one. The student's arms and legs should make alternating motions that are effective enough to move him or her 15 yards, with arms recovering in the water.
- Swim a back symmetrical paddle stroke (lead up for elementary backstroke) for 25 yards with an IFD or 20 feet without one. The arms and legs should move symmetrically and simultaneously and should remain underwater.

### Component 4: Water Games and Sports

- Do the tub with the hands only with an IFD.
- Jump into deep water and swim up from at least five to seven feet.
- Jump into the pool from a one-meter board and swim to the side with or without a flotation belt.
- Perform a surface glide, a surface glide to the bottom, and equalize pressure.

### Component 5: Rescue

- Be present for the activity, grasp an extended object, extend an object to someone, identify objects that can be used in a throwing rescue, and perform a throwing rescue to a victim no more than 2 to 4 feet away with two hands.
- Be present for and observe the demonstration of rescue breathing.

# Summary

## Starfish

### Component 1: Personal Safety

- Participate in the discussion of general diving safety rules and be able to name the four most important ones.
- Float for one minute or longer on the front and one minute or longer on the back without wearing an IFD.
- Tread water for 20 to 30 seconds without an IFD.
- Select, put on, secure, and take off a PFD.
- Jump in with or without an IFD, paddle stroke 15 yards, turn on the back, return to the pool side, and get out of the pool, and jump into deep water, paddle stroke 15 feet, roll to a back float for 10 seconds, then return to the pool side using a paddle stroke without wearing an IFD.
- Maintain the HELP position continuously for 2 minutes, and understand the purpose of the HELP position.
- Perform 10 bobs in deep water without an IFD, getting a breath each time.
- Get in and out of a boat safely and independently from the side of the pool using a three-point contact while wearing a PFD.
- Actively participate in the discussion and demonstrate the proper way to sit in and change position in a boat safely using a three-point contact balance.

### Component 2: Personal Growth

- Actively participate in the discussion and be able to discuss where dangers are in and around water, follow safety advice, and know how to help in case of a water emergency.
- Share a situation that demonstrates caring, honesty, respect, or responsibility.
- Participate in the discussion and show awareness of safety precautions through discussion in class

### Component 3: Stroke Development

- Swim a front alternating paddle for 25 yards with an IFD and 40 feet without one, using rudimentary rhythmic breathing. He or she should be able to swim with the face in the water and get a breath and return the face to the water. Arms alternate and can stay underwater or rudimentarily come out on recovery.
- Swim a front symmetrical paddle stroke for 25 yards with an IFD and 40 feet without one. The arms and legs should move roughly symmetrically and simultaneously and should remain underwater.
- Swim a side alternating paddle for 25 yards with an IFD and 40 feet without one. The arms and legs should make alternating motions and remain underwater.
- Swim a back alternating paddle stroke for 25 yards with an IFD and 40 feet without one. The student's arms and legs should make alternating motions that are effective enough to move him or her 25 yards, with arms recovering in or out of the water.
- Swim a back symmetrical paddle stroke (lead up for elementary backstroke) for 25 yards with an IFD or 40 feet without one. The arms and legs should move symmetrically and simultaneously. Legs should remain underwater, with arms recovering in or out of the water.

### Component 4: Water Games and Sports

- Do the tub with the hands only, move forward and backward, and circle left and right, with or without an IFD.
- Do a front and back somersault in the water without assistance.
- Demonstrate canoe sculling for 15 seconds without an IFD.
- Jump into deep water and swim up from at least 5 to 7 feet.
- Jump into the pool from a one-meter board and swim to the side with or without a floatation belt.
- Perform a surface glide and a surface glide to bottom and equalize pressure, perform a flying porpoise and a head-first surface dive, and perform a kneeling dive with assistance, glide, then paddle 15 feet without wearing an IFD.
- Throw the ball with one hand at least 5 feet and catch a tossed ball with two hands; pass a ball to a partner so the partner can catch it; throw a ball at least 10 feet between cones that are 10 feet apart 50 percent of the time; dribble the ball in front while paddling (with or without an IFD) for at least 75 feet.

### Component 5: Rescue

- Be present for the activity, grasp an extended object, extend one object to someone, identify objects that can be used in a throwing rescue, and perform a throwing rescue to a victim no more than 3 to 5 feet away with one hand.
- Be present for and observe the demonstration of rescue breathing.

# APPENDIX A

# Aquatic Program Guidelines for Children Under the Age of Three

## Statement of the YMCA of the USA Medical Advisory Committee:

The YMCA of the USA developed the following guidelines to provide the safest and highest quality early water experiences for under-three children and their parents. In brief, the objectives of the Parent/Child Aquatic Program are to promote water enjoyment and exercise for parents and their young children while also providing water and boating safety information as part of a larger parent and family Y education. Programs that follow these minimum guidelines are more likely to provide developmentally appropriate and safe classes for both child and parent.

1. Aquatic programs for children 6 to 36 months of age require the in-water participation of a parent, guardian, or other adult who is trusted by and legally responsible for the child.

The parent or guardian is the first and best teacher of the child. The Parent/Child Aquatic Program is directed to this parent or adult. The instructor provides guidance to the adult, who must accompany and supervise the child in the locker room, pool, and any other areas that are related to the aquatic program. Parents are responsible for their children and need to be educated on water safety and the importance of constant supervision of their child in or around all types of water environments.

An important objective of this program is to help strengthen and support families. The program offers an opportunity for the parent to spend uninterrupted time and to experience a closeness with the child. The program provides opportunities for parents to socialize, share their experiences, make new friends, and learn from other parents.

2. Participants enrolled in the Parent/Child Aquatic Program should be a minimum of six months old and have sufficient head control in a prone position to keep the face out of the water.

Infant motor development is marked by individual differences in the age of onset of developmental benchmarks. The ability to maintain head righting is a key marker indicating an infant's readiness for safe participation in an aquatic program. When infants can right their heads, they are less likely to accidentally submerge their faces while being held in a prone position by their parents.

3. The participating parent or guardian assumes responsibility for the child's health before, during, and after participation in the aquatic program.

It is recommended that parents discuss with the child's physician the possible benefits as well as any concerns they may have about participation in the Parent/Child Aquatic Program.

4. Terms such as *aquatic* or *water adjustment, familiarization, fun, readiness*, and/or *orientation* are appropriate and accurate to describe the Parent/Child Aquatic Program philosophy. Terms such as *drownproofing, waterproofing, watersafe*, or even *swimming* are inappropriate and misleading to describe the intent, philosophy, and content of the program.

Aquatic programs for children in this age range should employ developmentally appropriate practices that focus on adjustment to a water environment, exploration, child-centered learning, and enjoyment by both parent and child. Parent education should include information such as the proper use of flotation devices and appropriate progressions and water games. It must be emphasized to parents that aquatic programs alone do not prevent drowning.

Parents must learn to implement strategies for preventing a child's unsupervised access to water. In addition to constant supervision, homes with backyard pools or spas should have multiple passive barriers installed. These include four-sided fences, self-locking and latching gates, lockable spa covers, and door latches out of the reach of a toddler. Parents should also be aware that toilets, buckets, and bathtubs present a risk for drowning, and similar strategies for preventing unsupervised child access should be implemented.

5. Dropping, pushing, or tossing a child into the water is strictly prohibited. Submersions coerced or controlled by an adult should not occur. Voluntary face submersions and swallowing water by children under 24 months must be limited and carefully monitored by parents and instructors.

Ballistic movements resulting from dropping, pushing, or tossing a child in the water are dangerous and abusive to children and serve no educational purpose. As a child-centered program, The Parent/Child Aquatic Program also does not support or condone submersions coerced or controlled mainly by an adult. Instead, children in this age range should be

encouraged to mimic and explore others as they learn to control their breath in the water.

6. In-water class time for children in this age range should be limited to a maximum of 30 minutes per session but adapted individually for differences in water and air temperatures, skill level, experience, and enjoyment.

Sessions should not exceed the maximum in-water time of 30 minutes. Class time may vary based on the child's experience, enjoyment, skill level, and/or water and air temperature. It is preferable to end a water session early rather than late, when a child may become chilled, tired, or irritable.

Children six to twelve months old may do better in shorter sessions of 15 minutes or so. Babies tend to chill easily, and other factors such as body composition also influence the length of time any child may comfortably stay in the water. Generally, children can tolerate longer class periods in the water after the thermoregulatory system develops.

Another area of concern is a rare condition called *hyponatremia*, which can occur when a child ingests water to a point where the body's electrolytes are diluted and the kidneys fail to filter out the excessive water effectively. Ingested pool water plus the additional liquids from feedings before and after class may contribute to this condition. Numerous submersions, small body size, and/or long class sessions may increase the likelihood of hyponatremia. Symptoms may include lethargy, restlessness, nausea, vomiting, and/or convulsions. Hyponatremia is one of the reasons why it is important to monitor an infant's ingestion of water during the class as well as limit in-water sessions to a maximum of 30 minutes.

7. Parent/Child Aquatic Programs should be conducted by currently certified Parent/Child Aquatic Program instructors as well as supervised by a currently certified YMCA lifeguard.

The Parent/Child Aquatic Program is developed based on the overall philosophy of the YMCA plus the principles of child and motor development as they relate to swimming and water safety. Parent/Child Aquatic Program instructors receive developmental training plus teaching methods for parents in this program. The course also includes information about dispelling myths and providing realistic expectations of what the program can accomplish. The importance of a properly trained instructor and a class conducted in a lifeguarded pool helps ensure the quality of the program and the safety of participants.

8. Appropriate swimming apparel should be worn to prevent contamination of pool water and to avoid the spread of disease.

The contaminants (e.g., bacteria, viruses, parasites) that are found in fecal matter can be hazardous to participants. Infants must be clothed in appropriate attire to confine such matter. Plastic pants or other swimmingsuits that are lightweight and have snug, elastic-fitting leg and waist bands are best. Parents should monitor their child and be instructed to remove the child from the water should clothing become soiled. A child who is experiencing diarrhea should not participate in the program until the condition has been resolved.

9. Pool indoor water temperature should be in the range of 82 to 86 degrees Fahrenheit (27.5 to 30 degrees Celsius). Air temperature should range from three to five degrees Fahrenheit (1.5 to 2.7 degrees Celsius) higher than the water temperature.

Young children do not adjust to temperature extremes as effectively as do older children and adults. Parents and instructors must monitor the child for any signs of exposure to cold (e.g., shivering, bluish lips or skin), heat or sun (e.g., flushed, reddish skin), or behavioral changes (e.g., persistent crying or listlessness). The child should be removed from the water and/or sun if any of these warning signs or symptoms appear.

In the case of outdoor pools, water and air temperature are more difficult to control. Again, it is the parents and instructors who need to monitor the child's comfort and safety.

10. All state and local government laws and regulations applicable to the program facility, including those pertaining to water quality and sanitation, must be carefully followed.

In areas used by young children, sanitary conditions are of the utmost importance. Your Y bears the responsibility of keeping the surroundings as clean and comfortable as possible. This includes adhering to all state and local government laws and regulations applicable to facility and water quality requirements and the guidelines found in the course and text, *YMCA Pool Operator On Location*. Locker room areas must be kept clean and disinfected. Proper facilities include places for diapering, for proper disposal of diapers and human wastes, and for dressing.

*May 1990*

*Revised November 1996*

APPENDIX B

# Activities, Songs, and Games

**Young children often learn best when they are engaged in activities that they enjoy doing.**

**Exploration, play, and make-believe are part of their everyday lives, so we can take advantage of this to teach water skills with play and imaginary activities and active songs and games.**

This appendix provides you with many ideas for activities that can develop not only children's water skills but also their cognitive abilities and their values. It is divided into activity ideas and songs and games and character development activities. The songs and games section is further divided by skills: water adjustment, water entry and exit, buoyancy, breath control, balance, and locomotion.

## Activity Ideas

This section presents ideas that you can incorporate into your classes to make learning fun and exciting. It includes suggestions for play areas for children and parents and some game concepts and imaginative analogies to make water skill development entertaining for the children. A list of useful toys and equipment is offered, followed by ideas for specific class activities and activities that enhance children's development.

### Water Play Areas

Younger children (13 months and under) need adult assistance as they play near water. Older children can play more independently but should be supervised closely. Create areas in and around the pool where parents and children can play together:

- Suggest activities that can be done on deck as well as in the pool.
- Bring in a plastic pool or large tub filled with warm water for children to play in or beside. Provide floating boats and animals.
- Have on deck plastic containers of different sizes or unbreakable plastic toys that can hold water.
- Set up stations around the pool so parent/child teams can move in order from one to another:

  *Station 1.* A large mat a child can lie on or walk on

*Station 2.* Plastic inflatable objects to ride on or in, such as a boat

*Station 3.* Plastic hoops to go through, held on the surface by an adult

*Station 4.* Kickboards for riding across the pool

*Station 5.* Toys that can ride across the pool on a kickboard

*Station 6.* A small, smooth board that acts as a slide to ride into the pool, where the parent catches the child

*Station 7.* Floating colored objects that can be gathered into matching colored containers

*Station 8.* Horns, whistles, or bubble pipes to teach blowing (a bubble wand also can be used)

*Station 9.* A pole extended across a corner of the pool, which can be held by an adult; a child can hold on to the pole and "sleep" on his or her back

*Station 10.* Large balls or soft plastic balls to throw and go after

## Imaginative Games for Water Skills

### Bubbling

Blow soap bubbles on deck.

Play with bubble pipes in the pool.

Use straws in the pool for bubbling.

Blow large plastic whistles in the water.

### Poles

Have children pretend to be fire fighters climbing poles.

Have children pretend to ride an elevator by sitting in the curve of a shepherd's crook and being lowered under water.

Hold poles horizontally for children to kick and duck under.

### Imaginary Trips

Take trips to the gas station, motoring (kicking) and bubble blowing.

Drive your kickboard car in traffic through streets and alleys with red lights and green lights.

Take trips to the grocery store with "groceries" on kickboard carts.

Take a trip to Florida, flying there in a plane and driving kickboard cars to Busch Gardens to ride on the roller coaster and water flume. Imitate wild animals.

Drive to Disney World to take a submarine ride. Visit other attractions.

Drive to Cape Canaveral and pretend to be rockets.

Drive to Cypress Gardens and imitate the floating flowers and trick skiers.

Drive to Sea World and pretend to be a whale, an otter, and a seal, and then fly home.

Take a trip to the grandparents' house over the river and through the woods. Prepare a holiday table, eat a meal, sleep after the meal, and drive home.

Visit the farm or zoo and pretend to be animals.

Visit the pet store and pretend to be various kinds of dogs, such as retrievers who fetch, beagles who dig, or terriers who play tug of war.

Visit the circus and act out the various performers and animals.

Go on a fishing or camping trip.

Visit "Pooh Corner."

Visit the seashore.

### Props

Create an obstacle course.

Go treasure hunting for toys that sink.

Rescue a child in the water by extending an object.

Swim in, out, and around a swamped canoe or rowboat.

Make bridges with the arms or with large plastic hoops to go under.

### Pretending to Be Someone or Something Else

Be ducks getting into a pond.

Act out favorite stories like "Red Riding Hood" or "Peter and the Wolf."

Play at being deep sea divers.

Be frogs jumping into water from a log.

## Word Actions

Use these word actions to clarify your instructions and make them fun.

### Arm Strokes

Scoop the sand.

Reach for a cookie and put it in your pocket.
Dig for a bone.
Climb a ladder.
Crawl through the water.
Pretend you are a dog.
Make a whirlpool.
Wave at Mr. Sun.
Row your boat.

**Bubble Blowing**

Blow out birthday candles.
Let off your steam.
Get rid of the old air.
Talk to the fish.
Blow a hole in the water.
Blow up balloons.
Blow a whistle.

**Floating**

Be like a cloud.
Be light as a feather.
Be like whipped cream floating in hot chocolate.
Be a letter "T."
Take a nap.
Be a glider.
Be an airplane.
Be a rocket.
Be gentle in the water like a dry leaf floating on the lake.
Look for the birds in the sky.
Lie down on your waterbed.
Make your hands like wet spaghetti on a fork.
Touch your toes.
Be a puppet.
Be a rag doll.

**Kicking**

Run, run, run.
Start your motors.
Rev your engines.
Stretch yourself into a long person.
Bounce a ball off your toes (back).
Make a fountain.
Splash your neighbor.

## Toys and Equipment

Supply toys and equipment to help develop children's cognitive skills, provide support for the children in the water, and make being in the water fun! The following are some suggested items.

**Toys**

Sponges
Squeeze tubes
Water cans
Plastic cups
Stacking cups
Strainers
Scoops
Plastic bottles
Plastic buckets
Laundry baskets
Plastic hoops, with and without a weighted side
Playground-size plastic balls without needle-inflating air valves
Beach balls
Plastic flowers with weighted bottoms
Squirting toys
Spraying toys
Toys that make noise but have no removable parts or squeakers
Objects to pull and push in the water

**Equipment**

Floating Supports
Unicellular foam pads
Water logs
Kickboard
Surfboard
Inflatable rafts
Inflatable boats
Inner tubes
Canoes
Rowboats
Ring buoys
Rescue tubes
Rescue buoys
Swim Aids
Pull buoys
Fins
Kickboard
Water logs
Snorkels
Flotation belts
Large and small barbells
Diving rings and sticks

## Activities to Enhance Development

Incorporate these activities into playtime or interaction time during your classes.

### *Shrimps: 6 to 8 months*

- Do a warmup massage, stroking the baby's arms, legs, and torso. This is a lead up to stretching.
- Put a toy for the child to try to reach and grasp and hold



### *Kippers: 9 to 12 months*

- Give each child a set of colored nesting cups, and say the name of the color of the cup as the child stacks it.
- Show the child a plastic animal and say, "What does a (name of animal) say?" Then imitate the sound the animal makes, such as "quack, quack" for a duck or "ribbit, ribbit" for a frog. Have them repeat the words.
- Pair up and do activities with another parent/child team or other adult.
- Put a toy on the deck in front of each baby in the water. Encourage the babies to hold on to the side and climb out to get the toy. This activity encourages gross motor skill development.
- Pair actions with words. For example, when the babies move their feet up and down, say, "kick, kick, kick."
- Play Peek-a-Boo by hiding a toy underneath a bucket or cup and saying, "Where's the (name of toy)?" Then lift the bucket or cup and say, "Peek-a-boo, there it is!"

### *Inias: 13 to 18 months*

- Give your child a box or large plastic container. Put a number of toys and objects into the container, then show your child how to put them in and take them out.
- Play catch by rolling a large ball to your child. Show him or her how to push the ball and catch it.
- Put pictures of objects on storage containers, so babies can try to put the things in the container that match the picture.
- Provide the child with things to toss into a basket.
- Play with boats made out of aluminum pans. Let the child make passengers.
- Experiment with your child on making sounds by hitting things together, such as hitting objects with a spoon.
- Help your child wash a doll.
- Try pushing and pulling things with the child.
- Take a tour of the pool area and point out interesting things to the child.

- To increase the child's body awareness, say the name of the body part when you touch it or wash it.
- Try coordination activities such as clapping your hands, patting your head, or kicking your feet.
- Give the child two acceptable choices to make and then let him or her choose one.
- Play with sponges in the water.
- Play with a shape sorter, in which blocks are to be inserted in matching holes.
- Play games that require imitation, such as "Simon Says" or "Follow the Leader."
- Make bubbles.
- Play a ring toss game.
- Pour water into one object from another.
- Float and sink objects in the water.
- Count objects.
- Ask the child to find specific toys and bring them to you.
- Kick a beach ball.
- Play with sponges, squirt bottles, funnels, and cups in the water.
- Wash things with sponges.
- Match words with actions, such as through, in, under, or over.
- Look for colors.

### *Perch: 19 to 36 months*

- Do warm-up baby massage together before swimming. Include slow bending and stretching of the limbs
- Play make-believe games such as pretending to be animals, cars, or boats.
- Pretend to make cookies: Mix all the ingredients, put the cookies on the pan, pop them into the oven, smell them cooking, then take them out and gobble them up.
- Play games in which you help your child say the names of colors or objects or count objects.
- Help your child identify and say what he or she feels like. Is your child happy, sad, or angry?
- Practice jumping on two feet.
- Try jumping running, leaping, or galloping in the water.

## Songs and Games

Songs and games help children learn and make class enjoyable for both child and parent. Such activities can be used to break up the various components of the class as well as to begin and end the class. Choose each song and game with a purpose in mind; it should help to achieve an objective. Remember that the key words are *warm*, *loving*, and *happy* as you select and use songs and games. If you have more than one level of class in the pool at the same time, try to choose songs and games that are appropriate for all levels to minimize noise and confusion.

The songs and games are grouped under the following headings: water adjustment, water entry and exit, buoyancy, breath control, balance, and locomotion. Each song is introduced along with the suggested age group for the song and the object of the activity that goes with the song. Some songs also provide a description of the activity to do while singing the song; the activities that go with other songs will be obvious from the words.

### Water Adjustment

#### *Songs*

##### My Bonnie Lies Over the Ocean

**9 months to 18 months**

*To back float and to relax*

Have parents rock their children gently while the children are in a back floating position, or pull the children across the water, alternating from prone to back positions.

*My bonnie lies over the ocean.*

*My bonnie lies over the sea.*

*My bonnie lies over the ocean.*

*Oh, bring back my bonnie to me.*

*Bring back, bring back,*

*Oh, bring back my bonnie to me, to me.*
*Bring back, bring back,*
*Oh, bring back my bonnie to me.*

### Yankee Doodle

**9 months to 18 months**

*To learn to hang on to the parent's back while moving through the water*

Have parents walk through the water with their children on their backs, hanging on to the parents' shoulders.

*Yankee Doodle went to town a riding on a pony.*
*Stuck a feather in his hat, and called it macaroni.*
*Yankee Doodle keep it up,*
*Yankee Doodle Dandy,*
*Mind the music and the step, and with the girls be handy.*

### Here We Go 'Round the Mulberry Bush

**18 months and over**

*To reinforce skills*

*Here we go 'round the mulberry bush,*
*The mulberry bush, the mulberry bush,*
*Here we go 'round the mulberry bush,*
*On a cold and frosty morning.*

***Variations:***

*This is the way we wash our legs, etc.*
*This is the way we kick our feet, etc.*
*This is the way we row our arms, etc.*
*This is the way we jump up and down, etc.*

You also can use this song as a good-bye song, changing the last line to *"So early in the morning (or afternoon or evening)."*

### Rock-a-Bye Baby

**Under 18 months**

*To adjust to water while parents gently rock their babies in the water*

*Rock-a-bye baby*
*On the tree top.*
*When the wind blows,*
*The cradle will rock.*
*When the bough breaks,*
*The cradle will fall,*
*And down will come baby, cradle and all.*

### Merry-Go-Round Song

**Under three**

*To feel comfortable in the water*

*I'd like to go on a merry-go-round,*
*Round and round, round and round.*
*I'd like to go on a merry-go-round,*
*Round and round and round.*
(Parents walk their children in a circle.)
*I'd like to go on a merry-go-round,*
*Up and down, up and down.*
*I'd like to go on a merry-go-round,*
*Up and down with you.*
(Parents walk their children in a circle and go up and down with them at the same time.)

### Pat-A-Cake

**Under three**

*To adjust to water*

*Pat-a-cake, pat-a-cake, baker's man!*
*Bake me a cake just as fast as you can.*
*Pat it, and prick it, and mark it with a "B."*
*And put it in the oven for baby and me.*

## Swim Little Fishes

**Under three**

*To adjust to the water while being towed*

*Swim little fishes,*

*Swim if you can.*

*And they swam and swam*

*Right over to their Mom (or Dad)!*

## This Little Piggie

**Under three**

*To feel comfortable in the water*

As the children rest on their backs in the water on the front of their parents' bodies, the parents wiggle each of the children's toes, moving from the big toe to the little toe. This activity helps children become more comfortable with back floating and getting the ears wet.

*This little piggie went to market,*

*This little piggie stayed home,*

*This little piggie had roast beef,*

*This little piggie had none.*

*This little piggie cried wee-wee-wee*

*All the way home.*

## Head and Shoulders, Knees and Toes (Tune: There Is a Tavern in the Town)

**Three and over**

*To get faces wet*

Children touch parts of the body as they are named.

*Head and shoulders, knees and toes,*

*Knees and toes.*

*Head and shoulders, knees and toes*

*Knees and toes.*

*Eyes and ears and mouth and nose.*

*Head and shoulders, knees and toes,*

*Knees and toes.*

## Spin, Spin, Spin Your Top (Tune: Row, Row, Row Your Boat)

**Three and over**

*To adjust to the water*

Sing the song three times, the first time in a standing position, the second time crouching, and the third time crouching even lower.

*Spin, spin, spin your top,*

*Spin it all around.*

*Spin it, twirl it, spin it, twirl it,*

*Throw it on the ground.*

## Lift One Foot (Tune: Ten Little Indians)

**Three and over**

*To adjust to the water and to build confidence*

Children follow the movements in the song.

*I lift one foot and then the other,*

*I lift one foot and then the other,*

*I lift one foot and then the other*

*'Cause I'm a beautiful kid.*

*I squat real low, then up I go,*

*I squat real low, then up I go,*

*I squat real low, then up I go,*

*'Cause I'm a beautiful kid*

### Ring Around the Rosie

**All ages**

*To adjust to the water*

Have parents hold their children in a heartbeat hold and form a circle, then circle around. The children should be held above the water; on "all fall down," the children are dipped into the water but not submerged.

*Ring around the rosie,*

*Pocket full of posies,*

*Ashes, ashes (or water, water or splashes, splashes)*

*We all fall down!*

### Clap Your Hands Together

**All ages**

*To learn parts of the body*

*Clap, clap, clap your hands,*

*Clap your hands together.*

*Clap, clap, clap your hands,*

*Clap your hands together.*

***Variations:***

*Stamp, stamp, stamp your feet, etc.*

*Raise, raise, raise your arms, etc.*

*Tap, tap, tap your head, etc.*

Each verse can be led by a parent/child team, or you can lead each verse.

### The Eency, Weency Spider

**All ages**

*To relax in the water*

Have parents form a circle, holding their children on their forearms and facing the center. The parents can help young children do hand motions with the song. Older children can play without their parents as they sit on the side of the pool.

*The eency, weency spider crept up the water spout.*

*Down came the rain and washed the spider out.*

*Out came the sun and dried up all the rain.*

*And the eency, weency spider crept up the spout again.*

### Come and Go Away With Me

**All ages**

*To relax*

Parents may do any slow, relaxing movement through the water as they sing and carry the babies. The song can be sung as a round.

*Come and go away with me.*

*We shall sail across the sea.*

*Come and go away with me.*

*We shall sail across the sea.*

### Did You Ever See a Lassie?

**All ages**

*To feel comfortable in the water*

(You can substitute a child's name or the phrase, a laddie.)

*Did you ever see a lassie, a lassie, a lassie,*

*Did you ever see a lassie, go this way and that?*

*Go this way, and that way, and that way and this way.*

*Did you ever see a lassie, go this way and that?*

### Kookaburra

**All ages**

*To adjust to the water*

Have parents hold their children and form a circle in the water. Have the parents move around in a circle, lifting the children in the air on "when he eats a fish or two" and moving to the center of the circle on "ha, ha, ha" and out on "hee, hee, hee."

*Kookaburra has no work,*

*He has no work to do.*

*He sits out in the pool all day and eats a fish or two.*

*And when he eats a fish or two,*

*He laughs right out with glee.*
*Ha ha ha ha ha ha,*
*Hee hee hee hee hee.*
*Ha ha ha ha ha ha,*
*Hee hee hee hee hee.*

## Everybody Splash Your Hands (Tune: Mary Had a Little Lamb)

**All ages**

*To reinforce skills*

*Everybody splash your hands, splash your hands, splash your hands,*
*Everybody splash your hands in our swimming pool.*
*Everybody kick your feet, kick your feet, kick your feet,*
*Everybody kick your feet in our swimming pool.*
*Everybody turn around, turn around, turn around,*
*Everybody turn around; give a great big cheer!*
*YAY!!!!!!!!!!!*

## Hokey Pokey

**All ages**

*To explore movement*

Form a circle, sing, and use gestures.

*You put your right arm in,*
*You put your right arm out,*
*You put your right arm in,*
*And you shake it all about.*
*You do the Hokey Pokey and you turn yourself around.*
*That's what it's all about.*

Repeat the verse using the left arm, right and left legs, head, and whole self. You can also try other body parts, such as the nose, ear, shoulder, and so on.

## Good-Bye

**All ages**

*To say good-bye*

*Good-bye to you,*
*Good-bye to you,*
*Good-day, Good-day, Good-day.*
*So long to you,*
*So long to you,*
*Please come again and play.*

## If You're Happy and You Know It

**All ages**

*To orient to water*

Each parent/child team can do a verse as they sit on the deck. If the class is large, you can lead a few verses. These songs and rhymes are especially good for younger children. The parents play an active role in manipulating, tickling, or giving a ride to the children.

*If you're happy and you know it, clap (splash) your hands.*
*If you're happy and you know it, clap your hands.*
*If you're happy and you know it,*
*Then your life will surely show it,*
*If you're happy and you know it, clap your hands.*

***Variations:***

*If you're happy and you know it, nod your head, etc.*
*If you're happy and you know it, kick your feet, etc.*
*If you're happy and you know it, pat your tummy, etc.*

## I'm a Little Teapot

**All ages**

*To orient to water*

*I'm a little teapot, short and stout.*
*This is my handle.* (Put one hand on hip.)

*This is my spout.* (Extend opposite arm sideways, hand out.)

*When I get all steamed up, then I shout,*

*"Just tip me over and pour me out."* (Bend body toward extended arm.)

*S-S-S-S-S*

*I'm a clever teapot, it is true.*

*Here is something I can do.*

*I can change my handle and my spout.* (Change position of hands.)

*Just tip me over and pour me out.* (Bend body toward extended arm.)

*S-S-S-S-S*

***Another version for back floating:***

*I'm a little pancake on my back.*

*I'm a little pancake nice and flat.*

*I'm a little pancake on my back.*

*Just flip me over and flip me back.*

## Mary Was a Red Bird

**All ages**

*To feel comfortable in the water*

*Mary wore her red dress, red dress, red dress,*

*Mary wore her red dress all day long.*

Additional verses can be made up to describe actions the children are doing; for example, Julie was kicking or Tommy was jumping.

## The More We Get Together

**All ages**

*To feel comfortable in the water*

*The more we get together, together, together,*

*The more we get together, the happier we'll be.*

*'Cause your friends are my friends,*

*And my friends are your friends.*

*The more we get together, the happier we'll be.*

## Mr. Sun (Tune: Twinkle, Twinkle, Little Star)

**All ages**

*To feel comfortable in a group situation*

Have the children sit on the edge of the pool. Parents may help the children with movements. For Mr. Sun, they should make a big circle with the arms; they should follow with the other movements suggested by the actions in the song.

*Mr. Sun lights up the sky.*

*I sit right up and I rub my eyes.*

*I brush my teeth and I comb my hair.*

*I put on my swimsuit with the greatest of care.*

*Then off to swimming class I go,*

*To learn those things I ought to know.*

## Swing Low, Sweet Chariot

**All ages**

*To feel comfortable in the water*

*Swing low, sweet chariot,*

*Coming for to carry me home.*

*Swing low, sweet chariot,*

*Coming for to carry me home.*

*I looked over Jordan*

*And what did I see,*

*Coming for to carry me home.*

*A band of angels coming after me,*

*Coming for to carry me home.*

*Swing low, sweet chariot,*

*Coming for to carry me home*

*Swing low, sweet chariot,*

*Coming for to carry me home.*

### Teddy Bear, Teddy Bear

**All ages**

*To adjust to the water and to learn parts of the body*

*Teddy bear, teddy bear, turn around.*

*Teddy bear, teddy bear, touch the ground.*

*Teddy bear, teddy bear, show your shoe* (or substitute body part).

*Teddy bear, teddy bear, you better skiddoo!*

### Ten Little Indians

**All ages**

*To feel comfortable in the water*

As each numbered Indian is mentioned, the parent holds up one finger, until all fingers are up; then a finger is lowered as the number of Indians goes down. As children get older, they can try to do this, too.

*One little, two little, three little Indians,*

*Four little, five little, six little Indians,*

*Seven little, eight little, nine little Indians,*

*Ten little Indian boys.*

*Ten little, nine little, eight little Indians,*

*Seven little, six little, five little Indians*

*Four little, three little, two little Indians,*

*One little Indian boy!*

### Wheels on the Bus (Tune: Mulberry Bush)

**All ages**

*To explore body movement*

Have parents and their children form a circle. Have the parents help the children with motions, or children may do them independently.

*Wheels on the bus go round and round,*

*Round and round, round and round.*

*Wheels on the bus go round and round*

*All over town.*

*Motions:* Move the hands and forearms in a circular motion in the water. (Smaller children may turn around in circles.)

***Second verse:*** *Doors on the bus go open and shut.*

*Motions:* Parents push smaller children forward and pull them back, or parents push the children's hands together back and forth in the water.

***Third verse:*** *Windows on the bus go up and down.*

*Motions:* Parents raise smaller children up and down. Older children can jump up and down.

***Fourth verse:*** *Baby on the bus cries wah, wah, wah.*

*Motions:* Move the hand toward and away from the mouth.

***Fifth verse:*** *Mommy on the bus says sh, sh, sh.*

*Motions:* Put a finger to the mouth.

***Sixth verse:*** *Driver on the bus says move on back.*

*Motions:* Lay children on their backs if they don't protest.

***Seventh verse:*** *Horn on the bus goes beep, beep beep.*

*Motions:* Hit the water with a hand.

***Eighth verse:*** *People on the bus, they wave bye-bye.*

*Motions:* Wave good-bye.

### Where Is Thumbkin?

**All ages**

*To learn finger movements*

*Where is Thumbkin? Where is Thumbkin?*

(Put hands behind back.)

*Here I am,*

(Show one thumb.)

*Here I am.*

(Show other thumb.)

*How are you today, sir?*

(Bend one thumb.)

*Very well, I thank you.*

(Bend other thumb.)

*Run away, run away.*

(Put hands one at a time behind the back.)

***Variations:***

*Where is pointer?, etc.*

*Where is tall man?, etc.*

*Where is ring man?, etc.*

*Where is pinky?, etc.*

### Who Came to Swim Today? (Tune: Mulberry Bush)

**All ages**

*To say hello*

Have the children sit in a circle or on the edge of the pool.

*Who came to swim today, swim today, swim today?*

*Who came to swim today and what's his (or her) name?*

_______ *came to swim today, swim today, swim today.*

_______ *came to swim today and that's his (or her) name.*

### With My Hands I Clap, Clap, Clap

**All ages**

*To adjust to the water*

*With my hands I clap, clap, clap (splash, splash, splash).*

*With my feet I stamp, stamp, stamp (kick, kick, kick).*

*With myself I turn around.*

*Then one, two, three, we all fall down (blow bubbles).*

## Games

### Feel the Wind

**18 months and over**

*To blow bubbles in the water*

Have the children pick out their favorite toys and blow on them out of the water. Then place the toys in the water and have the children blow on them there.



Another way parents can do this is to ask children to "feel the wind." Parents place their hands in front of the children's mouths, out of the water, then lower their hands into the water, telling the children to make it rain (to blow bubbles). They can even pretend that their hands are clouds: The children's breath is the wind, and the bubbles are the rain.

### Ring Game

**Three and over**

*To open the eyes under water*

Equipment: Diving rings

Divide the children into two or more teams and have each team form a line. Put as many diving rings as there are children into the water. The first child in each line does a seat dive to pick up a ring, then brings it back to where the team stands and goes to the end of the line. This process is repeated with the next child in line. The first team to finish wins. (Don't stress winning. Say instead "You all tried," or "You all did well.")

### Bake Chocolate Chip Cookies

**Three and over**

*To put the face in the water*

Tell children that they are going to make chocolate chip cookies. Have them imitate the following motions:

1. *Soften the butter.* (Pound the water with fists.)
2. *Pour in the sugar and vanilla.* (Throw the water toward the middle.)
3. *Crack the egg.* (Chop the water with a karate chop.)
4. *Sift the flour and baking soda.* (Clap the hands together in the water.)
5. *Put in chocolate chips.* (Throw water into the air.)
6. *Mix everything together.* (Swirl around in a circle.)
7. *Put it in a pan.* (Throw water over the shoulders.)
8. *Put it in the oven.* (Shove the water with the hands.)
9. *Watch the cookies baking.* (Put the face into the water and open the eyes.)
10. *Take it out of the oven.* (Pull the water backwards with the hands.)
11. *Eat the cookies.* (Bring water to the face in cupped hands.)

## Bridge

**Three and over**

*To put the face in the water*

Have the children form a line. Then you and another instructor (or volunteer) place your hands together to form a bridge. The children go under the bridge, which is just enough above the water that they need to try to put their faces in the water. Adjust the height of the bridge to the comfort level of each child putting the face in the water.

## Choo-Choo Train With Waterfall

**Three and over**

*To relax in deep water, get the face wet, and swim in deep water*

Use a black line (at the side of the pool) as a railroad track. You pretend to be the train engine going around the pool. The children follow, holding on to the edge of the pool with their hands and moving themselves hand over hand around the side.

- The diving board may be a bridge or a place to stop and watch other children jump off.
- The ladders may be "gas-up" stations. Children can "gas up" by holding the side and kicking very fast.
- A person in the way may be a cow on the track; children have to let go and swim around it.
- A rope or hoop may be a tunnel to go under or through.
- An instructor pouring a cup of water slowly over the children may be a waterfall to go under.

## Diving Dolphins

**Three and over**

*To put the face underwater or swim underwater*

**Equipment:** Large plastic hoops, some weighted

Hold a hoop vertically with the top at water level or above. When the children go through the hoop, they have to duck underwater. Keep lowering the hoop as the children get better. (Adjust the height for each child.) Weights on the hoops make them sink under water and stand on their sides. Children can swim through one or more hoops, coming up between the hoops or swimming through more than one at a time.

## Follow the Leader

**Three and over**

*To reinforce various skills*

Let each child think up a different thing to do, do it, then have others imitate it. Give children ideas but only when needed. Each child, for safety reasons, needs to tell you first what he or she will be doing. This works very well using the diving board, with one turn for each child.

## Firefighter

**Three and over**

*To orient to deep water*

This may be done in deep or shallower water. You hold a pole, and, one at a time, each child wraps his or her legs and hands around it. The child climbs down the pole, hand over hand, to water level or beneath, and goes back up in the same manner.

## How Do You Do?

**Three and over**

*To practice letting go of the side of the pool*

Shake hands with each student and formally exchange names. Repeat, extending the handshake to pulling each child off the wall toward you, then returning the child to the wall. In later lessons, this game can include having the child push off the wall and go to you.

## Name Game

**All ages**

*To say hello*

Have parents and their children sit in a circle or on the edge of the pool. For each parent/child team, say the following:

*Names, names, what's in a name?*

*I've got a name and you've got a name.*

*What's your name?*

The parent or the child says the child's name along with a gesture, such as tapping the child's head. Then the whole group says that child's name three times, imitating the gesture. Use skills as gestures.

## Water Entry and Exit

### *Songs*

#### Jack Be Nimble

**Under three**

*To do standing jumps*

*Jack be nimble,*

*Jack be quick,*

*Jack jumped over*

*The candlestick!* (Jump after command.)

#### Little Speckled Frogs (Tune: Little Peter Cottontail)

**Under three**

*To enter the pool, turn, and get back to the wall*

Have the children sit on the edge of the pool pretending to eat bugs. On the word *jump* the parents assist the children into the pool and return them to the wall.

*Six little speckled frogs*

*Sitting on a speckled log*

*Eating most delicious bugs.*

*One jumped into the pool*

*Where it was nice and cool*

*Now there are five speckled frogs.*

#### Jack and Jill

**18 months and over**

*To practice falling into the water, turning, and getting back to the wall*

Have parents sit on the edge of the pool with their children. One at a time, the parents fall in and the children come tumbling after, then turn and go back to the wall. Older children (three and up) could do this all at the same time.

*(Parent's name) and (child's name) went up the hill*

*To fetch a pail of water.*

*(Parent's name) fell down and broke his crown (jumps in and makes a splash)*

*And (child's name) came tumbling after.*

Instructor Note: *Caution parents to make sure that children under three do not ingest water.*

#### Humpty Dumpty

**18 months and over**

*To enter the pool and turn back to the wall*

The children sit on the edge of the pool, and the parents rock the children from side to side as they say the rhyme. On "fall" the parents help the children into the water and to the parents' chests. Then the parents turn the children around and move them back to the wall.

*Humpty Dumpty sat on a wall.*

*Humpty Dumpty had a great fall.*

*Humpty Dumpty swam back to the wall.*

Instructor Note: *Caution parents to make sure that children under three do not ingest water.*

## Games

### Give Me Five

**18 months and over**

*To jump into the pool without holding on*

Have parents hold out their hands, palms up. Then have the children jump, hitting their parents' hands as they do so. This will slow down the children's fall and make their faces less wet.

### Jump Into My Circle

**18 months and over**

*To jump off the side of the pool*

Equipment: A large plastic hoop (optional)

Have the children line up. Place a hoop on the water or draw a circle on the water with your finger. Have each child try to jump through the hoop or circle.

If children have trouble with this, have them lean over and place their hands under the water. From this position they may find it easier to jump.

### Easter Egg Coloring Time

**Three and over**

*To practice jumping in the water*

Have the children line up beside the pool or on the diving board and think of a color. Tell them the pool water is magical at Easter time—it will dye the children an Easter egg color when they jump in. The children have to tell what color they are going to be before jumping into the water.

### Hickory, Dickory, Dock

**Three and over**

*To build strength and to go underwater*

Have a firefighter's pole ready. The class recites the rhyme. One at a time, each parent may help his or her child move up to the top of the pole on the first two lines; on "mouse ran down," the child slides down the pole and underwater.

*Hickory, dickory, dock,*

*(Child's name) ran up the clock.*

*The clock struck "one,"*

*And (child's name) ran down,*

*Hickory, dickory, dock.*

### Parachute

**Three and over**

*To jump off the side of the pool*

Have the children stand on the deck. Explain that they are in a big plane and that they are going to jump from the plane with a parachute onto the landing strip (black line). Take each child's arms and have the child jump. The second time hold only one of the child's arms. Finally, have the child jump without assistance.

### Popcorn

**Three and over**

*To get the face wet and jump off the side of the pool*

Have the children jump off the side into the pool one at a time, first holding both your hands; then one hand; then jumping into your arms; then slapping your hands (give me five); and, finally, without any contact. As they do this the class recites this rhyme:

*It's getting hot! It's getting hotter!*

*It's getting really hot! It's going to POP!*

### Rocket Booster

**Three and over**

*To dive and to swim underwater*

Have the children sit on the side of the pool with the soles of their feet on the pool wall, arms over their ears, and hands together over their heads. They blast off by diving into the water, their noses just missing their knees, and pushing off the wall with their feet. (This is their " rocket booster.")

### Submarine

**Three and over**

*To learn the standing dive*

Have the children line up at the deep end of the pool with their toes over the edge. Tell the children to stand tall and straight with their arms over their heads and their hands together. Say, "I am a submarine booster; wait until I come to boost you off." Then move behind the children, and, one at a time, place your hands on each child's waist and tell the child to bend forward at the waist with their hands pointing into the water. Guide the child into the water, saying, "Blast off!" as each diver is launched. Remind each child to steer up.

## Buoyancy

*Songs*

### Ride a Cock Horse

**18 months to 36 months**

*To gain confidence and to experience buoyancy*

Have the parents sit on the wall, with the children sitting on the parents' ankles and holding the parents' hands. The parents gently raise and lower their feet in the water as they sing the song.

Alternate version: The children sit, backs to parents, on the parents' ankles. The children lie back against the parents' knees. The parents open their knees to let the children's heads float when the parents' legs are level with the top of the water. (Purpose: To practice the back float without the parents holding the children with their hands.)

*Ride a cock horse to Banbury Cross*

*To see a fine lady upon a fine horse.*

*With rings on her fingers and bells on her toes,*

*She will make music, whenever she goes.*

### Pop Goes the Weasel

**Under three**

*To experience buoyancy*

Have the parents form a circle. Holding their children at their chests, the parents should turn them back and forth (like a washing machine) as they sing the song, then lift them up into the air on "POP!"

*All around the cobbler's bench*

*The monkey chased the weasel.*

*The monkey thought it was all in fun.*

*POP goes the weasel!*

*A penny for a spool of thread,*

*A penny for a needle.*

*That's the way the money goes,*

*POP goes the weasel!*

*I've no time to waste or cry,*

*Nor patience to wait till by and by.*

*Kiss me quick, I'm off, good-bye,*

*POP goes the weasel!*

### Sailing, Sailing

**Under three**

*To maintain back and front position in the water*

Have the parents sing while moving the children through the water, alternating from front to back position.

*Sailing, sailing,*

*Over the bounding main.*

*For many a stormy wind shall blow*

*'Til Jack comes home again.*

*Sailing, sailing*

*Over the bounding main.*

*For many a stormy wind shall blow*

*'Til Jack comes home again.*

### Row, Row, Row Your Boat

**All ages**

*To become accustomed to flotation devices*

Parents give their children a ride on kickboards as they sing, making a circle or a line that moves around the pool. This song is fun to sing as a round. On "dream," children three or over may go underwater.

*Row, row, row your boat*

*Gently down the stream.*

*Merrily, merrily, merrily, merrily,*

*Life is but a dream.*

***Variations:***

*Drive, drive, drive your car,*

*Gently down the street.*

*Merrily, merrily, merrily,*

*Life is but a treat.*

*Ride, ride, ride your bike,*

*Gently down the street.*

*Merrily, merrily, merrily, merrily,*

*Life is but a treat.*

## *Games*

### Timber

**Three and over**

*To learn to float*

Have the children stand in a line in the pool a sufficient distance from the side and pretend they are trees. First they raise their branches (arms) above their heads and stretch their trunks. When you say, "timber," the "trees" fall on their backs or fronts.

# Breath Control

## *Songs*

### Little Green Frog

**18 months and over**

*To blow bubbles and to put face in the water*

On "Roomp," the children blow bubbles; on "blink, blink, blink" they put their faces in the water three times instead of singing the words.

*Baa Roomp went the little green frog one day.*

*Baa Roomp went the little green frog.*

*Baa Roomp went the little green frog one day.*

*And his eyes went blink, blink, blink.*

### Hurry, Hurry, Hurry Up the Firepole (Tune: Ten Little Indians)

**Three and over**

*To develop strength going underwater*

Equipment: A long pole

Use a pole. The class sings this song as each parent helps his or her child to the top of the pole, then the child slides down and under the water.

*Hurry, hurry, hurry up the firepole,*

*Hurry, hurry, hurry up the firepole,*

*Hurry, hurry, hurry up the firepole,*

*Down, down, down, down, down.*

### London Bridge

**All ages**

*To move through the water*

Equipment: A large plastic hoop (optional)

You and another instructor or parents make a bridge by holding hands (a hoop may be used instead) and the class sings the song. The children go through the bridge until the end of the song, when the bridge is dropped down and a child is caught inside.

*London bridge is falling down,*

*Falling down, falling down.*

*London bridge is falling down*

*My fair lady (or gentleman).*

**Variations:**

*London bridge is all washed out, etc.*

*Here's a fish that we have caught, etc.*

*In the water it must go, etc.*

## Games

### Feel the Wind

**18 months and over**

*To blow bubbles in the water*

Have the children pick out their favorite toys and blow on them out of the water. Then place the toys in the water, and have the children blow on them there.

Another way parents can do this is to ask their children to "feel the wind." Parents place their hands in front of the children's mouths, out of the water, then lower their hands into the water, telling the children to make it rain (to blow bubbles). They can even pretend that their hands are clouds: The children's breath is the wind, and the bubbles are the rain.

### Hickory, Dickory, Dock

**Three and over**

*To build strength and to go underwater*

Have a firefighter's pole ready. The class recites the rhyme. One at a time, each parent may help his or her child move up to the top the pole on the first two lines; on "mouse ran down," the child slides down the pole and underwater.

*Hickory, dickory, dock,*

*(Child's name) ran up the clock.*

*The clock struck "one,"*

*And (child's name) ran down,*

*Hickory, dickory, dock.*

### Look and Listen

**Three and over**

*To learn breathing and blowing*

Have the children hold on to the wall (or kickboards). Tell them there are fish at the bottom of the pool. (Name the fish after the children if you wish.) Tell them the fish are "pretend" fish and the only way you can see them is to put your eyes in the water. Then tell them the fish are talking to them and they should listen, putting their entire ears in the water. Start by saying "Look at the fish; now listen." As they go on and become more comfortable just say, "look" and "listen."

For more advanced children, tell them to blow bubbles at the fish and then breathe. Then condense the activity to blow-breathe-blow-breathe (or talk to the fish and listen to the fish).

### Treasure Hunt (for advanced swimmers)

**Three and over**

*To follow directions, to listen, and to perform endurance swimming*

**Equipment:**

A large plastic hoop, objects that will sink (such as toys or coins)

Scatter objects that will sink on the bottom of the shallow area. Then have the children jump or dive off the side of the pool and swim through a hoop you hold to the shallow area to pick up the "treasures" (sunken toys, coins, etc.).

### Under—Over

**Three and over**

*To put the face underwater in the right way for bobs*

Have the children (not more than five to an adult) hold on to the lane line, facing you or another instructor on the other side of the line. Let the children go under the lane line while still holding on to it. Not letting go, the children should stop, then go back to the other side again. They may also blow bubbles or say "candy," "popcorn," or other words underwater.

## Balance

### How Do You Do?

**Three and over**

*To practice letting go of the side of the pool*

Shake hands with each student and formally exchange names. Repeat, extending the handshake to pulling each child off the wall toward you, then returning the child to the wall. In later lessons, this game can include having the child push off the wall and go toward you.

### Push Against the Wall

**Thirteen months and over**

*To practice the back float position and kicking with assistance*

Children lie back on their parents, with their heads resting on their parents' shoulders and feet touching the wall. The parents provide extra support under the shoulders and hips, as needed. The children push off the wall hard and begin kicking while the parent guides them to the other side of the swim area. Just before the children reach the wall, parents should encourage the children to roll over, push off from their parents' thighs, and grab the wall. Encourage the proper position by asking them to push up their hips and to look at the ceiling for some imaginary objects such as a spider, picture, or little man.

As the children become more comfortable, you can hand out kickboards and have parents place them under the children's heads and the parents' shoulders. This leads up to kicking on the back with a board and without parents' support.

## Locomotion

*Songs*

### Here We Go Round the Mulberry Bush

**18 months and over**

*To reinforce skills*

*Here we go round the mulberry bush,*
*The mulberry bush, the mulberry bush,*
*Here we go round the mulberry bush,*
*On a cold and frosty morning.*

***Variations:***

*This is the way we kick our feet, etc.*
*This is the way we paddle our arms, etc.*
*This is the way we blow bubbles, etc.*
*This is the way we do all three, etc.*
*This is the way we row our arms, etc.*
*This is the way we jump up and down, etc.*

### Everybody Splash Your Hands (Tune: Mary Had a Little Lamb)

**All ages**

*To reinforce skills*

*Everybody splash your hands, splash your hands, splash your hands,*
*Everybody splash your hands in our swimming pool.*
*Everybody kick your feet, kick your feet, kick your feet,*
*Everybody kick your feet in our swimming pool.*
*Everybody turn around, turn around, turn around,*
*Everybody turn around; give a great big cheer!*
*YAY!!!!!!!!!!!!*

### Noble Duke of York

**Three and over**

*To move through the water, bobbing*

*The Noble Duke of York,*
*He had ten thousand men.*
*He rode them up the hill*
*And he rode them down again.*
*When you're up, you're up.*
*And when you're down, you're down.*
*And when you're only halfway up*
*You're neither up nor down.*

### Open Them, Shut Them

**Three and over**

*To learn arm and hand movements*

The children do the hand movements as they are described in the song.

*Open them, shut them, open them, shut them,*
*Give a little clap, clap, clap.*
*Open them, shut them, open them, shut them,*
*Lay them in your lap.*

*Creep them, crawl them, creep them, crawl them*
*Right up to your chin.*
*Open up your little mouth,*
*But do not let them in.*

*Open them, shut them, open them, shut them,*
*Give a little clap, clap, clap.*
*Open them, shut them, open them, shut them,*
*Lay them in your lap.*

*Creep them, crawl them, creep them, crawl them*
*Right up to your cheeks.*
*Cover up your little eyes*
*And give a great big peek!*

*Open them, shut them, open them, shut them,*
*Give a little clap, clap, clap.*
*Open them, shut them, open them, shut them,*
*Lay them in your lap.*

*Open them, shut them, open them, shut them,*
*To your shoulders fly.*
*Let them like the little birdies*
*Flutter to the sky.*

*Falling, falling, falling, falling,*
*Nearly to the ground.*
*Quickly raising all your fingers*
*Twirl them round and round.*

### We're Going for a Walk (Tune: Farmer in the Dell)

**Three and over**

*To reinforce skills*

Move in a circle or across the pool.

*We're going for a walk,*
*We're going for a walk,*
*Hi ho and away we go,*
*We're going for a walk.*
*Variations:*
*We're going for a swim, etc.*
*We're going to do a bob, etc.*
*We're going to blow bubbles, etc.*

### Swimming, Swimming (Tune: Sailing, Sailing)

**Three and over**

*To practice skills*

Form a circle while singing.

*Swimming, swimming, in the swimming pool.*
*When days are hot, and days are cold, and days are just like ice.*
*Kicking, arm stroke, fancy diving too.*
*Don't you wish you never had anything else to do?*

### Touch Your Toes (Tune: Frere Jacques)

**Three and over**

*To reinforce skills*

Children perform the designated motions as they sing.

*Touch your toes, touch your toes.*

*Turn around, turn around.*

*Do a little jumping, do a little jumping.*

*Squat real low, up you go.*

*Touch your toes, touch your toes.*

*Turn around, turn around.*

*Do a little hopping, do a little hopping.*

*Squat real low, up you go.*

Substitute any action in underlined parts.

### Clap Your Hands Together

**All ages**

*To learn the parts of the body*

*Clap, clap, clap your hands,*

*Clap your hands together.*

*Clap, clap, clap your hands,*

*Clap your hand together.*

***Variations:***

*Stamp, stamp, stamp your feet, etc.*

*Raise, raise, raise your arms, etc.*

*Tap, tap, tap your head, etc.*

Each verse can be lead by a parent/child team, or you can lead each verse.

### Kicking Is Fun

**All ages**

*To learn kicking and other skills*

The children kick on the last line.

*Kicking is fun, kicking is fun,*

*Kicking is fun for everyone.*

*The more you kick, the better you swim,*

*So everybody kick, kick, kick.*

Additional verses may include any action such as running, hugging, jumping, or waving.

### I Can Make My Arms Go Up and Down (Tune: Mulberry Bush)

**All ages**

*To practice body movements*

Bubble and breathe up and down (do bobs).

*I make my arms go up and down,*

*I make my arms go up and down,*

*I make my arms go up and down,*

*JUST LIKE THIS!*

***Variations:***

*I make my arms go round and round, etc.*

*I make my legs go up and down, etc.*

## Games

### Motor Boat

**18 months and over**

*To experience excitement and to explore*

Form a circle, with the parents holding children in the prone position, moving slowly, then faster, and then very fast. The parents and children may put their faces in the water and blow bubbles after "step on the gas." This can be varied for older children.

*Motorboat, motorboat, go so slow,*

*Motorboat, motorboat, go so fast,*

*Motorboat, motorboat, step on the gas!*

### Touch Your Beautiful

**Under three**

*To learn the parts of the body*

*I touch my beautiful head, head, head.*

*I touch my beautiful chest, chest, chest.*

*I touch my beautiful elbows, elbows, elbows.*

*I touch my beautiful ankles, ankles, ankles.*

Sing about body parts that the children may have trouble identifying, or ask them which ones they want to sing about.

### Let's Go for a Bicycle Ride

**Three and over**

*To tread water or to learn the paddle stroke*

Have the children pretend they are going on a bicycle ride, but they can't move around. Have them stay in one place and tell you where they are going. Show them how to move their hands for treading water or paddle stroking.

### Barge Boat

**Three and over**

*To get the arms straight and the chin in when using a kickboard*

Put a toy on the edge of each child's kickboard. (Make sure the toy is not round, or it will roll off.) Tell the children to stretch out their arms and move their chins in, and explain that if they lean on the kickboards, their toys will fall off. Make a game of it, if you wish, but don't stress winning. Tell each child how well he or she did. (If the toy falls off 206 times, you should have told them to try next time each of the last 205 times.)

### Relay Races

**Three and over**

*To line up better and faster and to learn various skills*

Have two or more teams line up at the end of the pool, choosing fast and slow swimmers for each team. Then have the teams race across the pool, one child from each team swimming at the same time. As each child finishes, he or she gets out of the pool and lines up. The team that swims well and is first to line up gets a round of applause. The other team gets big smiles and words of encouragement.

**Try these variations:**

- Bob across the pool.
- Swim across the pool.
- Swim backwards across the pool.
- Swim on the back across the pool.
- Make up your own.

### Shape Toss

**Three and over**

*To experience independence in the water and to learn shapes and colors*

Sit down with the children on the deck. Hand them each a shape (a toy). Then take their shapes back and hold them up, one at a time, asking whose shape it was so that there will be no confusion later when they retrieve their shapes from the water. (Children this age are still learning shapes and colors, and they may need help. Never criticize a child if he or she doesn't know the shape or color.) Have the children close their eyes, then throw the toys a reasonable distance into the water. Ask the children to swim to their own toys, then let them continue the lap.

If the children need to work on their backs, have them first swim on the front and, once they have the toys, turn over on their backs. If a great deal of work is needed on the back position, throw the toys only 10 to 20 feet so that the children have to turn over sooner.

### Superman

**Three and over**

*To learn to kick better and to streamline the body*

Ask the children how Superman flies. Ask if he flies with bent arms; they'll say no. Ask about bent legs; they'll say no. Tell them, then, to pretend that they're Superman and to stretch out, using the wall or kickboards. You can use other favorite TV heroes

### Wave to the Fishes

**Three and over**

*To get the finning motion of the hands correct*

Have the children stand in the pool. Tell them, "We are going to lie on our backs and kick to the other end. But we're going to pretend there are fishes at the bottom of the pool." (Name the fish after the children, if you wish.) Tell them to wave to the fishes. You may have to move their hands for them the first time. Remember, they are still developing motor skills and coordination.

### Diving Dolphins

**Three and over**

*To put the face underwater or swim underwater*

Equipment: A large plastic hoop, one or more weighted plastic hoops

Hold a hoop with the top at water level or above, and ask the children to swim through it, one at a time. When the children go through the hoop, they have to duck underwater. Keep lowering the hoop as the children get better. (Adjust the height for each child.)

Weighted hoops sink underwater, standing on their sides. Place one or more weighted hoops for the children to swim through, either by coming up between the hoops or swimming through more than one hoop at a time.

### Follow the Leader

**Three and over**

*To reinforce various skills*

Let each child think up a different skill to do, do it, then have others imitate it. Give children ideas but only when needed. Each child, for safety reasons, needs to tell you first what he or she will be doing. This works very well using the diving board, with one turn for each child.

### Imitation

**Three and over**

*To reinforce skills*

Have the children imitate different animals jumping off the diving board into the water (monkeys, bears, seals, chickens, etc.).

### Simon Says

**Three and over**

*To jump, to listen, and to practice different skills*

Play this game as it is traditionally played, but use swimming skills to challenge the children.

### Red Light, Green Light

**All ages**

*To learn to kick*

Have children hold on to the wall. Tell them to kick their feet when you say, "green light," and to stop kicking when you say, "red light." When you say, "yellow light," they should slow their kicking.

### Bubble Train

**Three and over**

*To learn to blow bubbles*

Give each child a barbell. Then have the children put the barbells underneath their armpits and hold on to the ankles of the child in front of them to form a "train." You hold the first child's hand and pull the whole "train" through the water, saying, "Blow your bubbles; it's a bubble train." Keep an eye on all the children throughout this activity, and allow those who need one to wear a flotation belt.

## Character Development Activities

This section contains character development activities that you can include in your classes. They are divided into activities appropriate for the Parent/Child levels and activities for the Preschool levels.

### Parent/Child Activities

#### Hug, Please (children 6 to 36 months old)

***Value:*** *Caring*

Have the babies sit on the side of the pool with the parents standing just in front of them. Say, "It's time to send love. Give your baby a hug and say, 'Hug, please.' Hold your baby closely for a minute and say, 'I love you.' Release your child and say, 'Hug, please,' then hug him or her again. Repeat this as long as you and your baby are having fun."

### Love Ball (children 19 to 36 months old)

**Value:** *Caring*

Equipment: Balls that can be squeezed, one for each parent

Have the children on the side of the pool (sitting or standing). Give each parent a ball, and ask the parents to squeeze their balls as if they were hugging them. Tell the parents to say, "I'm going to toss the ball to you and send my love to you." Before tossing the ball, they should say, "Here comes my love." The children should catch the balls. The parents should ask the children if they got their love. After the children respond, the parents should say, "Can you put love in the ball and send me your love?"

After the parents and children play the game together for a while, expand the game to sending love to other parent/child teams and to you, the instructor.

### Heart Toss (children 19 to 36 months old)

**Value:** *Caring*

Equipment: A basket with a heart inside it, a ball or another toy

Put a basket with a heart inside it in the pool or on the deck. Then hold a ball or toy to your heart and say, "I'm filling this with love, and I'm going to toss it into the heart basket." Then ask the children if they can fill the ball with love and toss it into the heart basket. You can ask them to name someone (baby, mommy, daddy, grandma, brother, sister, etc.) they love before tossing their love into the basket.

### Instilling Honesty

**Value:** *Honesty*

Discuss why it is important to instill honesty at such a young age. Ask parents who have older children to share how they have responded when kids tell little white lies and how they've taught their older children to be honest.

### Welcome Circle

**Value:** *Respect*

Have a welcome circle on the first day of class. Pair up a parent who has already participated in a class with a new parent. During class the more experienced parent can tell the new parent what to expect in class.

### Clean-Up

**Value:** *Responsibility*

Equipment: Toy barrels or whatever toys are stored in

Have all the children put their toys away at the end of class. Explain to parents that this is a good way for their children to learn about responsibility.

### Showering

**Value:** *Respect and responsibility*

Have all participants shower before class, and ask parents to instill the habit in their children as part of their responsibility to keep the pool clean.

### Boating Safety

**Value:** *Responsibility*

Equipment: Life jackets for adults, children, and infants

Discuss boating safety with parents. Demonstrate what to look for in a good life jacket and how it should fit. Discuss why children need to learn the importance of wearing life jackets through watching their parents wearing life jackets.

### Missing Class

**Value:** *Caring*

Ask parents to call you ahead of time if their children will miss a class; then you can let everyone know why. Make it a point to call each child that misses a class. Report to the rest of the class why the child isn't there if he or she misses again.

### Safety Day

**Value:** *Caring*

Equipment: Classroom or deck space, CPR class list

Have a safety day and teach rescue breathing to parents. Discuss how this knowledge could save a baby's life and how important it is to know how to do it. Bring a list of infant CPR classes and encourage class members who have not been certified to sign up together.

### If You're Honest and You Know It

**Values:** *Caring, honesty, respect, and responsibility*

Sing to the tune of "If You're Happy and You Know It."

*If you're honest and you know it, splash your hands.*
*If you're honest and you know it, splash your hands.*
*If you're honest and you know it, then your life will surely show it.*
*If you're honest and you know it, splash your hands.*

**Variations:**

*If you're caring and you know it, kick your feet, etc.*
*If you're respectful and you know it, turn around, etc.*
*If you're responsible and you know it, jump up and down, etc.*

## Preschool Activities

### Trust Me

**Level: Pike**

**Value:** *Honesty*

Talk to the class about the concepts of honesty and trust. Tell them that whenever you say you'll hold them or they'll swim to a certain distance, you'll never let go or move back. Say, "You can always trust me." Ask them if they would be able to tell if you were ever dishonest with them.

### Bobbing

**Level: Pike**

**Value:** *Respect*

Demonstrate bobbing and have the students watch. Then have the students work on bobbing; they should not stop on top of the water and should blow all their air out underneath. As each child accomplishes the skill, all the other children clap for him or her.

### Little Fish Who Cried "Hook"

**Level: Ray**

**Value:** *Honesty*

Tell the story about the little boy who cried wolf, but change the boy to a fish who cries, "hook," and who finally gets caught by a fisherman.

### Being Proud

**Level: All**

**Value:** *Respect*

To teach self-respect ask each student, "What did you do well today and what are you most proud of?" This should give each student the opportunity to feel good about that day's accomplishments.

### Showers

**Level: All**

**Values:** *Respect and responsibility*

Before getting into the pool on the first day, discuss why we take showers before entering the pool. Say, "We are respecting everyone's right to swim in a clean pool. What other rules should we respect during swim lessons?"

### Respecting Rules

**Level: All**

**Value:** *Respect*

On the first day of class, discuss the rules for the class and the pool. Tell students why the rules are important and what the appropriate behavior is. Explain the consequences if someone does not follow the rules.

Be sure to enforce the rules and to acknowledge the students when they are following the class and the pool rules.

### Pool Rules

**Level: Pike**

**Value:** *Responsibility*

Assistance: Lifeguard

Discuss the pool rules and how all of us are responsible for following them. Introduce the lifeguard to the class and have him or her talk about what the guard is responsible for doing at the pool.

### Love Bobs

**Level: Pike**

**Value:** *Caring*

Have each student tell you how many people they love and who these people are. Have them do that many bobs.

### Ball Pass

**Level: Pike and Eel**

***Value:*** *Caring*

Equipment: Beach ball or small playground ball

Show students how to pass the ball in the water and how to catch it. After passing to each student, have them pass to each other a few times. Ask if everyone got a turn to pass and catch. Explain that making sure everyone got a turn is a way of showing caring for each other.

### Boating Safety

**Level: Ray and Starfish**

***Values:*** *Caring, honesty, respect, and responsibility*

Equipment: Boat, PFDs (preschool, youth, and adult sizes)

Discuss how we demonstrate our values by learning about boating safety:

- *Caring:* Check that everyone is wearing a PFD correctly, especially your buddy.
- *Honesty:* Speak up if you notice something is wrong, like someone's life jacket is not on correctly.
- *Respect:* We follow instructions from the "captain" of the boat (mom or dad) when he or she tells us we need to stay seated or to put on our life jackets.
- *Responsibility:* You have a responsibility for yourself to wear a PFD whenever you are on a boat.

### Treading Water

**Level: Starfish**

***Value:*** *Caring*

Have the students tread water. When they can think of a nice thing they did for someone, they raise their hands. As you tap them, they can stop and hold on to the side of the pool and tell the class their act of kindness.

### Clean-up Monitors

**Level: All**

***Value:*** *Responsibility*

Equipment: Equipment storage bins or areas, gold star stickers

Choose two clean-up monitors for each class. After class is over, they must stack up the kickboards or whatever equipment was used. Each monitor gets a star sticker after class if everything is put back neatly.

### Boating Safety

**Level: All**

***Value:*** *Responsibility*

Equipment: Plastic bottle with message; boat; PFDs, one for each student

On Boating Safety Day have all the students put their life jackets on and get in the boat in the pool. (Be sure you have your life jacket on, too!) Throw a plastic bottle with a message inside it into the middle of the pool. Pretend you are on the high seas, and row out to the bottle. Inside the bottle have placed a value statement about boating safety and being responsible near boats, lakes, and oceans.

### Recognizing Caring for Others

**Level: All**

***Value:*** *Caring*

By the age of three, children can show caring or empathy. Make a point to recognize students whenever they demonstrate these qualities to another student. For example, Sally sees a classmate is scared and tells him, "It's okay, kicking to the teacher will be fun." You bring the statement to the attention of the other students after the activity by saying, "Sally showed she cared about Ricky by showing concern for what Ricky was feeling."

## Beads

**Level: All**

***Value:*** *Caring, honesty, respect, and responsibility*

Equipment: Colored beads and plastic lanyards, one for each student

Give each student a plastic lanyard and a colored starter bead representing the class level (Pike = white, Eel = purple, etc.) to tie onto his or her swim bag. Each day you discuss a value, give the students different colored beads to put on their lanyards. When you have talked about all four core values and the students can tell you what the four values are, they get multicolored beads. (The standard colors for the values are these: Respect is gold or yellow, red is caring, blue is honesty, and green is responsibility.)

# Index